The PBS special *Jane Goodall: Reason for Hope* was inspired by this book.

AN OUTPOURING OF PRAISE FOR JANE GOODALL AND
∂ REASON FOR HOPE ∂

"An important book. . . . REASON FOR HOPE is part memoir, part scientific theorizing, part theological musing, and part challenge. . . . This statement of faith becomes not only extraordinary but also humbling."
—*Philadelphia Inquirer*

"When Goodall describes her work as a scientist and her sincere efforts to make the world a better place, I stand in awe."
—*Washington Post Book World*

"Subtle. . . . Nobody will read her profound, delicate, and accessible confessions without identifying with her."
—*New York Times Book Review*

"Moving . . . morally thrilling . . . will be treasured by all concerned about the fate of the planet and its inhabitants . . . compelling and inspiring."
—*Publishers Weekly* (starred review)

"An inspirational story of faith and love from the amazing life of Dr. Goodall."
—*Indianapolis Star*

"An important message, and the way she tells it is particularly valuable. . . .Goodall is one of the few to tell us there is, indeed, reason for hope."
—*Salon.com*

"Thrilling to read. . . . Part memoir, part educational venture, part spiritual testimony . . . alive with scenes from Gombe, Tanganyika. . . . REASON FOR HOPE gives us a startling look backward at where we, the chimpanzees, and the whole 'green movement' have come from."
—*Los Angeles Daily News*

"Jane Goodall is that rare thing, a celebrity scientist, and now she has given us a rarer thing, an inspirational book that is truly inspiring. . . . Striking . . . a powerful message."
—*Cincinnati Enquirer*

"A very thought-provoking and wonderful read. . . . Goodall blends a disarming humility and sense of wonder at the natural world with a determined belief that humankind is capable of doing better."
—*Library Journal* (starred review)

more . . .

P9-CEH-841

"A poignant, highly readable memoir, the book is a quiet treasure."
—*Atlanta Journal-Constitution*

"Surprisingly optimistic...part memoir, part science, part spiritual and both enjoyable and stimulating."
—*Milwaukee Journal Sentinel*

"By the middle of the book I was hooked and by the time I finished I was convinced that I had just read one of the best books I would encounter for a long time."
—*Louisville Courier-Journal* (KY)

"A charming, often passionate account of her work with chimpanzees, her spiritual journey, and her conflicted feelings of the despair and hope for a troubled world."
—*Hartford Courant*

"Goodall is a rare creature accomplishing great things. . . . Honest and often elegant. . . . Goodall, with the help of religious scholar Berman, sets down the spiritual and ethical lights that serve as guides in her rather extraordinary life."
—*Kirkus Reviews*

"A poignant, highly readable memoir."
—*Fort Worth Star-Telegram*

"The greatest pleasures of REASON FOR HOPE are the passages about the chimpanzees and her insights into spirituality . . . brimming with emotional and philosophical views. . . . What makes her book such a delight is her unbridled, intelligent optimism. . . . She is a beautiful role model for these sometimes ugly days."
—*BookPage*

"Even if you have read her other books, this book offers a fresh perspective and offers 'reasons for hope' for all of us that we must develop our own alternatives to aggression and social disorganization."
—*Southern Pines Pilot* (NC)

"It's hard not to be impressed with her moral and intellectual integrity and her lucid, easy-to-read, and logical prose. . . . Anyone interested in nature and the world of animals will be fascinated by Goodall's REASON FOR HOPE."
—*Grand Rapids Press*

"Takes readers along with her to a cathedral in the wilderness. . . . Well worth reading for the thrilling world of the Gombe preserve, for the honesty and huge heart of this woman who spends her days working to keep the wild alive. It takes its place among a burgeoning library of books on our relationship to wildness, to our fellow creatures and the connection between them and the holy."
—*San Jose Mercury News*

"A remarkable surprise. . . . She writes of her life's work and loves and of her own philosophical journey in her trademark no-nonsense yet often lyrical style."
—Hamilton Spectator (Ontario, Canada)

"The most important aspect of the book is its deft and timely message of the compatibility between religious faith and scientific knowledge. . . . The chimpanzee material is fascinating, delving into the personal lives and quirks of our nearest evolutionary relatives. Recommended."
—Austin American-Statesman

"Without preaching, REASON FOR HOPE is inspiration to take action now to save the planet."
—Winnipeg Free Press

"Shines in numerous places. Mrs. Goodall has lived an exciting life."
—World

"A powerful book that will change the mind of anyone who has felt one person cannot make a difference."
—Winston-Salem Journal (NC)

"A scalding indictment of rich nations whose greed and waste are depleting the earth."
—Springfield Union-News (MA)

"It's thrilling to read. . . . Goodall's role in radically altering our perception of human and animal life is presented clearly."
—Book

"The extraordinary scientist of the chimpanzee studies explores her extraordinary life."
—Sullivan County Democrat

"Soul-baring. . . . Throughout her 39-year career, the eminent chimpanzee researcher has risked her scientific reputation . . . by recording simple truths. . . . Today Goodall challenges the prevailing notion that the pursuit of science precludes a belief in God. . . . In so doing, she reveals her own religious beliefs, inspiration, despair, and explorations of worlds beyond the one we know."
—New Age

"A wonderful glimpse into an extraordinary life, a life some may only dream of living."
—Satya

Also by Jane Goodall

Books for Adults
The Chimpanzees of Gombe: Patterns of Behavior
In the Shadow of Man
Innocent Killers (with Hugo van Lawick)
Through a Window
Visions of Caliban: On Chimpanzees and People
(with Dale Peterson)

Books for Children
The Chimpanzee Family
The Chimpanzee Family Book
Grub the Bush Baby
My Friends the Wild Chimpanzees
My Life with the Chimpanzees
With Love

REASON
FOR HOPE
A SPIRITUAL JOURNEY

JANE
GOODALL

WITH PHILLIP BERMAN

GRAND CENTRAL
PUBLISHING

NEW YORK   BOSTON

Copyright © 1999 by Soko Publications Ltd. and Phillip Berman
Epilogue copyright © 2003 by Soko Publications Ltd.
All rights reserved. Except as permitted under the U.S. Copyright Act of 1976, no
part of this publication may be reproduced, distributed, or transmitted in any form or
by any means, or stored in a database or retrieval system, without the prior written
permission of the publisher.

Grand Central Publishing
Hachette Book Group
1290 Avenue of the Americas
New York, NY 10104

www.HachetteBookGroup.com

Printed in the United States of America

Originally published in hardcover by Hachette Book Group.

First Trade Edition: October 2000
23

Grand Central Publishing is a division of Hachette Book Group, Inc.
The Grand Central Publishing name and logo is a trademark of Hachette Book Group, Inc.
The publisher is not responsible for websites (or their content) that are not owned by
the publisher.
The Library of Congress has cataloged the hardcover edition as follows:

Goodall, Jane
    Reason for hope : a spiritual journey / Jane Goodall with Phillip
Berman.
        p.   cm.
    ISBN 978-0-446-52225-0
        1. Goodall, Jane, 1934–   . 2. Spiritual biography—England.
I. Berman, Phillip L. II. Title.
QL31.G58A3   1999
590'.92—dc21
    [B]   99-25611
                                                                     CIP

ISBN 978-0-446-67613-7 (pbk.)

Book design by Giorgetta Bell McRee
Cover design by Jackie Merri Meyer and Flag
Cover photo illustration by Franco Arcornero
Photo reference by Michael Neugebauer

For Vanne, Judy, and all my wonderful family.

And in vivid memory of Danny, Derek, Louis, Rusty, and David Greybeard.

©Steve Bloom

ACKNOWLEDGMENTS

Before moving on to the beginning of my story I want to express my heartfelt gratitude to the hundreds of people who have helped me along the way. When we were small my sister, Judy, and I had a story read to us every night. There was one that I loved about the time when the birds decided to have a competition to see who could fly the highest. Well, of course the mighty eagle was sure that he would win. He flew slowly, gradually gaining height. Higher and higher he rose until he had passed all the others, until even he could fly no higher. And at just that moment a little jenny wren, who had hidden in the feathers on his back, flew up—and won the competition.

What a marvelous allegory. For I too have ridden on the back of an eagle—an eagle whose every feather is someone who has helped me. My nanny. My teachers and friends at school, the students and field staff at Gombe, the board members and staff of the Jane Goodall Institute, all my wonderful friends around the world.

ACKNOWLEDGMENTS

The people who have been there to reach out a helping hand, to comfort and encourage when things went wrong, those who have provided inspiration and helped me to find the energy to continue. And there are so many whose names or even faces I do not know. For one's attitude can be changed by a passing conversation, a passage in a book. Hundreds—no, thousands—of human beings, yes, and animals too, have helped me to reach this point in time and space. How grateful I am to each and every one of them, and I only wish I had the space to list the names of all those who have helped me so much throughout the years.

At the very heart of everything I've done is my remarkable family: my grandmother Danny, my sister Judy, and my amazing mother, Vanne. Vanne has been there for me from the start, helping, comforting, and encouraging me to new endeavors.

I would also like to thank those who have played a specific role in the making of this book: Phillip, for his idea and all his hard work; Jamie Raab, our editor, for her patience and understanding; Jonathon Lazear, our agent, for his wisdom and good advice; and Catherine Allan and her staff at KTCA and the generous people at Tom's of Maine, who have worked so diligently to make possible the companion public broadcasting television special based on this book.

So many feathers on the eagle. For my eagle, of course, is the symbol of the great spiritual power that I believe carries us all. That supports us when our commitment and determination are put to the test. From which, if we will, we can gain strength and new energy even when we are at our most exhausted. If we have faith, and if we ask.

CONTENTS

(Courtesy of the estate of Michio Hoshino)

This photo was taken by Michio Hoshino, who visited Gombe to plan an extended photographic study. Tragically, he was killed by a bear in Russia before he could realize this dream.

INTRODUCTION

Many years ago, in the spring of 1974, I visited the cathedral of Notre Dame in Paris. There were not many people around, and it was quiet and still inside. I gazed in silent awe at the great Rose Window, glowing in the morning sun. All at once the cathedral was filled with a huge volume of sound: an organ playing magnificently for a wedding taking place in a distant corner. Bach's Toccata and Fugue in D Minor. I had always loved the opening theme; but in the cathedral, filling the entire vastness, it seemed to enter and possess my whole self. It was as though the music itself was alive.

That moment, a suddenly captured moment of eternity, was perhaps the closest I have ever come to experiencing ecstasy, the ecstasy of the mystic. How could I believe it was the chance gyrations of bits of primeval dust that had led up to that moment in time—the cathedral soaring to the sky; the collective inspiration and faith of those who caused it to be built; the advent of Bach himself; the brain, his brain, that translated truth into music; and the mind that could, as mine did then, comprehend the whole inexorable progression of evolution? Since I cannot believe that this was the result of chance, I have to admit anti-chance. And so I must believe in a guiding power in the universe—in other words, I must believe in God.

I was taught, as a scientist, to think logically and empirically, rather than intuitively or spiritually. When I was at Cambridge University in the early 1960s most of the scientists and science students working in the Department of Zoology, so far as I could tell, were agnostic or even atheist. Those who believed in a God kept it hidden from their peers.

Fortunately, by the time I got to Cambridge I was twenty-seven years old and my beliefs had already been molded so that I was not influenced by these opinions. I believed in the spiritual power that, as a Christian, I called God. But as I grew older and learned about different faiths I came to believe that there was, after all, but One God with different names: Allah, Tao, the Creator, and so on. God, for me, was the Great Spirit in Whom "we live and move and have our being." There have been times during my life when this belief wavered, when I questioned—even denied—the existence of God. And there have been times when I have despaired that we humans can ever get out of the environmental and social mess which we have created for ourselves and other life-forms on the planet. Why is the human species so destructive? So selfish and greedy and, sometimes, truly evil? At such times I feel there can be no underlying meaning to the emergence of life on earth. And if there is no meaning, doesn't this suggest, as a bitter New York skinhead once put it, that the human species is simply an "evolutionary goof"?

Still, for me those periods of doubt have been relatively rare, triggered by a variety of circumstances—such as when my second husband died of cancer; when the ethnic hatred erupted in the little country of Burundi and I heard terrible tales of torture and mass killings that reminded me of the unspeakable evils of the Holocaust; when four of my students studying in Gombe National Park in Tanzania were kidnapped and held for ransom. How, I asked myself on such occasions, how can I be expected to believe in some divine plan in the face of so much suffering, so much hatred, so much destruction? Yet somehow I overcame those periods of doubt; most of the time I am optimistic about the future. There are, however, many people today who have lost whatever faith and hope they had, whether in God or human destiny.

Since 1986 I have been traveling almost constantly. I do this to raise funds for the various conservation and educational projects of the Jane Goodall Institute, and to share with as many people as possible a message that I feel is desperately important. A message that concerns the nature of human beings and our relationship to the other animals with whom we share the planet. And a message of hope—hope for the future of life on earth. These tours are exhausting. During a recent (and typical) seven-week tour in North America, for example, I went to twenty-seven cities, climbed on and off a total of thirty-two airplanes (on which I tried to catch up on the ever increasing mounds of paperwork), and gave seventy-one lectures—speaking directly to about 32,500 people. In addition I gave 170 media interviews and had many business meetings, lunches, dinners—even breakfasts. All my lecture tours have similarly crazy schedules.

In the course of my travels, one thing detracts from my enjoyment of meeting people. I suffer from an embarrassing, curiously humbling neurological condition called *prosopagnosia*, which, translated, means I have problems in face recognition. I used to think it was due to some mental laziness, and I tried desperately to memorize the faces of people I met so that, if I saw them the next day, I would recognize them. I had no trouble with those who had obvious physical characteristics—unusual bone structure, beaky nose, extreme beauty or the opposite. But with other faces I failed, miserably. Sometimes I knew that people were upset when I did not immediately recognize them—certainly I was. And because I was embarrassed, I kept it to myself.

Quite by chance, when talking to a friend recently, I found that he suffered from the same problem. I could not believe it. Then I discovered my own sister, Judy, knew similar embarrassment. Perhaps others did, also. I wrote to the well-known neurologist Dr. Oliver Sacks. Had he ever heard of such an unusual condition? Not only had he heard of it—he suffered from it himself! And his situation was far more extreme than mine. He sent me a paper, titled "Developmental memory impairment: faces and patterns," by Christine Temple.

Even now that I know I need not feel guilty, it is still difficult to know how to cope—I can hardly go 'round telling everyone I meet that I probably won't know them from Adam next time I see them! Or maybe I should? It is humiliating, because most people simply think I'm making an elaborate excuse for my failure to recognize them and that, obviously, I don't really care about them at all—so they are hurt. I have to cope as best I can—usually by pretending to recognize everyone! And while that can have its awkward moments too, it's not nearly as bad as the other way around.

People (whether I recognize them or not!) are always asking where I find my energy. They also comment on how peaceful I seem. How can I be so peaceful? they ask. Do I meditate? Am I religious? Do I pray? Most of all they ask how I can be so optimistic in the face of so much environmental destruction and human suffering; in the face of overpopulation and overconsumption, pollution, deforestation, desertification, poverty, famine, cruelty, hatred, greed, violence, and war. Does she really believe what she says? they seem to be wondering. What does she really think, deep down? What is her philosophy of life? What is the secret ingredient for her optimism, her hope?

I wrote this book to address these questions; because maybe the answers will be helpful. It has required a lot of soul searching, reawakened periods of my life that I prefer not to think about, caused pain. But I have tried to write my story honestly—else why write the book at all? If you, the reader, find some aspect of my own personal philosophy and faith that is at all useful or enlightening to you as you travel your own unique path, then my labor will not have been in vain.

Chapter 1

BEGINNINGS

THIS IS A STORY ABOUT A JOURNEY, the journey of one human being through sixty-five years of earth time: my journey. Traditionally, a story begins at the beginning. But what is the beginning? Is it the moment when I was born, with all the charming ugliness of the newborn human baby, in a hospital in London? The first breath I drew so that I could yell about the pain and indignity of my forced expulsion from the womb? Or should we start earlier, in the dark, moist secret place where one little wiggling sperm—one out of millions—managed to burrow into one little ovum—the fertile egg that was biologically, magically, transformed into a baby? But that, really, is not the beginning. For the genes that were handed down to me by my parents were created long, long ago. And my inherited traits were molded by the people and the events surrounding my early years: the characters and position of my parents, the country into which I was born, and the era in which I grew up. So should the story start with my parents, with the historical and social events that shaped Europe in the 1930s, that molded Hitler and Churchill and Stalin? Or perhaps we should go back to the first truly human creature that was born of ape-men parentage, or back to the first little warm-blooded mammal? Or should we go back and back through the mists of unknown time to when the first speck of life appeared on planet earth—as a result of some divine purpose or cosmic accident? From there we could start my story, tracing the strange paths that life has taken: from amoeba, through apes, to minds that can contemplate the existence of a God, and strive to understand the meaning of life on earth and beyond the stars.

I do not want to discuss evolution in such depth, however, only touch on it from my own perspective: from the moment when I stood on the Serengeti plains holding the fossilized bones of ancient creatures in my hands to the moment when, staring into the eyes of a chimpanzee, I saw a thinking, reasoning personality looking back. You may not believe in evolution, and that is all right. How we humans came to be the way we are is far less important than how we should act now to get out of the mess we have made for ourselves. How should the mind that can contemplate God relate to our fellow beings, the other life-forms of the world? What is our human responsibility? And what, ultimately, is our human destiny? It will serve my purpose to begin, simply, from the time when I drew my first breath and screwed up my face to cry my first cry, on April 3, 1934.

Through the years I have encountered people and been involved in events that have had huge impact, knocked off rough corners, lifted me to the heights of joy, plunged me into the depth of sorrow and anguish, taught me to laugh, especially at myself—in other words, my life experiences and the people with whom I shared them have been my teachers. At times I have felt like a help-less bit of flotsam, at one moment stranded in a placid backwater that knew not, cared not, that I was there, then swept out to be hurled about in an unfeeling sea. At other times I felt I was being sucked under by strong, unknowing currents toward annihilation. Yet somehow, looking back through my life, with its downs and its ups, its despairs and its joys, I believe that I was following some overall plan—though to be sure there were many times when I strayed from the course. Yet I was never truly lost. It seems to me now that the flotsam speck was being gently nudged or fiercely blown along a very spe-cific route by an unseen, intangible Wind. The flotsam speck that was—that is—me.

Without a shadow of a doubt my upbringing, the fam-ily into which I was born and the events that unfolded in the world around my childhood, shaped the person I would become. I grew up, with my sister, Judy (four years younger than I to the day), in an atmosphere that had become gently permeated by the ethics of Christian-ity. Our family's religion was never rammed down our throats, we were never forced to attend church, and we did not say grace before our meals (except at school). However, we were expected to say our prayers at night, kneeling on the floor at the side of the bed. From the be-ginning we were taught the importance of human values such as courage, honesty, compassion, and tolerance.

Like most children before the age of TV and computer games, I loved being outside, playing in the secret places in the garden, learning about nature. My love of living things was encouraged, so that from the very beginning I was able to develop that sense of wonder, of awe, that can lead to spiritual awareness. We were by no means a wealthy family, but money was not important. It didn't matter that we couldn't afford a car, or even a bicycle, or expensive holidays abroad—we had enough to eat, some clothes to wear, and an abundance of love, laughter, and fun. Indeed, mine was the very best kind of childhood: because every penny mattered, everything that was extra such as an ice cream, a journey on a train, a cinema, was a treat, exciting, to be treasured and remembered. If only everyone could be blessed with such a childhood, such a family. How different, I believe, the world would be.

As I look back over the sixty-five years of my life to date it seems that things just fell into place. I had a mother who not only tolerated but also encouraged my passion for nature and animals and who, even more important, taught me to believe in myself. Everything led in the most natural way, it seems now, to that magical invitation to Africa in 1957, where I would meet Dr. Louis Leakey, who would set me on my way to Gombe and the chimpanzees. Indeed, I have been extraordinarily lucky—although as my mother, Vanne, always says, luck was only part of the story. She has always believed, as did *her* mother, that success comes through determination and hard work and that "the fault . . . is not in our stars but in ourselves that we are underlings." I certainly believe that is true. Yet though I have worked hard all my life—for who wants to be an "underling" if it can be avoided!—I must admit that the "stars" seem to have played their part too. After all, I didn't strive (so far as I know) to be born into my own wonderful home. And then there was Jubilee, bought for me as a present by my father (Mortimer "Mort" Goodall), when I was just over one year old. Jubilee was a large, stuffed chimpanzee toy, created to celebrate the birth of Jubilee, the first chimpanzee infant ever born at the London Zoo. My mother's friends were horrified by this toy, thinking it would frighten me and give me nightmares. But Jubilee instantly became my most cherished possession and accompanied me on nearly all my childhood adventures. To this day, old Jubilee is still with me, almost hairless from all the loving, spending most of his time in my bedroom in the house where I grew up in England.

I was always absolutely fascinated by animals of all sorts. Yet I was born right in the heart of London, where animals were limited to dogs and cats, sparrows, pigeons, and some insect life in the small garden shared by the inhabitants of the mews where we lived. Even when we moved to a house just outside the city, from where my father would commute each day to his engineering job, nature was subjugated to pavement, houses, and manicured gardens.

My mother, Vanne, now aged ninety-four, has always loved to tell stories about my early fascination with animals and concern for their welfare. One of her favorites is of the time when, around the age of eighteen months, I collected a whole handful of earthworms from the London garden and took them to bed with me.

"Jane," she said, staring at the wriggling collection, "if you keep them here they'll die. They need the earth."

So I hurriedly collected up all the worms and toddled back with them into the garden.

Soon after this, we went to stay with some friends who had a house near a wild rocky beach in Cornwall. When we went down to the sea I was enthralled by the tide pools and their teeming life. No one realized that the seashells I carried back to the house in my bucket were all alive. When Vanne came up to my room she found little bright yellow sea snails crawling everywhere—the bedroom floor, up the walls, behind the wardrobe. When she explained that the snails would die when taken from the sea, I became hysterical. The entire household, she says, had instantly to drop what it was doing and help me collect the snails so that they could be rushed back to the sea.

One story has been told many times because it shows how, even as a four-year-old, I already had the makings of a true naturalist. Vanne had taken me to stay with my father's mother, Mrs. Nutt (I called her Danny Nutt because I could not say "granny"), at the family farm. One of my tasks was to collect the hens' eggs. As the days passed, I became more and more puzzled. Where on a chicken was there an opening big enough for an egg to come out? Apparently no one explained this properly, so I must have decided to find out for myself. I followed a hen into one of the little wooden henhouses—but of course, as I crawled after her she gave horrified squawks and hurriedly left. My young brain must have then worked out that I would have to be there *first*. So I crawled into another henhouse and waited, hoping a hen would come in to lay. And there I remained, crouched silently in one corner, concealed in some straw, waiting. At last a hen came in, scratched about in the straw, and settled herself on her makeshift nest just in front of me. I must have kept very still or she would have been disturbed. Presently the hen half stood and I saw a round white object gradually protruding from the feathers between her legs. Suddenly with a plop, the egg landed on the straw. With clucks of pleasure the hen shook her feathers, nudged the egg with her beak, and left. It is quite extraordinary how clearly I remember that whole sequence of events.

Filled with excitement I squeezed out after her and ran home. It was almost dark—I had been in that small stuffy henhouse for nearly four hours. I was oblivious of the fact that no one had known where I was, and that the whole household had been searching for me. They had even called the police to report me missing. Yet despite her worry, when Vanne, still searching, saw the excited little girl rushing toward the house, she did not scold me.

She noticed my shining eyes and sat down to listen to the story of how a hen lays an egg: the wonder of that moment when the egg finally fell to the ground.

Certainly I was lucky to be provided with a mother wise enough to nurture and encourage my love of living things and my passion for knowledge. Most important was her philosophy that her children should always try their very best. How would I have turned out, I sometimes wonder, had I grown up in a house that stifled enterprise by imposing harsh and senseless discipline. Or in an atmosphere of overindulgence, in a household where there were no rules, no boundaries drawn. My mother certainly understood the importance of discipline, but she always explained *why* some things were not allowed. Above all, she tried to be fair and to be consistent.

When I was five years old and my sister, Judy, was one, we all went to live in France, as my father wanted very much for us to grow up speaking fluent French. But this was not to be, for, within a few months of our arrival, Hitler occupied Czechoslovakia, an act that would lead to World War II. It was decided that we should return to England, and since our house near London had been sold we went to stay with Danny Nutt in the old manor house where my father had grown up. Built of gray stone, it nestled into the Kent countryside, surrounded by fields of grazing cows and sheep. I passionately loved my time there. On the grounds of the manor house were the ruins of a castle where King Henry VIII had held one of his wives—crumbling blocks of gray stone filled with spiders and bats. Inside the manor house itself there was always the faint smell of the oil lamps that were lit each evening, for there was no electricity. Even now, more than sixty years later, the smell of oil lamps always takes me back to those magical days. But they did not last long. The impending horror of war was coming closer and, knowing my father would join the army at the first opportunity, Vanne took Judy and me to stay with her own mother at the Birches, an 1872 Victorian red-brick house in Bournemouth.

On September 3, 1939, it happened: England declared war on Germany. I was only five and a half years old at the time, yet I remember the occasion. The whole family was in the drawing room. The atmosphere was tense as everyone listened to the news on the wireless; after the announcement there was silence. Of course I didn't understand what was going on, but that silence, the sense of impending doom, was very frightening. Even now, half a century later, I cannot hear the chiming of Big Ben— which always preceded the BBC news—without an involuntary shock of apprehension.

As expected my father enlisted immediately, so the Birches, just a few minutes' walk from the English Channel, became my home. It was there, on the south coast of England, that I would spend the rest of my childhood and adolescence. Indeed, this much loved house is still my home, my refuge, when I am in England. It is where I am writing this book.

My maternal grandmother, known to all as Danny (again because I could not pronounce "granny"), was the undisputed head of the extended family that shared the Birches. She was a strong, self-disciplined, iron-willed Victorian who ruled over us with supreme authority and had a heart big enough to embrace all the starving children of the world. Her husband, a Welshman, had been a Congregational parson and had died before I was born. He had also been a brilliant scholar, receiving degrees in theology from three universities—Cardiff, Oxford, and Yale. And Danny, who survived him by more than thirty years, kept all his letters, tied up in red ribbon, and often read them before she slept. Also, she told us, she counted her blessings every night as she lay in bed, waiting for sleep. Above all, she had a horror of going to bed without making peace with those around her. There are always little upsets, minor rows, when many people live together—these should be resolved before bedtime; "Let not the sun set on thy wrath" she would quote. And to this day I hear her voice, when I quarrel with a friend: "How terrible you would feel if he (or she) should die before you made it up, before you said *sorry*." I think that is why the words of Walter de la Mare strike home when he bids us "Look thy last on all things lovely every hour."

We shared the Birches with my mother's two sisters, Olwen—immediately dubbed Olly by me—and Audrey, who preferred to be called by her Welsh name, Gwyneth. Their elder brother, Uncle Eric, who was a surgeon, came home from his hospital in London most weekends. And soon after the start of the war we took in two single women who, like hundreds of others, were left homeless by the ever-spreading chaos and destruction in Europe. All households were asked to find space for such unfortunates. And so the Birches, at that time, was an active place, filled with people of all sorts. We simply had to learn to get along with each other. The house had (and still has) a warm atmosphere; it was full of character and, despite the number of people, filled with peace. Best of all there was a big garden or backyard with many trees, and a green lawn and lots of secret places behind the bushes where, of course, gnomes and fairies lived and danced in the moonlight. My love for nature grew as I watched birds making their nests, spiders carrying their egg sacs, squirrels chasing each other round the trees.

My memories of childhood are almost inseparable from memories of Rusty, an endearing black mongrel dog with a white patch on his chest. He was my constant companion, and he taught me so much about the true nature of animals. There were other pets too at different times. A succession of cats, our two guinea pigs, a golden hamster, various tortoises, a terrapin, and a canary, Peter, who slept in a cage but was free to fly about the room in the daytime. For a while Judy and I each had our own "racing" snails with numbers painted on their shells. We kept them in an old wooden box with a piece of glass on the top and no bottom so they could eat the dandelion leaves as we moved the box around the lawn.

In one part of the garden there was a little clearing behind some thick bushes where Judy and I established a "camp" for the meetings of our club, a club which had just four members, we two and our best friends Sally and Susie Cary, who came to stay every summer holiday. In the camp we kept an old trunk containing four mugs, small supplies of cocoa and tea, and a spoon. We would light a fire and boil water in a tin can balanced on four rocks. Sometimes we went there for midnight "feasts"; during the war years almost everything was rationed, so we seldom had more than a biscuit or a crust of bread saved from our meals. It was the excitement, the silent creeping from the house, the lawn and trees ghostly in the moonlight, that we loved. Our feeling of achievement as we defied the rules provided the fun, not the insignificant bits and pieces that we gathered to eat. To this day, food is supremely unimportant to me.

Like most children who grow up in happy homes, I never had cause to question the religious beliefs of my family. Did God exist? Of course. God was as real to me then as the wind that rustled through the trees in our garden. God somehow cared for a magical world, full of fascinating animals and people who were mostly friendly and kind. It was an enchanted world for me, full of joy and wonder, and I felt very much a part of it.

Danny went to church every Sunday and at least one

of us always went with her. Indeed, Audrey never missed a service, and Olly sang in the choir. But we children were never forced to go with them, nor did we go to Sunday School. Nevertheless, Danny tried to make sure that our beliefs weren't limited to the animistic worship of nature and animals. She believed deeply in God the Father, God the Son, and God the Holy Spirit. She wanted Judy and me to share her belief for the comfort it would bring. And so she did her best to ensure that the ethics and wisdom of Christ's teachings influenced our lives. The rules that we had to obey were the simple ones contained in the Ten Commandments. She would sometimes quote texts from the Bible. Her very favorite, which I took as my own, was: "As thy days, so shall thy strength be." This has helped me through the hardest times of my life. Somehow we *shall* find the strength to get through a day of unhappiness, of suffering, of heartache. Somehow, I always have.

As a child I was not at all keen on going to school. I dreamed about nature, animals, and the magic of far-off wild and remote places. Our house was filled with bookshelves and the books spilled out onto the floor. When it was wet and cold, I would curl up in a chair by the fire and lose myself in other worlds. My very favorite books at the time were *The Story of Dr. Dolittle, The Jungle Book,* and the marvelous Edgar Rice Burroughs Tarzan books. I also loved *The Wind in the Willows,* and, to this day, I remember the beautiful and mystical experience shared by Ratty and Mole when they found the missing otter cub curled up between the cloven hoofs of the sylvan god, Pan. And I was enthralled by one other book: *At the Back of the North Wind*—a story full of Victorian moralizing that would make no sense to the children of today. Little Diamond, its boy hero, slept in a loft above Big Diamond, the cab horse upon whom the family, which was poor, de-pended for its livelihood. The icy north wind blew into Little Diamond's loft, and then appeared to the boy as a beautiful woman, sometimes small as a tinkerbell, sometimes tall as an elm tree. Then she would take him to see the world, safe in the still place behind the wind, curled into a nest that she made for him in her beautiful, long, thick hair. It was magic, mystical, and it introduced me to human suffering in story form, preparing me, in a way, for the real-life suffering of war. For the war was raging in Europe and, all too soon, it would make itself felt even in sleepy Bournemouth.

More and more often we would hear the drone of a German plane and the thunder of an exploding bomb. We were fortunate, as nothing fell close enough to do damage. But the windows rattled loudly, and some panes of glass were cracked. How well I still remember the wailing of the air-raid warnings. They usually sounded sometime in the night for that was when the bombers came over. Then we had to leave our beds and huddle together in the little air-raid shelter that was erected in our house in the small room (once a maid's bedroom) that, even today, is known as the "air-raid." It was a low, steel-roofed cage about six feet by five feet and only four feet high. Thousands of these were issued to households who were living in potential danger zones. And there we had to stay—sometimes as many as six adults as well as we two children—until the welcome sound of the "All Clear."

By the time I was seven I was used to news of battles, of defeats and of victories. Knowledge of man's inhumanity to man became more real as the newspapers and radio hinted at unspeakable horrors perpetrated on the Jews of Europe and the cruelties of Hitler's Nazi regime. Although my own life was still filled with love and security, I was slowly becoming aware of another kind of world altogether, a harsh and bitter world of pain and death and human cruelty. And although we were among the luckiest, far away from the horror of massive bombings, nevertheless, signs of war were all around: Our own father, far away and in uniform, somewhere in the jungles of Singapore. Uncle Eric and Olly setting off on air-raid duty, out into the dark night when the air-raid warning sounded. Audrey working as a land girl. The blackout that dominated our lives every evening. The American soldiers with their tanks who occupied the road outside the Birches. One of them became a real friend, but then went off to the front with his regiment and was, like so many hundreds, killed.

Even we had one narrow escape. It was during the fourth summer of the war. Judy and I, with our best friends Sally and Susie, were spending a week's holiday a few miles along the coast where one could actually get onto the sand (England was prepared for a possible German invasion, so most of the coastline was barricaded by miles and miles of barbed wire). One day, as our mothers sat on the sand and we children played, Vanne suddenly decided to take a different route back to our little guest house—a very long way around that meant we would miss lunch. But she was determined. Ten minutes after we set off, and as we were walking over some sand dunes, we heard the faint sound of a plane flying very high, heading south toward the sea. I can still remember, absolutely vividly, gazing up and seeing two tiny black objects, looking no bigger than cigars at that height, dropping from the plane into the blue, blue sky. German bombers often dumped their bombs along the coast if they had not managed to get rid of them on designated targets. It was safer when they met our planes on their way home. I can still remember the two mothers telling us to lie down, then trying to shield us with their bodies.

I can still recall the terrifying explosions as the bombs hit the ground. And one of them made a deep crater halfway up the lane—exactly where we would have been but for Vanne's premonition.

When the war finally ended in Europe on May 7, 1945, the grim rumors about the Nazi death camps were confirmed. The first photographs appeared in the newspapers. I was eleven years old at the time, very impressionable and imaginative. Although the family would like to have spared me the horrifying Holocaust pictures, I had never been prevented from reading the newspapers and they did not stop me then. Those photographs had a profound impact on my life. I could not erase the images of walking skeletons with their deep-sunk eyes, their faces almost expressionless. I struggled to comprehend the agony of body and mind these survivors had gone through, and that of all the hundreds of thousands who had perished. I still remember seeing, with shock, a photo of dead bodies piled on top of one another in a huge mound. That such things could happen made no sense. All the evil aspects of human nature had been given free rein, all the values I had been taught—the values of kindness and decency and love—had been disregarded. I can remember wondering if it was really true—how could human beings do such unspeakable things to other human beings? It made me think of the Spanish Inquisition, and all the medieval tortures that I had once read about. And the terrible suffering that had been inflicted on black slaves (I had once seen a picture of rows of Africans chained in the galleys, a brutal-looking overseer standing with an upraised whip in his hand). I began to wonder, for the first time, about the nature of God. If God was good and all powerful as I had been led to believe, how could He allow so many innocent people to suffer and die? Thus the Holocaust dramatically introduced me to the age-old problem of good and evil. This was not an abstract theological problem in 1945; it was a very real question that we had to face as the horror stories mounted.

I found that things were not as clear-cut as they once had seemed; that life was full of ambiguity and contradictions. The Holocaust unsettled me deeply. All my life I have felt compelled to buy books about the Nazis and the death camps. How could people behave that way? How could anyone endure and survive such torture? It seems I have been asking these questions my entire life.

Uncle Eric, Audrey, Danny, Jane, Olly, and Judy

Chapter 2

PREPARATIONS

W<small>HEN</small> I <small>WAS</small> <small>TWELVE</small> <small>YEARS</small> <small>OLD</small> my parents divorced. Vanne, Judy, and I simply went on living at the Birches. Since I had seen my father only a few times during the long war years, and then just for a couple of days at a time when he returned on leave, nothing really seemed to change. By then, after all, the Birches had been my home for seven years.

I was working hard at school, for I enjoyed learning—at least, learning about the subjects that interested me such as the English language, English literature, history, Scripture, and biology. And I went on reading out of school as well. Among the hundreds of volumes at the Birches were many philosophy books that had belonged to my grandfather. I was fascinated by these ancient tomes, many of which were printed in a lovely old Gothic typeface. As well as reading I loved writing stories, and I also wrote a lot of poetry, mostly about nature and the joy of being alive. I lived for the weekends and the school holidays because then, with Rusty, I could be outside, roaming the cliffs that rose from the seashore, with their sandy, pine-covered slopes. In the late spring they were bright yellow with gorse bushes in bloom, and in the summer, a blaze of mauve and crimson rhododendrons. There were squirrels and all manner of birds and insects. And the freedom of it!

I shall never forget the thrill when, one day in early spring, I saw a weasel hunting mice in the heather on the cliffs above the sea. Or the hot summer evening when I watched a hedgehog, with much grunting and snuffling, courting his prickly mate. One magical afternoon in late autumn, I came upon a squirrel gathering and burying beechnuts. They would provide her with food when she periodically woke from her winter sleep. At least, that was the intention. But a jay, perched above her, flew down after each careful burial and robbed the cache. The sequence was repeated seven times; twice the squirrel actually watched the theft, then continued her profitless labor with unabated zeal. Once I glimpsed the russet coat of a fox, found his tracks in the January snow, saw how he had chased, and missed, a rabbit.

Although I loved being on my own with Rusty, I was by no means antisocial and sometimes I went out with a few girlfriends—coed schools were rare in those days, and mine was for girls only. I don't remember the exact games we played, but they all involved being outside on the cliffs or the beach. We loved to dare each other to perform somewhat dangerous acts, such as scrambling along a sandy slope above a steep drop. Once this almost resulted in tragedy. One girl started to slip, causing a little avalanche of sand to go tumbling down the cliff. She froze. She stopped sliding down but was unable to move in any direction for what seemed hours until, somehow, we talked her into taking the next step. We were all chastened by that experience and became a little less foolhardy. Although I could not know it at the time, all of this was, of course, perfect training for Gombe.

Most Saturdays I went to a riding school in the country owned by the remarkable Selina Bush, known as Bushel. Vanne could not afford to pay for me to ride every week so I used to clean the saddles and bridles, and muck out, and help on the farm. I worked so hard and so enthusiastically that I was often rewarded with a free ride. Most of Bushel's animals were small, hardy New Forest ponies who had been taken, as foals, from the herds that ran wild in the nearby forest. On them I gradually learned the art of horsemanship. One day, to my enormous delight, I was allowed to ride a show pony. Sometimes I went in for jumping competitions at local gymkhanas. And then I was offered the chance of going hunting. Fox hunting. How exciting! It meant that I would ride with the huntsmen in their "pink" coats, which in fact are red as red can be. There would be huge hedges and fences to jump; there would be the sound of the hunting horn. Most important, Bushel clearly believed my riding was good enough for such a challenge. I determined that I would not let her down.

I didn't think about the fox. And then, after three hours of hard riding, I saw him, bedraggled and exhausted, just before the hounds seized and tore him up. All the excitement was gone in that moment. How could I for even one moment have wanted to be part of this murderous and horrible event with a whole lot of grown-up people riding on horses, following in cars and on bicycles, while a great pack of baying dogs chased after one poor little fox? I remember lying awake that night thinking of the fox I had seen on the cliff, and of the other fox—the pathetic victim of the hunt. Certainly my cliff fox had been hunting too, but only because he needed food. Not for sport.

I have wondered a lot about that hunt. The very fact that I, an animal lover, had wanted to take part seems extraordinary now. What if I hadn't seen the fox at all? Would I have wanted to go again? What if we had lived in the country, and had horses of our own, and I had been expected to go hunting from an early age? Would I have grown up accepting that this was the thing to do? Would I have hunted foxes again and again, and watched dispassionately their suffering, "all pity choked by custom of fell deed"? Is this how it happens? We do what our friends do in order to be one of the group, to be accepted? Of course there are always some strong-minded individuals who have the courage of their convictions, who stand out against the group's accepted norms of behavior. But it is probably the case that inappropriate or morally wrong behaviors are more often changed by the influence of outsiders, looking with different eyes, from different backgrounds. Fortunately, I was not put to the test. None of my family's friends were of the hunting set, who are mostly from the landed gentry; I could drop out of the picture without causing even a lifted eyebrow. But I continued to love riding horses, and I did, to my shame, go hunting one more time many years later in Kenya.

Throughout my school days I spent many hours in the garden, often taking my homework into our little wooden summerhouse, or even up into the top of my favorite tree, Beech. I loved that tree—so much that I persuaded Danny to sign a piece of paper leaving it to me in her will! There, high above the ground, I could feel a part of the life of the tree, swaying when the wind blew strongly, close to the rustling of the leaves. The songs of the birds sounded different up there—clearer and louder. I could sometimes lay my cheek against the trunk and seem to feel the sap, the lifeblood of Beech, coursing below the rough bark. And I would read up there, in my own leafy and private world. I think I went through all the Tarzan books thirty feet or so above the ground. I was madly in love with the Lord of the Jungle, terribly jealous of his Jane. It was daydreaming about life in the forest with Tarzan that led to my determination to go to Africa, to live with animals and write books about them.

I also went up Beech simply to be by myself, to think. The horror of the war days, the Holocaust, the dropping of the atomic bombs had affected me deeply. I could not reconcile such evil with the existence of an all-good, all-powerful God, and so I had pushed religion out of my mind. I found more nourishment for my soul in nature than on the occasions—increasingly rare—when I went to church on Sundays. Then, suddenly, everything changed. A new parson was appointed to the Richmond Hill Congregational Church, the Reverend Trevor Davies, DD. He was highly intelligent, and his sermons were powerful and thought-provoking. Yet the message was always expressed with utmost simplicity. I could have listened to his voice for hours, with the underlying musical lilt of his native Welsh. I fell madly in love with him. I was fifteen years old, and in those days one could still be a child at that age. Although I imagined all manner of romantic adventures with the object of my passion, these did not include physical sex. It was platonic love, but no less powerful for all that. I flung myself into this new phase of my life with enormous enthusiasm. Suddenly no one had to encourage me to go to church—indeed, there were never enough services for my liking. And in order to get through the six bleak days between one Sunday and the next I would make excuses to walk at night past the Manse, past the lighted square of his study window, and, with luck, glimpse the top of his head as he wrote his sermons—at least, I presumed that was what he was doing.

Trevor held several theological degrees, and I felt I should try to learn something about the interests of my beloved. And so once again I dug out some of my grandfather's books and began to struggle with the writings of

Plato, Socrates, and other philosophers. Of course it was important that Trevor should know of my efforts and so, every so often, I rang the doorbell of the Manse to ask his advice and borrow one of his books. Then, clutching whatever he deemed suitable, I would return, ecstatic, with one of *his* very own books. One of those was about the philosophy of sensationalism. Outside your mind, I was informed, nothing existed, nothing was real. Chairs, tables, trees, other people: there was no way to prove that any material object existed; therefore we should assume it did not. My sixteen-year-old mind found this utterly absurd. I immediately wrote a humorous little poem on the subject and put a copy in the book when I gave it back to Trevor. To my huge disappointment he never mentioned it—he probably never opened the book.

REDUCTIO AD ABSURDUM

(Lines written after reading the philosophy of Hume)

Now if you take an orange
    And hold it in your hand,
It isn't really there at all—
    Or so I understand.
A sensationalist will prove to you
    That though you know it's there,
It's only just sensations
    Of which you are aware.
Seeing, feeling, tasting, smelling,
    Sensations he will call,
And all these things exist in you
    Not in the fruit at all.
"Now eat it!" he may say to you,
    "Sensation once again."
(Though since he says it isn't there
    To eat would seem in vain!)

But still you feel he must be wrong
  And so you will persist,
And tell him plainly you're quite sure
  That matter does exist.
"It can't be seen or touched or heard
  And so it can't be known,
So why assume it's there at all
  When truth can ne'er be shown?"
Thus he'll reply, and after that
  Maybe he will declare
That you are only his sensation
  And so you can't be there.
"But I'm as real as you!" you cry—
  To this he must agree,
And so maintains that he himself
  Is unreality.
It follows thus that everything
  Which you would say exists,
Is non-existent and unreal
  To the sensationalists.
And therefore I will cease to write
  Since I cannot be here,
And none can ever read these lines
  For nobody is there!

At the Birches, this new phase of my life created a good deal of fun. I was teased unmercifully—as we always teased each other. And I enjoyed the teasing and played up to it too. I refused to wash my hand when Trevor had shaken it after a service. Once, when the text of his sermon was "the second mile" I did everything twice for the next week or so. I fetched not one, but two, buckets of coal. Made two pots of tea. Said good night to everyone twice over. Even had two baths, one after the other. I drove the family quite mad—especially Uncle Eric, who always stayed somewhat aloof from our fooling around.

Trevor was, without any doubt, a major influence in my life. The Christian religion came alive as I listened to his sermons; and once again I allowed thoughts of God and religion to permeate my life. I felt very close to Jesus, and I prayed to Him a good deal. I felt that He cared, and that He knew what I was up to. Jesus of Nazareth, the Lamb of God, the Light of the World, the Good Shepherd, the Messiah. And the Son of God. What did that mean? Again and again Jesus himself says that we are *all* sons and daughters of God. Even then I think I had a glimmering of what that meant. He told us to open our hearts and minds to the power of the Holy Ghost; and He told us that this would be difficult for those preoccupied with material possessions and the acquisition of power and wealth on earth, which wasn't very relevant to me. So, in the fervor of adolescence, I did my best to let the Holy Ghost creep into my being: in the church, as I listened to Trevor's sermons and gazed past him at the beautiful picture of Jesus with a lamb in his arms; as I sat high in Beech, close to the birds while the wind whispered in the leaves; as I lay in bed and looked at my favorite picture—of the Good Shepherd reaching down a steep precipice, at great danger to himself, to seize hold of one sheep, stuck on a rocky ledge. Yes, I believed in Jesus. And I believed in the miracles, for even then I had faith in the tremendous power of the human mind. I was sure that if I had known Jesus when He was on earth I would have been cured (if I had been sick) because I would have believed, implicitly, in His power to cure. And it is that absolute, unquestioning faith which can result in miracles. I could not put this to the test at that time of my life, however, for no sickness, no real sickness, came my way.

When I was sixteen my love for Jesus was so strong, my conviction that His presence was close by so vivid, that I was haunted by the agony of the Crucifixion, and His mental torment in the Garden of Gethsemane. I remember walking through the center of town, in Bournemouth, on a Good Friday and seeing people playing tennis. I was horrified: How could they possibly play tennis on the anniversary of Jesus' suffering and death? There was nothing remotely sanctimonious in this thought. I was so upset myself, and so convinced that Jesus would be saddened, that I was genuinely angry. I felt sure that they were mostly Christians, and should have understood.

I was, at the time, preoccupied with torture. Would I have the strength of mind to endure what Jesus and the martyrs suffered? How would I have withstood torture in the war? Could I have kept quiet to protect those I loved, those in my group, if nails pierced my flesh, if I was beaten, if I was on the rack? I didn't think I could endure, and I spent hours agonizing about it. Would I sacrifice my life for what I believed? There was, of course, no way I could be sure. To paraphrase what Eleanor Roosevelt once said: people are like tea bags; you never know how strong they are until you dump them in boiling water.

Something of my anguish shows in a long narrative poem I wrote at the time. Take these lines, for example:

> Eyes mad with fright, their lids torn off
> That, helpless, they must watch the red-hot iron
> Creep closer, closer, through the oozing blood
> Each fiber tight with horror for the end,
> The angry hiss as deep into each vital orb
> The red-hot metal bores. The scream that issues
> From the womb of agony herself.

Yet this was my idea of hell:

The margins of my Soul pressed each on each
And I was naught. And yet assigned, as *nothing*,
Existence to the end of time.

Sometimes I fantasized about becoming a martyr. We heard so much about Stalin and the cruelty of his dictatorship that I decided I would go to give support to the Christians in communist Russia, organize small groups of believers in secret, and help keep alive the flame of faith. And, of course, the communists would imprison and torture me for my beliefs. Imagining myself in a heroic role, enduring torment for my faith, helped me to stop worrying so much about how I would perform in real life. This daydreaming was part of my attempt to come to terms with human brutality and evil, human suffering, courage, idealism, and faith.

It was during this period that I started to read the Bible extensively and carefully—and was quite unable to believe everything I read there. For one thing there were parts that seemed downright illogical. I mean, why devote an entire chapter to tracing the lineage of Joseph, who, if the story of the virgin birth is to be believed, had absolutely nothing whatsoever to do with begetting Jesus? What was the point? It just didn't make any sense. And while I was willing to believe in the reality of some things that could not be proven, such as God—because I *knew* in my heart that God existed— I was unable to believe other things, such as the creation of the world in seven days, or Eve developing from Adam's rib. I could not believe that Communion bread and wine could become, literally, the flesh and blood of Christ, although I believed that if a person *did* believe that, then for that person it would really *seem* to be the flesh and blood of Christ. But did Jesus intend his words to be taken literally? Surely not—surely Jesus meant the eating and drinking to be symbolic? And so I came to realize that my belief in God and in Christ had its own meaning for me, personally, outside the words of the Bible; which, for the very devout, is tantamount to heresy. I once read that Thomas Jefferson came to the conclusion that the Bible was simply a compilation of the memories and thoughts of any number of people, some of whom had far more knowledge and far more wisdom than others. So he excerpted from the four Gospels all those passages he considered to be the most worthy and compelling, and used this considerably shortened version for his inspiration.

Despite my reservations I enjoyed reading the Bible, especially some of the marvelous stories in the Old Testament. Danny had what she called a blessings box: you took off the lid and there, inside, were neat little rolls of paper. With a special pair of tweezers you selected one, unrolled it, and read your text from the Bible. There were no more than thirty of these and whoever selected them had obviously intended they should soothe and comfort the reader. Only a few of them were challenging or called you to action. So I decided to make another box myself. This project took far longer than I had anticipated. "If you are going to do something, do it as well as you possibly can." I'm not sure who said that, but the words were part of our lives. And so I had to work hard on my Bible box. In order that my selection of texts should be comprehensive, I read through the entire Bible, Old and New Testaments, from cover to cover, picking out the verses that I felt were suitable. I wrote these neatly on little strips of paper about one quarter of an inch high and three to four inches long. When they were done I rolled them up tightly and arranged them in six matchboxes. I glued these together to form a little chest with six drawers, each of which could be pulled open with a tiny brass ring. There were some twenty texts in each of the drawers. Finally I covered the outside of the chest with dark blue paper and stuck a tiny, exquisite nativity scene on the top.

I well remember making this box. Much of it was done in bed, late at night, so as to keep it a secret from the rest of the family, for I have always loved surprises. It was ready just in time for Christmas and I put it in Danny's stocking at the end of her bed. Judy and I, when eventually we had realized that Father Christmas was not for real, used to make, or save up and buy, little gifts so that each member of the family could have a Christmas stocking. We would take them each a cup of tea very early in the morning and quietly lay their filled stockings at the end of their beds. Of course Danny loved her Bible box, and wept over it as she wept over everything that moved her. My whole family always has. We call it "kinking"—a Yorkshire expression from Danny's childhood.

We still have that little box, and frequently we open one of its six drawers, pull out a scroll at random, and read it. I love the element of surprise—you never know what gift of comfort, inspiration, or admonition you'll pull out. I picked one out this morning: *Stand still and consider the wondrous works of God* (Job 13, verse 4). I asked Olly to pick one, and hers was *Are not five sparrows sold for two farthings, and not one of them is forgotten before God* (Luke 12, verse 6). And then Vanne's *Let him that is athirst come. And whosoever will, let him take the water of life freely* (Revelation 22, verse 17).

One of the reasons I enjoyed reading the Bible was, I think, because of the sheer poetic beauty of much of the prose—much of which is lost in the modernized version. I loved poetry and read a great deal. I had catholic tastes, but at that time I was especially enamored of the works of Francis Thompson, Keats, Shakespeare, Milton, Robert Browning, and Alfred Noyes. And the war poets such as Rupert Brooke and Wilfred Owen. I was also in love with the poetry of Walter de la Mare. Because we could never afford new books, I used to spend hours in secondhand bookshops, browsing in the poetry section. I loved the feel of those with soft leather covers, and bought as many as I could find—and afford. I had an entire row of them—my "squidgy poets"—in my room. (They are in the sitting room of the Birches today.) Many evenings I stayed up late reading these poets—or working on a poem of my own, for one of my dreams then was to become, one day, Poet Laureate of England. The themes of my early poems ranged widely. Some were playful, but many, like "The Duck," combined my love for the natural world with my interest in spiritual topics.

THE DUCK

A duck that flew across the sun
    Flew on past me,
Winging his solitary way
    Towards the sea.

I saw the brightness of his eye
    So close he flew;
His feathers in the sunset gleamed
    With lustrous hue.

I heard the music of his wings,
    The song of flight
Stirring the stillness of a world
    Awaiting night.

I sensed the warm life in his breast
    So close to me
And in my heart the pain of joy
    That such could be.

The lovely dunes; the setting sun;
 The duck—and I;
One Spirit, moving timelessly
 Beneath the sky.

Clearly, at that time, I was starting to feel myself a part of a great unifying power of some kind. Certain things caused feelings of such profound happiness that tears would come to my eyes—"and in my heart the pain of joy that such could be." I never knew when such emotions would be triggered: an especially beautiful sunset; standing under the trees when the sun suddenly burst from behind a cloud and a bird sang; sitting in the absolute hush of some ancient cathedral. At moments such as those, I felt strongly that I was within some great spiritual power—God. And as I moved through life I would gradually learn how to seek strength from this Power, this source of all energy, to bolster my flagging spirits or my exhausted body in times of need.

In the meantime, this aspiring poet and martyr was about to leave school. What would I do next? We did not have enough money for university fees, and unless you were good at a foreign language (which I was not, and still am not) you could not get a scholarship. So, although my exam results were excellent, university was not an option. One of my father's sisters and her husband invited Vanne and me for a short visit to Germany, where Uncle Michael worked in the administration of the British sector of the defeated country. I think Vanne hoped the trip would teach me there were many ordinary Germans who were full of kindness and love, despite the bitter feelings of hatred toward Germany that gripped England in the aftermath of the two world wars.

While there, we went to the city of Cologne. Like so many other German cities it had been destroyed by the heavy bombing of the Allied forces during the war. As I gazed, horrified, at the ruins, I suddenly saw the great spire of Cologne Cathedral rising undamaged from the rubble of the surrounding buildings. To me it was a message symbolizing the ultimate power of good over evil. At the same time, the once beautiful city, reduced to ruins because one man's lust for power had plunged Europe into a brutal war, was a compelling reminder of human evil. I shall never forget that sight—it meant quite as much to me as all the sermons I had listened to in Bournemouth, so powerful was the symbolism.

When I returned to England, Vanne convinced me I should train to be a secretary because, she said, secretaries could get jobs anywhere in the world. And I still wanted to travel and to work with animals in some far-off place. I continued to read books about animals in between the poetry and philosophy. And still Africa was where I most wanted to go. I realized that Vanne was right—secretarial training could get me there. So off I went to London. I was nineteen, a very naive nineteen by modern standards. Living in London was a fantastic— and innocent—experience. I spent hours in art galleries, especially the Tate, and I went to classical music concerts. I roamed the Natural History Museum during many lunch hours. And I met young men with whom I flirted deliciously and who took me out to dinner and the theater. In those days if a man invited a girl to go out with him, he would have been horrified if she had tried to pay her share. That helped a lot, as I was desperately short of money; it meant that when I was taken out to dinner I could do without lunch—which was seldom anything more extravagant than a sausage roll anyway. On the evenings when I didn't go out my meal often consisted of a quarter of a boiled cabbage (the cheapest vegetable) and an apple, or a Penguin biscuit.

Despite the fun of London, and all that I was learning from art galleries and museums, I wanted to get a more formal education. I think I felt slightly inferior because so many of my school friends had gone off to university, as I had dreamed of doing. So I enrolled for some free evening-school classes provided by the London School of Economics. I took a course in journalism, and one in English literature that taught me to appreciate the poetry of Dylan Thomas and T. S. Eliot. I also began to attend courses held once a week on the teachings of Theosophy. I was especially drawn to the concepts of karma and reincarnation, because I was still trying very hard to make sense of the horrors of the war. If karma was operating, Hitler and the Nazis would pay for their crimes in some future life, while those who were killed in battle or tortured in the death camps may have been paying for former transgressions. They would then either be reborn to a better life or go to some kind of heaven or paradise. I had never been able to believe that God would give us poor frail humans only *one* chance at making it—that we would be assigned to some kind of hell because we failed during *one* experience of mortal life. After all, one human life span measured against eternity—it is gone faster than a millionth of a second. So the concepts of karma and reincarnation made logical sense to me.

The woman who taught our Theosophy course was charismatic. Most of the young men were semi in love with her and I thought she was brilliant. She would take a little idea and develop it in a thousand different directions. She constantly emphasized the need to stop what she called "circling thought" so that we could become more aware of things going on around us. Circling thought, she explained, is the constant flow of thoughts that go through one's mind, almost all the time. Trying to make my mind a blank, thought-less, was perhaps the hardest task of all. Much of what I learned in those classes was very helpful to my own constantly evolving personal beliefs about God and the universe. I wrote quite a lot of poetry at the time: the following is a good example.

THE OLD WISDOM

When the night wind makes the pine trees creak
And the pale clouds glide across the dark sky,
Go out, my child, go out and seek
Your soul: the Eternal I.

For all the grasses rustling at your feet
And every flaming star that glitters high
Above you, close up and meet
In you: the Eternal I.

Yes, my child, go out into the world; walk slow
And silent, comprehending all, and by and by
Your soul, the Universe, will know
Itself: the Eternal I.

After a session some of us would go to a coffeehouse and talk for hours and I learned a great deal about life during those late-night sessions. We were a motley collection, representing all strata of society. There was the "Worm Lady," who jumped to her feet repeatedly during the classes to offer pearls of wisdom, her points invariably illustrated by reference to earthworms because of the symbolism of such lowly creatures who yet aerated the soil, that all might live. It was amazing how many times worms were mentioned thanks to the Worm Lady. And there was an utterly fascinating Dutchman who had been part of the Dutch resistance. He was much older than I and I fell in love with him. We came close to having an affair. However he was married, and our morals were very different in those days.

Theosophy captivated me—but my deep love of Jesus remained. I remember a girl from secretarial college who came up to me during this time and said, "You so often have a little smile on your face, you always look as if you have a wonderful secret." I did—I felt that I had a personal relationship with Jesus. But it was a private thing and I did not want to talk about it.

After receiving my secretarial diploma I got my first job—at my aunt's clinic. Olly was a physiotherapist, and she worked almost entirely with children who had limbs paralyzed by polio or some kind of accident, or who had cerebral palsy or muscular dystrophy or some other tragic affliction. My job was to take down the doctor's comments on each case and type them up afterward. Ever since that time I have felt great empathy with people who are disabled by disease or accident. My first real boyfriend was in a plaster cast from ankles to waist when first I met him, the result of a terrible car crash. My second husband, Derek Bryceson, was left with semiparalyzed legs when his plane was shot down by a German pilot during the war.

My months at the clinic, and also the times when Uncle Eric let me watch him at work in the operating theater, taught me a great deal about human resilience, both physical and mental; and made me appreciate my own extraordinarily healthy body. I know how lucky I am, and I do not, not ever, take it for granted.

After working at the clinic I got a job in Oxford, where I was able to learn something about the life of an undergraduate—at any rate I experienced a good deal of the fun of university life with none of the academic burdens. Then I got a fascinating job in London doing music selections for a documentary film studio. It was a small organization and I was able to learn a great deal about almost all aspects of filmmaking. And then, suddenly, everything changed. On Wednesday morning, December 18, 1956, I received a letter from Marie Claude Mange. Clo, as she was known, had been my best friend at school. I hadn't heard from her for a while, and was surprised when I saw that her letter was from Africa. I still remember the Kenyan stamps—there was an elephant on one and two giraffes on the other. Her parents, she wrote, had just bought a farm in Kenya. Would I like to join them for a visit? Would I ever!

But first I had to earn enough money to pay for my fare. And it had to be a round-trip ticket. The authorities wouldn't let people in on a single ticket unless they had someone responsible for them there. And anyway, Vanne would never have allowed me to go without a return ticket. It meant a lot of money; and my job, fascinating as it was, paid poorly, as did many jobs in postwar England. So the very day I got the letter I handed in my notice and returned to Bournemouth. There I could live at home while I saved up. I got a job as a waitress. I saved my wages and my tips—every penny I could. Each weekend I put my earnings under the carpet in the drawing room of the Birches (this was where Danny always kept her petty cash). And then, one evening, after I had worked for five months, the entire family gathered round; we drew the curtains so that no one could look in, and counted my savings. Added to the small amount of money I had been able to save when I worked in London, I had enough. I could go to Africa—and my life would be changed forever.

With Louis Leakey, 1957

Chapter 3

AFRICA

Vanne and Uncle Eric came to the docks in London to see me off. We inspected the cabin I would share with five other girls; we looked out of its little porthole. We met the steward who would look after me. We walked round the ship that would be my home for the next three weeks. I was twenty-three years old and I was leaving all that I knew—my home, my family, my country. I must have been a little apprehensive. I'm sure I felt sad to be parting from Vanne and Uncle Eric, Danny and Olly and Judy. But I don't remember anything except a feeling of absolute amazement. It was actually happening. I was sailing off to Africa, into the unknown where the only person I would know would be a school friend I had not seen for at least five years.

The blast of the ship's horn signaled that visitors must leave. The last hugs and kisses. Last messages and wishes of good luck. I'm sure there were tears. I remember standing by the railing, watching the waving figures get smaller and smaller; then the White Cliffs of Dover were all that I could see of England and finally they too vanished. The adventure, the voyage to Tarzan's Africa, to the land of lions, leopards, elephants, giraffes, and monkeys, had actually begun. I would give anything to be able to remember, forty years later, exactly what my thoughts were that night when, after my first shipboard dinner, I finally climbed into my little bunk and lay down, soothed by the gentle, reassuring throb of the engines. But those thoughts have vanished, along with the youth of the girl who thought them.

The ship in which I sailed was a large passenger liner, one of the famous Castle Line's fleet. This was the *Kenya Castle*—the best of them all so far as I was concerned—the only one that was not divided into steerage and first class. When I originally booked my ticket the ship was taking the shortest—and cheapest—route: through the Red Sea and southward down the African coast to Mombasa in Kenya. But because of the Egyptian war, the Suez Canal was closed just a week before we were due to sail. I was terrified that my trip would be postponed, but the company decided to sail anyway, avoiding the Suez Canal by routing us down the west coast of Africa, around the Cape of Good Hope, and up to Mombasa—an extra week at sea. And although I had to part with a little more of my precious savings, that fabulous voyage was well worth it. My excitement increased as the cool days of an English spring gradually gave way to days filled with warm tropical sun.

Of the many wonders, the best was to stand in the bow with the sea all around and stretching away as far as the eye could see. I used to spend hours on the deck, behind one of the lifeboats where I could be alone. We passed schools of flying fish and dancing dolphins, as well as the occasional sinister triangular fins of sharks. I loved it when it got wild and stormy, when the spray drenched the decks. Most of the passengers retreated to their cabins so that I felt quite alone with the elements raging around me while our ship climbed the huge waves and plunged, crazily, down from the top. Of course when it got really rough I had to go below. The sailors did not want foolish landlubbers getting washed overboard, or getting in their way as they did the things sailors do.

That long, glorious voyage was a riotous mixture of pure ecstasy over the wonder of the new sea world around me and all the excitement of life on board an ocean liner. A number of romantic, innocent shipboard flirtations, drinking gin and tonic under the tropical night sky, the fun of crossing the equator with a splendid Neptune who threw water over us novices—or did he throw us in the swimming pool? Now, all these years later, my memories of the fun I had on board are hazy. I don't even remember the names of the girls with whom I shared my cabin, though we became good friends during the voyage. But the hours I spent in the company of the ocean and all its moods, the sense of being a part of a limitless world of water and air, sun and stars and wind—that is still vivid in my mind. For those were the times that nurtured my spirit, allowed my inner self to grow and expand in understanding. My belief in a great Power was strengthened—a Power outside, yet including each one of us and all the wonders of the world. I think it was then, sailing along just out of sight of land, that I made an unconscious commitment to Africa. The days of my childhood, and of my adolescent preoccupation with philoso-

39

phy and the meaning of life, of time, of eternity, had come to an end.

Looking back, I see clearly that my own personal philosophy was gradually molded during those first two decades by my family, my schooling, my living through the war, my years of listening to extremely powerful sermons; also by the books I read, the hours I spent outside in the natural world, and by the animals who shared our house. Now the *Kenya Castle* was carrying me forward into a new world, where the lessons would be taught by life itself in all its wonderful, sometimes tragic, often harsh, inconsistencies and surprises. And I could move into this new era without fear, for I was equipped, by my family and by my education, with sound moral values and an independent, free-thinking mind.

We dropped anchor in only four ports during the journey to Mombasa: the Canary Islands, Cape Town, Durban, and Beira. Going ashore in those exotic places was romantic—after all, the farthest afield I had been before was drab, war-torn Germany. I remember the warm air of the tropical nights, the colorful markets, the dark faces of the people and their bright clothes. Yes, and the scents, the exotic mix of tropical blossoms, and fruit, and bits of food grilled over charcoal, and dust, and animal dung, and urine, and sweat.

I remember, too, rounding the Cape of Good Hope and pulling into the harbor at Cape Town. This is one of the most beautiful cities on earth, but it is not the beauty that I remember; it is the shock of my first encounter with apartheid. Everywhere I went were grim reminders of the deliberate denigration of one group of human beings by another. SLEGS BLANCS was written in bold letters on notices pinned to shops, benches, buses, lavatories, parks, beaches, hotels: *slegs blancs* is Afrikaans for *whites only*, and the signs were everywhere.

When we stopped in Durban a few days later it was even worse. I had a friend there, Peter Gordon, who had been one of Trevor's curates at Richmond Hill. I spent a day with Peter, and his stories of apartheid in action took me straight back to the horrors of Nazi Germany, the dehumanization of one race by another. One of his stories I have never forgotten. As he was walking along the road, an old African woman ran past him to catch her bus. One handle of her overloaded shopping bag broke and all her purchases tumbled onto the ground. When Peter stooped to help her pick everything up she blanched, terrified, and begged him to stop. She would get into terrible trouble, she said, if she allowed a white man to help her. Peter told me he did not think he could stand it much longer; I never heard from him again so I don't know how he made out.

When the *Kenya Castle* finally steamed into Mombasa I was so much a part of life on the boat that I never wanted the journey to stop. Many of us felt that way, for an ocean voyage creates seemingly close friendships—most of which do not last. At the time, though, I felt I could not bear to leave all my new friends, all the fun, and the relaxed atmosphere in which one never had to make any decisions. But the engines throbbed, the boat moved relentlessly across the smooth waters of the harbor—and we docked. Two days in a train, from the coast to Nairobi, gave us time to adjust gradually to life on the ground. I shared a compartment with three of my cabin mates and slowly the floating world we had left came to seem unreal, far away. The rhythm of wheels took the place of the gentle throbbing that had lulled me to sleep for three weeks, and out of the window, instead of the endless seascape, was the landscape of East Africa. I had arrived.

Clo and her parents were there to meet me when, finally, the train stopped in Nairobi. The drive to their farm up in the Kinangop—part of what was then known as the White Highlands—was absolutely magical. As the quick tropical dusk fell we passed a lone male giraffe, right beside the road. When we stopped short, I looked up at that amazing face with the long eyelashes and supercilious-seeming expression, and wondered at the extraordinary gait as he turned and cantered away, tail curling up, seemingly in slow motion. I still am amazed by giraffes, even today, and I shall never forget that first sight. And then, later when it was dark, Clo's father braked again to avoid hitting an aardvark, or antbear—another creature out of my books—who ambled across the road and vanished into the night. Had I known how seldom they are seen I would have been even more excited.

I spent the next few weeks with the Manges on their farm, exhilarated by the clear mountain air, the icy streams, the unfamiliar birds with their strange cries. I was shown the pug marks of a huge leopard. It was all so new and exciting and beautiful. And yet once again the knowledge of human hatred and cruelty lay just below the surface, for many of the people I met had been involved in the bloody uprising of the Mau Mau in the early 1950s when so many of the white settlers and Kikuyu moderates had been ruthlessly slaughtered— men, women, and children. Almost everyone had some tale to share of human brutality: for instance the European doctor who was captured, then left to die, slowly and in agony, buried up to his neck in an underground nest of vicious army ants. The bite of even *one* is excruciatingly painful. Mercifully, he suffered from diabetes and soon lapsed into a coma. There were many tales of bravery too, especially concerning loyal Kikuyu servants who risked death, and worse, to help their white families.

It was at that time, to my shame, that I went hunting again—for the second and last time in my life. How on earth could I have done such a despicable thing? It is hard for me to put myself in the mind of the headstrong and foolish young girl who hurled herself into the fray without a thought. It came about when I met Bob, an attractive young man who had an enormous horse who was said to be very dangerous. The horse had thrown a number of people and no one would ride him. So of course, when Bob offered me a ride over the wild bush country, I begged to be allowed that particular horse. At first Bob adamantly refused, but I persisted, and wheedled, and (as usual!) got my way. The ride turned out to be a hunt and I think the quarry was probably a jackal. I rode the horse (despite his rearing up so high that he fell over backward the first time I mounted) and he was quite wonderful, all 17.2 hands of him. For the nonhorsey, a hand is four inches, so he was nearly six feet tall at the withers (that's the shoulders), the biggest horse I've ever ridden. So much for all my sanctimonious condemnation of fox hunting. Fortunately nothing was caught—and that really was my last hunt.

After my holiday I went to Nairobi to start working as secretary to the manager of the Kenya branch of a British company. Uncle Eric had arranged this job through one of his contacts long before I left England—for it had been drummed into us that we should never "sponge" off friends. A few weeks with Clo, and then I must make out for myself. The job itself was boring, but it earned me enough money to stay in Africa until I could find an occupation that would bring me into contact with animals.

I did not have to wait long. It began after a dinner party when I was being given a lift back to my quarters. "If you are interested in animals," someone said, "you should meet Louis Leakey." So I made an appointment and went to see the famous paleontologist/anthropologist at the Coryndon Museum of Natural History (which is now called the National Museum). We met in his large, untidy office, strewn with piles of papers, fossil bones and teeth, stone tools, and all sorts of other things. Louis then took me around the museum and asked me question after question about the various exhibits; fortunately, because I had gone on reading about Africa and animals, I was able to answer most of them. And even when I couldn't, at least I knew enough to know what he was talking about. I think he was impressed that someone with no degree understood the meaning of words like *ichthyology* and *herpetology*.

Louis was fifty-four years old when we met, and a true giant of a man; a real genius with an inquiring mind, enormous energy, great vision—and a marvelous sense of humor. He could also, as I learned later, be short-tempered and impatient with people he considered fools—which often meant people whose thinking did not agree with his! From the moment we met he enchanted me with his knowledge of Africa and its people and animals. Fortunately I apparently enchanted him too with my youthful enthusiasm, my love of animals, and my determination to get to Africa, which had resulted in our meeting. At any rate, he offered me a job as his personal secretary. And so, for the next year, I learned about the animals of East Africa at the museum. I also learned about the various tribes, especially the Kikuyu. Louis knew more than any other white man about them, since his missionary father had encouraged him to grow up within the culture of the tribe. As a newborn he had been set outside the house in a basket and, in accordance with Kikuyu custom, all the elders of the tribe had walked past to give him their blessing: each of them had spat on him! And later, as an adolescent, he had endured the terrifying and painful initiation ceremony, along with the boys with whom he had grown up. During circumcision, Louis told me, they had all sat in a circle on the ground with their knees drawn up, a little pebble placed on each knee. If a pebble fell off during the ceremony, that boy would be branded a coward for the rest of his life. I learned much of this because Louis dictated to me a book he was writing about Kikuyu history and customs.

Soon after I began working for Louis, he and his wife, Mary, invited me and another English girl, Gillian Trace, who also worked at the museum, to go on their annual dig at Olduvai Gorge in Tanganyika. In 1957, Olduvai was unknown except to the Masai who lived their nomadic lives on the vast plains of the Serengeti. In those days, before the opening of the Serengeti to large-scale tourism, the area was utterly remote; the roads and tourist buses and light aircraft that pass there regularly today were undreamed of. There was no road leading to Olduvai, not even a track. So when we left the trail from Ngorongoro Crater to Seronera (a trail that is now a well-marked road across the Serengeti), Gillian and I had to sit up on the roof of the overloaded Land Rover to look for what remained of the faint tire marks left by the Leakeys the year before.

For several years Louis and Mary had been going to Olduvai for three months each year to look for fossils, and they already knew a great deal about the prehistoric creatures that had roamed the Serengeti in bygone days. But although they had found many simple stone tools, they had yet to find the remains of the apelike humans who had made and used them. It was this quest for the bones of our ancient ancestors that took the Leakeys back year after year. Two years later, in 1959, their persistence was rewarded: it was their eldest son, Jonny, who found the skull of an apelike creature, eventually described as *Australopithecus robustus* but known familiarly as Dear Boy or George or, because of his large strong jaws and massive teeth, Nutcracker Man.

We arrived at Olduvai just as the sun was setting. We quickly set up our tents and built a campfire. I regret that I did not keep a journal, as it would be wonderful to have a written record these many years later. Exactly how did I feel during those first days at Olduvai? For about fourteen years—since I was eight or nine years old—I had dreamed of being in Africa, of living in the bush among wild animals. And suddenly, when I woke in the morning, I found I was actually living in my dream; the dream had become my reality, for the animals were there, all around our little camp. At night, as we sat by the campfire after supper, we often heard the distant, grunting roar of a lion. And later, as we lay on our small camp beds in our shared tent, Gillian and I would sometimes hear the strange, high-pitched giggling sounds, the catlike yowls, and the distinctive whooping calls which, we learned, constituted the varied repertoire of spotted hyenas.

Every day, after work was finished, Gillian and I were free to wander off on our own. Sometimes we explored the floor of the gorge among the acacia trees and the dag-gerlike leaves of the sanseveria, or wild sisal plants. At other times we climbed the steep slopes to walk on the plains, where the grass, burnt by the hot dry-season sun, was pale gold except where it was coated with gray dust by the relentless wind. The great herds of wildebeests, zebras, and Thomson's gazelles that migrate across these plains during the rains were long since gone, following the water that they need. Yet we discovered that there were many animals still living in and around the gorge, getting enough water from succulent leaves or roots. We often startled pairs of dik-diks, enchanting miniature an-telopes scarcely larger than a hare. Sometimes we came across a small herd of Grant's gazelles, and occasionally we saw a few giraffes wandering through.

There were a couple of real adventures, such as when we encountered a black rhino. Rhinos are very short-sighted, yet this one sensed our presence even though, fortunately, the wind was blowing toward us. He snorted and pawed the ground, peering around with his little, piggy eyes, then turned and trotted off, tail held high in the air. I was so excited that, afterward, my legs felt weak and my heart was hammering like a crazy thing in my rib cage. Our own rhino, and we were on foot! On another occasion, when Gillian and I were down among the thorn bushes at the bottom of the gorge, I had that prickling sensation that one sometimes feels if one is being watched. I turned to find a young male lion about forty feet away. He gazed at us with great interest. Gillian wanted to hide from him in the thick undergrowth at the bottom of the gorge, but I felt that we should climb up onto the plains, keeping in the open. Carefully we backed away from the lion, then turned and walked slowly to the side of the gorge. The lion was about two years old, with a mane starting to sprout in wispy clumps from his shoulders. Lions are intensely curious at this age and almost certainly this one had seen nothing like Gillian and me in his entire life. He followed us for at least a hundred meters, then watched as we climbed up the side of the gorge onto the plains. Later, Louis told us it was lucky we hadn't run—very likely he would have given chase, unable to resist hunting us in play, like a kitten after a ball of wool.

I spent the bulk of my time at Olduvai digging for fossils. It was hard work under the hot tropical sun, but it was fascinating. The site was first prepared by the small team of Africans that always accompanied the Leakeys. They used picks and shovels to remove the topsoil. Once they got down near the layer of fossils, Mary insisted on doing the last of the heavy work herself. She felt strongly that if an important fossil got broken by a pick, it was better that she should do it than one of the Africans. Since I was young, strong, and healthy, Mary was glad to have my aid, and we got on well together, sweating away as we swung the heavy implements.

When we finally got down to the fossil bed, we chipped away at the hard soil with hunting knives, searching for bones. When we found something, we used dental picks for the last part of the job. For at least eight hours a day we dug for fossils, pausing for a cup of coffee at eleven o'clock and a three-hour rest period in the midday heat during which we gathered under the shade of a tarpaulin to sort and mark our finds. The digging was monotonous most of the time but there were periods of intense excitement when the bones of some unusual creature were unearthed. And, of course, there was always the hope that one would be the very first to discover the remains of early man at Olduvai.

Then, too, there were those moments when, without warning, as I held a bone in my hand, I would be filled with awe by the sight or the feel of it. This—this very bone—had once been part of a living, breathing animal that had walked and slept and propagated its species millions of years ago. It had belonged to a creature with a personality, with eyes and hair and its own distinctive scent, its own voice. What had it really looked like? How had it lived? The first time this happened I was holding part of the tusk of one of the giant pigs that once roamed the plains. Almost I could feel myself back in that primeval world; there was the vast dark bulk of the pig, covered with coarse hair, his eyes glaring, his monstrous tusks gleaming. Almost I could smell his rich scent and hear him grinding his teeth. Several times I was thus transported back in time, my imagination colored by artists' reconstructions of life-forms long since vanished from our planet.

Olduvai was a world far removed from my childhood garden at the Birches in England and my sandy cliffs above the tamed seafront. Yet the child that I had been had dreamed of the life I was now living. The teasing, loving time with my family, the Sundays listening to Trevor preach, the first steps into adult life in postwar England had molded the very same mind that now explored the new and exciting world of Olduvai. The continuity of my thought processes linked the child that I once was to the young woman I had become. During those precious three months at Olduvai the mystery of evolution was all around us, and there's no doubt I was powerfully influenced. My experiences there helped to shape my own later philosophy regarding the progress of our species through time, the emergence of morality, our purpose in the overall scheme of things—our ultimate destiny.

A very strong influence at that time was Louis Leakey himself. We had countless opportunities to talk, especially after dinner as we sat under the clear African sky—the stars brilliant and amazingly close overhead—and watched the reassuring flickering of the campfire's flames, appreciating their warmth in the cold night air, aware of the sounds of animals. Our conversations were comprised of a mixture of storytelling, discussion of the events of the day, and a whole variety of topics that cropped up in any of our minds. I remember one evening when Louis talked about the Kikuyu religion. Many aspects of their ritual were, he said, uncannily like the ritual of the Old Testament. Even the color and age of goats, or chickens, for sacrifice were the same. He wrote to his brother, a bishop in Mombasa, with a whole list of similarities. But his brother, perhaps feeling that this was not an appropriate line of inquiry, never replied.

Louis never understood why so many people felt that science and religion were incompatible. I have never understood that either and it is surprising to me that so many scientists are atheists or agnostics. The science of quantum physics, which has come close to substantiating at least some religious beliefs, had not at this time emerged into mainstream thinking, nor had anyone proposed the Big Bang theory for the creation of the universe. Instead we discussed the gradual modification, through the process of evolution, of the human animal, its ever more sophisticated brain, the emergence of language that enabled our species to depend, ever more heavily, on cultural evolution. And, when compared with the ponderous crawl through time of physical evolution, cultural evolution leads to change with lightning speed. In storytelling mode one evening I remember describing how I imagined God, looking down on his creation, evaluating human progress, and deciding the time had come when these sons and daughters of His were ready to be made aware, truly aware, of who they were. They were ready to receive the Holy Ghost.

It was bigotry that was the greatest evil, Louis believed. I suppose he had loved his father, but he had hated his narrow-minded Scottish Presbyterian outlook. He told many stories about this. One concerned a powerful Kikiyu chief. If only this chief could be converted to Christianity, all the tribe would follow suit, his father thought. And that would be a feather in the cap of any missionary. After many months of persuasion, the chief finally made up his mind. He would be baptized. Smiling happily, Louis's father arranged a date, but then had a sudden terrible thought. "You do realize," he said, "that as a Christian you will be allowed only one wife?" The chief, who had at least eight wives, stared at him. He would think it over. The following Sunday the chief again went to the little church. "I will not be baptized," he said firmly. "My wives have served me faithfully. They are good wives. If I cast them out they will live in shame. I believed your god was a just god, but now I know differently. Your god is not my God." And he walked away. Stories like that cut right through the layers of ritual, of the packaging in which we wrap the spark of Truth.

Louis loved to discuss the probable behavior of our earliest ancestors. He had taught himself how to make stone tools, and loved to demonstrate the construction of hand axes, arrowheads, and other implements. He used to speculate on exactly how stone age man used these tools, how he hunted, what sort of society he lived in. Louis was a revolutionary thinker. He felt strongly that anyone who hoped to understand the origins of man needed to be familiar not only with the fossilized bones and artifacts of the past, but also with the living descendants of prehistoric creatures. He had, for example, instigated a detailed study of the limb bones and locomotor patterns of a number of modern antelopes; the functions of varying bone structures of their legs could then be ascertained. Then, from the structure of fossil antelope bones it should be possible to reconstruct their movements. Suddenly, the many fossil antelope bones we found at Olduvai seemed more exciting, and I looked with a new fascination at the little bumps for muscle attachment and at the grooves for sinews.

Toward the end of our three-month stay at Olduvai Louis began to talk to me about his great interest in chimpanzees, gorillas, and orangutans. Chimpanzees are found only in Africa, with a range extending throughout the equatorial forest belt from the west coast eastward to western Uganda and Tanzania. Louis had heard of some recent sightings of chimpanzees near Kigoma in the rugged mountainous country on the eastern shore of Lake Tanganyika—about six hundred miles southwest of Olduvai. These, he explained, were the eastern or long-haired variety, *Pan troglodytes schweinfurthii*. He was interested in all the Great Apes because they are our closest living relatives and because it made sense to him that an understanding of their behavior in the wild would help him to better guess how our stone age ancestors may have behaved. And this would provide another strand in his lifelong quest to unravel the mysteries of our prehistoric past. Already he had a good idea of what our stone age ancestors had looked like from the reconstructions made by skilled anatomists. The size and wear of their teeth suggested the type of diet they enjoyed. And he could make informed guesses as to the use of the various stone tools and other artifacts found at their living sites. But behavior does not fossilize. Louis reasoned that any behavior common to chimpanzees and humans today might well have been present in the apelike humanlike common ancestor which we shared, he believed, several million years ago. And if this was so, then those same behaviors were probably present also in the earliest true humans. This line of reasoning, new at that time, is widely accepted today, particularly as the geneticists tell us that our genetic material, our DNA, differs from that of chimpanzees by only a little over 1 percent.

Louis was anxious to initiate a scientific study of these chimpanzees. It would be difficult, he emphasized, for nothing was known; there were no guidelines for such a field study; and the habitat was remote and rugged. Dangerous wild animals would be living there, and chimpanzees themselves were considered at least four times stronger than humans. I remember wondering what kind of scientist he would find for such a herculean task.

When we returned to Nairobi from Olduvai I continued working for Louis at the museum. But I wasn't really happy being surrounded by dead animals, or all the killing that went on in order to get specimens for the scientific collection. The worst experience, for me, was when I went along on a collecting expedition to the Kakamega Forest, where countless animals were trapped, killed, and skinned for specimens. I loved the forest but I hated the collecting. I understood that the dedicated staff felt that it was important to create a permanent record of life-forms that might one day vanish altogether. But why was it necessary to have so many specimens of the same species of bird or rodent or butterfly? Look in the back rooms of any natural history museum—there are drawers and drawers full of stuffed birds and small mammals and literally thousands of insects of all kinds. It represents a horrifying slaughter of the innocents.

I was swept up by my first real love affair at that time. And how utterly ironic it was. For Brian was a hunter—a White Hunter—who would take clients out to shoot animals. How could this have happened? I was attracted to him partly because of his courage in the face of adversity. Recently he had been in a terrible car accident that had almost cost him his legs. He was in plaster from his toes to his waist when I first met him, and he seemed very brave. He had suffered a good deal and was lame throughout the year that I knew him. He had a sweet and gentle side; he was very kind to all domestic animals, and to wild-animal pets too. And he took me to some wild, beautiful, and utterly remote places. But he hunted and he killed the very animals I had come to Africa to live with and learn about. In my youthful naïveté, I suppose I thought I could change him. Of course I couldn't, and the affair was doomed to failure. But it was exciting and passionate while it lasted, and it taught me a lot about human nature—especially my own.

Louis still talked about the chimpanzees from time to time. If only I could do something like that, something that involved observing and learning, and not killing.

One day I blurted out: "Louis, I wish you wouldn't keep talking about it because that's just what I want to do."

"Jane," he replied, his eyes twinkling, "I've been waiting for you to tell me that. Why on earth did you think I talked about those chimpanzees to you?"

I'm sure I stared at him open-mouthed. How could I possibly be considered suitable for such an important study? I had no training, no degree. But Louis didn't care about academic credentials. In fact, he told me, he preferred that his chosen researcher should go into the field with a mind unbiased by scientific theory. What he had been looking for was someone with an open mind, with a passion for knowledge, with a love of animals, and with monumental patience. Someone, moreover, who was hardworking and would be able to stay long periods away from civilization, for he believed the study would take several years. When he put it like that, of course, I had to admit that I was the perfect choice!

In fact he had been watching me carefully ever since our trip to Olduvai. And then, having decided that I was the person he had been seeking for some time, he wanted to make sure that I knew how difficult, perhaps dangerous, the assignment would be before I agreed to tackle it. Whereas I, of course, the very moment he had chosen me, was eager to set off. Little did I realize, in my youthful enthusiasm, how long it would take before I could get started. Louis had to find the necessary money, and get the necessary permission.

While Louis tackled these problems I returned to England to prepare myself as best I could for the task ahead. I read everything I could get my hands on about chimpanzees. Almost nothing was known about their behavior in their natural habitat. In 1923 Dr. Henry W.

Nissen had gone to French Guinea to try to observe wild chimpanzees. He stayed in the field for only two and a half months, and he traveled about the forest with a trail of porters carrying his equipment. Not surprisingly the chimpanzees fled at his conspicuous approach. There were two other published field studies of nonhuman primates. In both cases, the investigators first collected what behavioral data they could—on gibbons and red-tail monkeys—and then killed their subjects to check on their age, sex, reproductive condition—and even stomach contents. More slaughter of the innocents. I got far more useful information from two other detailed accounts of the behavior of colonies of chimpanzees in captivity. Wolfgang Köhler and Robert Yerkes were psychologists and their observations yielded fascinating insights into the intelligence of the apes they studied. I spent time observing the chimpanzees in London Zoo—but there were only two bored psychotic individuals in a tiny cement cage with iron bars. I could learn little there—and I was shocked at the conditions they were in. I vowed that one day I would help them.

Meanwhile Louis was struggling to overcome the prejudices of the time. Who would finance a study that most people believed was doomed to failure? Leakey must be out of his mind, they said, else how could he think of sending a young untrained girl to undertake such a potentially dangerous project. It was amoral. Luckily Louis never cared what anyone thought. He persisted and eventually found a backer in Leighton Wilkie from Illinois. His company manufactured tools, and he had become interested in the Leakeys' collections of prehistoric artifacts. He had funded other projects for Louis and he agreed to provide seed money for this one, unlikely as it seemed—a sum sufficient to cover a small boat, a tent, airfares, and the other costs related to sustaining me in the field for six months. This was exciting, but another stumbling block lay ahead. At that time, in 1960, Tanganyika (now Tanzania after its merger with Zanzibar) was a British protectorate, and the government authorities were horrified at the thought of a young white woman going off into the bush. Louis, however, simply refused to take no for an answer, and eventually they gave in. However, they were adamant on one score—I had to take a European companion. Who should it be? Louis was concerned that the wrong person might ruin my chances of success. It must be someone with whom I was relaxed, someone who would not compete, and would leave me to do the study as I thought best. Who better than Vanne? I was overjoyed when she agreed to join me.

And so, after an adventurous journey in an overloaded Land Rover driven by Bernard Verdcourt, the botanist from the Coryndon Museum (who subsequently admitted that he had thought he would never see either of us again), Vanne and I arrived in Kigoma. Only a short boat ride along the lake separated us from the forested hills that would soon become my home.

(Hugo van Lawick)

Writing field notes by the light of a kerosene lamp
during my early days at Gombe

Chapter 4

GOMBE

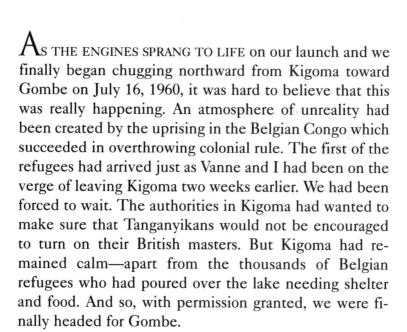

As THE ENGINES SPRANG TO LIFE on our launch and we finally began chugging northward from Kigoma toward Gombe on July 16, 1960, it was hard to believe that this was really happening. An atmosphere of unreality had been created by the uprising in the Belgian Congo which succeeded in overthrowing colonial rule. The first of the refugees had arrived just as Vanne and I had been on the verge of leaving Kigoma two weeks earlier. We had been forced to wait. The authorities in Kigoma had wanted to make sure that Tanganyikans would not be encouraged to turn on their British masters. But Kigoma had remained calm—apart from the thousands of Belgian refugees who had poured over the lake needing shelter and food. And so, with permission granted, we were finally headed for Gombe.

For the twelve-mile journey Vanne and I were accompanied by game ranger David Anstey in the government launch. Our own tiny boat, which would be our sole link with the outside world, was stowed on board. There was a strong wind and the lake was rippled with waves, each with its crest of white spray. To the west the hills of the troubled Congo were invisible in the dry-season haze, and the lake stretched on ahead toward Burundi in the north, as far as the eye could see. It was like being on a crystal-clear, freshwater ocean. We kept close to the eastern shore. The steep slopes of the rift escarpment, rising some nine hundred feet above the lake, were thickly forested except up on the top where it was bare and brown with sun-dried grass, since it was too rocky, the topsoil too sparse, for many trees to grow up there. There were little villages nestled in the valleys, with a few clearings cut for growing crops. Where the beaches were sandy they shone silver with the bodies of thousands of tiny sardine-sized fish drying in the hot sun. David Anstey explained that they were known as *dagaa,* caught at night when they were attracted to Aladdin lamps in the fishermen's canoes, then scooped up with what looked like giant butterfly nets. Some of the fishermen waved. After about an hour we arrived at the southern boundary of the game reserve (it did not become a national park until 1966). Today it is easy to tell when you reach the park because almost every tree outside has been cut down, but the boundary was not obvious four decades ago. I gazed at the rugged terrain and tried to imagine myself living and working there. I remember wondering how on earth I would manage to find the chimpanzees.

Soon we arrived at the ranger post where David Anstey had decided we should camp. I jumped onto the sand and pebble beach, the first of a thousand landings. I recall feeling neither exhilaration nor anxiety, simply a curious sense of detachment. But once the boat was unpacked and the tents were up, I left Vanne and David to sort out supper, and set off, on my own, up the forested slope opposite camp. Then the excitement, the sheer magic of it all, overwhelmed me. I remember sitting on a rock, looking out over the valley and up into the blue sky, and hoping that this is what it might be like in heaven. I met some baboons, who barked at me. I heard a variety of birds. I breathed in the smell of sun-dried grass, and dry earth, and the heady scent of some kind of ripe fruit. The smell of Gombe. And then, as the sun began to drop down toward the now calm, smooth lake, I scrambled down to join Vanne and David for that first enchanted evening. By the time I lay down to sleep on my camp bed under the twinkling stars, with the wind rustling softly through the fronds of the oil nut palm above, I already felt that I belonged to this new forest world, that this was where I was meant to be.

David Anstey stayed with us a couple of days, helping to organize our little camp with its single tent that Vanne and I would share for the next four months, and its makeshift kitchen, made of a few poles with a straw roof, that would be the domain of Dominic, the cook we had hired in Kigoma. He had his own tiny tent, set apart from ours. Then David left the two crazy English women, convinced—as were most people—that we would quit after a few weeks. Little did he know! Before he went he made me promise not to climb in the hills on my own, at least not until I knew my way around. He appointed one of the game rangers, Adolf, to accompany me, and a local man, Rashidi Kikwale, to be my guide.

I had known, of course, that there were dangers at Gombe. Nonetheless it was a shock when, during our very first week, two excited fishermen led Adolf, Rashidi, and me to a tree not far from the lake. Its bark was gashed and scored in a hundred places. Apparently a lone bull buffalo had charged one of the fishermen the night before. The man had managed to climb up the tree to safety, but the buffalo had stayed below for more than an hour, ramming the tree and trying to dislodge his terrified victim. These fishermen were obviously trying to warn me of the great hazards of living in the African bush, and it certainly made a powerful impression on me.

I remembered that battered tree on many occasions during the following weeks as we moved through the thick undergrowth of the lower slopes, often crawling along animal trails. There were quite a few buffalo at Gombe in those days. Once (some time later, when I had dispensed with the company of Adolf and Rashidi) I almost bumped into a buffalo—a huge animal, lying and chewing his cud in the dark before dawn, no more than six yards from me. Fortunately the wind was strong, its sound covering the small noise I made, and it was blowing from him to me. I was able to creep away undetected. On another occasion much later on when I was sleeping up in the hills, I heard the strange sawing call of a hunting leopard close by in the dark. Of course I was frightened—I was really scared of leopards in those days. But I told myself that the leopard would not hurt me because I was supposed to be there and I had a job to do. I would be protected. I put the blanket over my head and hoped for the best. I'm not sure, now, whether this was fatalism or whether I really thought that I had some kind of pact with God. "I'll do this job, God, and You look after me." In any event, the leopard, clearly, was not interested in sampling this strange white ape, though he was probably intensely curious. Leopards are.

And then there was the time when, as I was walking back to camp along the lakeshore, wading in the water to get around a huge rock, I suddenly saw the sinuous black body of a snake. I stopped dead in my tracks. It was about six feet long, and from the slight hood and dark stripes at the back of the neck I knew it was a Storm's water cobra—a deadly snake with a bite for which there was, at the time, no antivenin. It moved toward me, riding an incoming wave, and part of its body actually settled on one of my feet. I stared at it and it stared right back with bright, black eyes. I stood motionless, not even breathing, until the wave rolled back into the lake, drawing the snake with it. Then I leaped out of the water as fast as I could, my heart hammering. It was fortunate that my snake was not a female with eggs in her, for, as I discovered later, this is the one time when these snakes, normally quite calm, become aggressive and will attack anything that invades their territory. (The few human deaths caused by water cobra bites, however, typically occur when a snake gets tangled in a fisherman's net. If it is still alive when the net is pulled into the boat, then the snake, not surprisingly, bites.)

In fact, at that time, my fears of being harmed by a wild animal were almost nonexistent. I truly believed that the animals would sense that I intended no harm and, in turn, would leave me alone—as had been the case with the young male lion at Olduvai. Louis had encouraged this belief, at the same time making sure that I had a reasonable understanding of how I should behave if I came upon some creature unexpectedly. And he impressed on me that I should never take unnecessary risks. The most dangerous thing is to get between a mother and her young, or to encounter some animal that has been wounded and cannot run away, or one that has, for some reason, learned to hate man. But those were hazards no more dangerous—and probably even less dangerous—than those that could beset one in any city, and I was not concerned.

Much more worrisome during those early months was the fact that the chimpanzees were so afraid that they ran off as soon as they saw me. I was an intruder, and a strange one at that. I knew they would get used to me eventually—but how soon? Would I succeed in learning anything really significant before the funding ran out? I knew perfectly well that if results didn't come through, Louis wouldn't be able to raise further money. I was terrified of letting him down. That was the only thing that detracted from the extreme delight I experienced as I gradually became familiar with my new world.

Six weeks after we arrived at Gombe, Vanne and I fell ill with malaria. What a pathetic sight we must have been as we lay side by side on our two small camp beds in our army surplus tent, alternately raging with fever, then shivering with cold. We had been told there was no malaria at Gombe (a strange piece of misinformation coming from the local Italian doctor), so we had no medication. Our entertainment consisted of occasionally, weakly, taking our temperatures and comparing notes. Vanne was lucky to survive—for four days successively she ran terribly high temperatures up to 105 degrees and for a short while lacked the strength to walk.

As soon as I began to feel better I was desperate to continue my search for the chimps. And so, one morning early, when it was cool, I climbed, slowly and with many pauses, the steep slope opposite our tent. It was a red-letter day, a turning point, for I discovered the Peak and from that day on, my luck changed.

The Peak is a rocky outcrop, halfway up one of the ridges that run between the valleys from the top of the escarpment down to the lake. From this marvelous vantage point, about five hundred feet above the lake, I was able to overlook two valleys: Kakombe, where our camp was situated, and Kasakela to the north. And, as I sat there, too weak to travel farther after the effort of the climb, I heard chimps in the valley below. I watched them feeding in a large fig tree; I followed their progress with my binoculars as they moved off, calling noisily from time to time. And when they had quite gone, and all was quiet, I rushed down, fever forgotten, to share the magic with poor sick Vanne.

And so began one of the most exciting periods of my life, the time of discovery. Not a day went by that I did not learn some fascinating new fact about the chimpanzees. My life fell into a rhythm. I would set my alarm at about 5:30, eat a slice of bread, make coffee with hot water from a thermos, then climb to the Peak, still in the dark. Vanne called a sleepy goodbye, though I tried not to wake her. After I had watched a group of chimps, or a single chimp, I sometimes climbed down to collect whatever foods they had been eating and, in this way, I gradually became familiar with the terrain. And even as I was, bit by bit, piecing together something of their way of life, so they were getting used to the sight of this strange white ape—though it would be almost a year before I could approach most of them closer than a hundred yards or so.

While it was rare for a whole day to pass without at least one chimpanzee sighting, sometimes I had to wait hours and hours for the privilege. It was very important, during those periods of waiting, to stay watchful, because the chimpanzees were often in small groups, or even alone, and completely silent. It was the movement in a tree or the snapping of a branch that would alert me—though as often as not it would turn out to be baboons or monkeys and not chimps at all. One scientist who visited me during those early months was surprised that I did not take a supply of books up to the Peak, so that I could while away the hours of waiting. How much I would have missed!

During those days on the Peak I gradually began to piece together something of the daily life of the Gombe chimpanzees, and my fear of failure began to subside. But three months had passed before I made the first really significant and tremendously exciting observation. It had been a frustrating morning. I had tramped up and down three different valleys in search of chimps but had found none. At noon, weary from crawling through the dense undergrowth, I headed for the Peak. I stopped when I saw a dark shape and a slight movement in the long grass about forty yards ahead. Quickly focusing my binoculars, I saw that it was a single chimpanzee, and soon recognized the adult male, less fearful than the others, whom I already knew by sight. I had named him David Greybeard because of the distinctive white hair on his chin.

I moved a little, so I could see him better. He was sitting on the red-earth mound of a termite nest, repeatedly pushing a grass stem into a hole. After a moment he would withdraw it, carefully, and pick something off with his mouth. Occasionally he picked a new piece of grass and used that. When he left I went over to the termite heap. Abandoned grass stems were scattered around. Termites were crawling about on the surface of the nest, already working to close up the openings into which David had poked his grasses. I tried doing as he had done, and when I pulled out my grass termites were clinging to it with their jaws.

Just two weeks before I had been told that if only I could observe a chimpanzee using a tool, then the whole study would be more than worthwhile. And here was David Greybeard using a tool. A few days later, I observed the tool-using behavior again—and clearly saw how a small leafy twig was picked, and then stripped of its leaves. That was object modification—the crude beginning of tool*making*. It was hard for me to believe what I had seen. It had long been thought that we were the only creatures on earth that used and made tools. "Man the Toolmaker" is how we were defined. This ability set us apart, it was supposed, from the rest of the animal kingdom.

When I telegrammed the news to Louis Leakey, he responded with the now-famous remark: "Ah! We must now redefine man, redefine tool, or accept chimpanzees as human!" My observations at Gombe challenged human uniqueness, and whenever that happens there is always a violent scientific and theological uproar. On this occasion there were some who tried to discredit my observations because I was untrained, and therefore could not possibly produce reliable information. But the photographs that I eventually obtained proved the truth. Some scientists then actually suggested I must have taught the chimps to fish for termites! The result of it all, however, was that it was deemed necessary to redefine man in a more complex manner than before—heaven forbid that we should lose any aspect of our human uniqueness! I was unaware of all the controversy and speculation that was going on, as I was just living my simple life and continuing to learn more about the chimpanzees.

These observations of tool using were important not only because of their value to science. Even more important, for me, was that because of them Louis was able to obtain a grant from the National Geographic Society, which would enable me to continue my study. He wrote to tell me this exciting news just before Vanne, having stayed with me for five months, had to return to England.

I knew I was going to miss Vanne very much. She had been a wonderful companion, helping in so many ways. She was always there when I got down from my days in the mountains, eager to hear what I had been up to. We talked around the campfire, exchanging our news. She told me about her day. She described the fishermen who had come to the little clinic she had set up under a thatched roof where she dispensed the medicines provided by Uncle Eric, and demonstrated how a simple saline drip, regularly administered, could cure even the most ghastly tropical ulcer. In fact, as I learned many years later, she had been known as White Witchdoctor—and people had traveled long distances for the aspirins, Epsom salts, and such like that she had brought. I owe her a huge debt, not only for daring to venture into the wilderness with me, but also for the wonderful relations she established with the local people, relations that I and my staff and students have built on and developed ever since.

And there was another quality of Vanne's that I did not appreciate at the time. Often, in my eagerness to learn, I spent the night out in the forest, especially if the chimpanzees nested near the Peak. I carried a small tin trunk up there in which I kept a little tin kettle, some coffee powder and sugar, and a blanket. I would take the blanket to a place from where I could hear if the chimps called at night, and from which I could see them early in the morning. And there I slept. Always I went down, first, to have supper with Vanne. But then, in my youthful selfishness, I left her. I climbed up the well-known trail to the Peak in the moonlight, or with my little flashlight, totally happy. And I left Vanne in camp. I never thought of how she might feel, alone in such a strange new world. And she never complained. Now, looking back, I realize how truly incredible her contribution was.

After Vanne left, I would stay on for another year. She was apprehensive about leaving me alone, but was somewhat appeased when Louis promised to send Hassan, his trusted boat driver from Lake Victoria, to Gombe. He would collect my supplies and mail from Kigoma. Dominic, now joined by his wife and daughter, would continue to cook my food and together they would guard the little camp.

(Hugo van Lawick)

David Greybeard, 1960: The breakthrough observation of toolmaking

Chapter 5

SOLITUDE

I MISSED VANNE FOR HER COMPANIONSHIP, for the long talks we had enjoyed by the campfire, the discussions of new observations. Yet I did not feel lonely after she left: always I have enjoyed aloneness. Day after day, in the sun and the wind and the rain, I climbed into the hills. And gradually I was able to penetrate farther and farther into a magic world that no human had explored before— the world of the wild chimpanzees. There were days when I could not find them at all. But with the new grant, the pressure was off, and I could give myself up to the sheer pleasure of being on my own in the rugged terrain that I was coming to know as well as I had known the Bournemouth chines and cliffs as a child.

It was a time of exhilarating discovery, for I learned something new each day, if not about the chimpanzees then about other denizens of the forest. Perhaps I would encounter a troop of red colobus monkeys traveling noisily overhead along their arboreal pathways through the canopy. Or the lithe, sleek red-tail monkeys who moved almost silently through the trees. The baboons were fascinating, with the constant activity in the troop as infants romped and cheeky juveniles were firmly disciplined by their elders. The adult males were magnificent with the thick, almost manelike hair on their necks and their huge canines—capable of injuring a leopard—which they bared in warning if I incautiously stared into their eyes. Then there were birds and lizards and a whole host of fascinating insects—from the sometimes stunningly beautiful butterflies and moths to the cumbersome scarab beetles rolling their precious balls of dung.

I became totally absorbed into this forest existence. It was an unparalleled period when aloneness was a way of life; a perfect opportunity, it might seem, for meditating on the meaning of existence and my role in it all. But I was far too busy learning about the chimpanzees' lives to worry about the meaning of my own. I had gone to Gombe to accomplish a specific goal, not to pursue my early preoccupation with philosophy and religion. Nevertheless, those months at Gombe helped to shape the person I am today—I would have been insensitive indeed if the wonder and the endless fascination of my new world had not had a major impact on my thinking. All the time I was getting closer to animals and nature, and as a result, closer to myself and more and more in tune with the spiritual power that I felt all around. For those who have experienced the joy of being alone with nature there is really little need for me to say much more; for those who have not, no words of mine can ever describe the powerful, almost mystical knowledge of beauty and eternity that come, suddenly, and all unexpected. The beauty was always there, but moments of true awareness were rare. They would come, unannounced; perhaps when I was watching the pale flush preceding dawn; or looking up through the rustling leaves of some giant forest tree into the greens and browns and the black shadows and the occasionally ensnared bright fleck of blue sky; or when I stood, as darkness fell, with one hand on the still-warm trunk of a tree and looked at the sparkling of an early moon on the never still, softly sighing water of Lake Tanganyika.

The longer I spent on my own, the more I became one with the magic forest world that was now my home. Inanimate objects developed their own identities and, like my favorite saint, Francis of Assisi, I named them and greeted them as friends. "Good morning, Peak," I would say as I arrived there each morning; "Hello, Stream" when I collected my water; "Oh, Wind, for Heaven's sake, calm down" as it howled overhead, ruining my chance of locating the chimps. In particular I became intensely aware of the being-ness of trees. The feel of rough sun-warmed bark of an ancient forest giant, or the cool, smooth skin of a young and eager sapling, gave me a strange, intuitive sense of the sap as it was sucked up by unseen roots and drawn up to the very tips of the branches, high overhead. Why, I used to wonder, did our human ancestors not take to the trees, like the other apes? Or, if we started as arboreal primates, why did we ever come down? In particular I loved to sit in the forest when it was raining, and to hear the pattering of the drops on the leaves and feel utterly enclosed in a dim twilight world of greens and browns and soft gray air.

And there were the enchanted nights when I stayed up on the Peak in the moonlight. Below me the silvery light was reflected from the myriads of leaves that formed the upper canopy of the forest, glistening brightly on the smooth, shining palm fronds. Often the moonlight was so bright that only the most brilliant stars shone, and the gray mist of the sky clung around the mountain peaks and spilled down into the valley below. I was awed by the beauty. Eventually, though, the moon would sink down behind the mountains on the far side of the lake, and gradually even its lingering afterglow faded from the sky. Then the night seemed very different—inky black and sinister with rustlings, and crackling twigs everywhere. It was easy to imagine a leopard slinking through the tall grass, a herd of buffalo browsing the undergrowth. Yet nothing ever harmed me.

And all the time I was learning more and more about the chimpanzees. As I got to know them as individuals I named them. I had no idea that this, according to the ethological discipline of the early 1960s, was inappropriate—I should have given them more objective numbers. I also described their vivid personalities—another sin: only humans had personalities. It was an even worse crime to attribute humanlike emotions to the chimpanzees. And in those days it was held (at least by many scientists, philosophers, and theologians) that only humans had minds, only humans were capable of rational thought. Fortunately I had not been to university, and I did not know these things. And when I did find out, I just thought it was silly and paid no attention. I had always named the animals in my life. Moreover, Rusty and a series of cats, and assorted guinea pigs and golden hamsters, had taught me well. They had made it abundantly clear that animals had personalities, could reason and solve problems, had minds, had emotions—I thus felt no hesitation in ascribing these qualities to the chimpanzees. How right Louis had been to send someone to the field with a mind uncluttered by the theory of reductionist, oversimplistic, mechanistic science.

Once you become familiar with them, chimpanzees look very different, one from another. The easiest one to recognize at that time was Mr. McGregor, a somewhat belligerent old male whose shoulders were bald, as was his head save for a slight frill like a monk's tonsure. He reminded me of the crusty old gardener in Beatrix Potter's *Peter Rabbit.* There was Flo, with her bulbous nose and ragged ears, along with her infant daughter, Fifi, and her two sons, Faben and Figan. William, with his long, sad-looking face, and timid Olly with her elfin daughter, Gilka. There was Mr. Worzle, with his strange humanlike eyes that had white sclerotics instead of the usual brown. And then my favorite of all time, David Greybeard, with his calm and dignified personality. Because he lost his fear of me so soon, he helped me to gain the trust of the others. His acceptance of the white ape meant that, after all, I could not be as terrifying as they had first presumed. Whenever I saw his handsome face and well-marked silvery beard I was always delighted. And often, very often, he was accompanied by the slightly older male whom I named Goliath—not because of his size, which was normal, but because he had a bold and courageous personality. He was, as I eventually learned, the top-ranking male at the time.

And so the weeks became months and all the time I learned new and exciting things about the amazing chimpanzees; and the more I learned, the more I realized how like us they were in so many ways. I observed how they could reason and plan for the immediate future—as when one would sit, look around, scratch deliberately, then suddenly assume a purposeful demeanor, walk over to a clump of grasses, carefully select and trim one, and then, holding it in his or her mouth, set off to a termite mound that was absolutely out of sight. The chimp, upon arrival there, would inspect the mound and, if it yielded termites, a fishing session would commence. I saw chimps use and modify other objects as tools, such as crumpled leaves to sop rainwater from a hollow in a tree. Stones could be missiles; some of the males threw with good aim. And then there were the postures and gestures that complemented the sounds they made—their communication repertoire. Many of these were common to human cultures around the world—kissing, embracing, holding hands, patting one another on the back, swaggering, punching, kicking, pinching, tickling, somersaulting, and pirouetting. And these patterns appeared in the same kind of contexts and seemed to have the same kind of meaning as they do for us. I gradually learned about the long-term affectionate and supportive bonds between family members and close friends. I saw how they helped and cared for each other. I also learned that they could bear grudges that could last for more than a week. I found that their society was complex. They spent much time wandering about in small groups, the membership of which was always changing; and so they were always having to make decisions: whether to travel alone or in a group? with David Greybeard or with Flo? to climb to the high slopes to feed on delicious *muhande hande* or to move down in the cool valleys in search of figs?

Sometimes David let me follow him, and this taught me much. On one typical occasion I arrived below his night nest at dawn. He had slept alone. As it got lighter he climbed down, then sat for a while as though wondering where to go. Then he seemed to make up his mind and set off, quite fast, in a southerly direction. I followed, keeping a respectful distance, pushing through the thick undergrowth, struggling to keep up. We reached a grassy ridge that ran between two valleys and here David stopped, looked down into the trees below, and gave a series of pant-hoots in his deep, distinctive voice. Then he listened, waiting to see if there would be a reply. Almost immediately, from the bottom of the valley, came a chorus of pant-hoots; among the calls I heard Goliath's unmistakable voice.

David set off toward the group and as we got close I could hear the small grunts of pleasure that accompany the eating of good food, the sound of breaking branches, and the pattering of discarded peelings falling to the ground. Suddenly, David pant-hooted again, a different sound this time. He was announcing his arrival, and it provoked an answering chorus. David climbed into one of the trees and I was just in time to watch as he swung toward Goliath and, hair bristling with excitement, they flung their arms around each other in an embrace. They groomed for a short time, then Goliath resumed his feeding and David joined in.

The chimpanzees fed for a couple of hours on the succulent *mtobogolo* figs, one of some fifteen varieties at Gombe. Then, one by one, they climbed to the ground. Some youngsters started to play, chasing and tickling, while the adults settled down to groom each other. It was cool under the shade of the tall trees, and by midday most of the group were stretched out on the ground resting, some actually asleep. In the late afternoon David wandered off with Goliath and I left them, feeling I had intruded enough.

In order to collect good, scientific data, one is told, it is necessary to be coldly objective. You record accurately what you see and, above all, you do not permit yourself to have any empathy with your subjects. Fortunately I did not know that during the early months at Gombe. A great deal of my understanding of these intelligent beings was built up just *because* I felt such empathy with them. Once you know *why* something happens, you can test your interpretation as rigorously as you like. There are still scientists around nowadays who will raise supercilious eyebrows if you talk of empathy with animals, but attitudes are beginning to soften. At any rate, I felt very much as though I was learning about fellow beings in those early days—animal beings who bridged the supposed gap between human beings and the rest of the animal kingdom.

The time I spent in the forests following and watching and simply being with the chimpanzees provided not only scientific data but also gave me a peace that reached into the inner core of my being. The huge, gnarled, and ancient trees; the little streams, chuckling their way through rocky pathways to the lake; the insects; the birds; the chimpanzees themselves; all unchanged in form from the days of Jesus of Nazareth.

One day, among all the days, I remember almost with a sense of reverence. I lay on my back, stretched out on the dead leaves and twigs of the forest floor. I could feel the smooth stones where they pressed into me and I inched my body this way and that until it fitted snugly between them. Way above me David Greybeard was feeding on figs. Occasionally I saw a black arm reaching out to pluck a fruit, a dangling foot, a dark shape moving skillfully through the branches.

I remember I was struck by the harmony of color in the forest, shades of yellow and green deepening to the browns and purples. And the way the vines curled up through the trees, clinging to twigs and branches, twined around each other. I noticed where they embraced an old dead limb and dressed it again with life and color. The midday chorus of the cicadas was loud and strident, breaking out into the forest air in waves as different groups of the insects started up, then dropped out, like

The Birches, the
nineteenth-century
Victorian house in
Bournemouth that
I've called "home" for
most of my life.

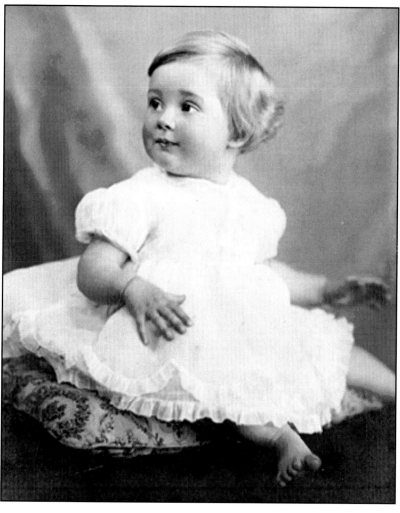

Here I am, one year old and all dressed up.

With my father, mother Vanne, and sister Judy.

(W.E. Joseph)

A pensive shot.

My lifelong love of animals started early.

With Figaro.

(W.E. Joseph)

With Daniel at Bushel's riding stables.

With Nanny, Judy, and Jubilee.

The family in 1947: Judy, Olly, Danny, Audrey, me, Uncle Eric, and Vanne.

Uncle Eric and Danny, with Audrey, Vanne, and Olly.

Reverend John Trevor Davies, the great "love" of my adolescence.

Jane and Rusty: The Inseparables.

With my father, prior to leaving for Africa.

Louis Leakey, 1972.

My mother in Gombe, with our
wonderful boat driver Hassan.

(Hugo van Lawick)

My mother Vanne, the "white witchdoctor," in the clinic she set up in Gombe, 1960.

(Hugo van Lawick)

(Judy Waters)

Vanne and walkie-talkie—when I was staying out all night with the chimps, 1960.

David Greybeard on a termite heap. He has just collected a fresh grass stem for use as a tool.

(Hugo van Lawick)

With David Greybeard, the chimpanzee who lost his fear of me before the others and introduced me to his forest world.

(Judy Waters)

(Judy Waters)

The bride and her father.

Newly wed to Hugo van Lawick, 1964.

(Hugo van Lawick)

With Grub at Gombe, 1971.

shrill choristers singing endless round songs without words.

One of the tasks that I had found most difficult during my Theosophy classes was the suppression of circling thought, the first step on the road to experiencing true awareness. There was a time when I had practiced often; then, in the press of life, I had lost the art. But on this day I felt the old mystery steal over me—the cessation of noise from within. It was like getting back into a beautiful dream.

I lay there, part of the forest, and experienced again that magical enhancement of sound, that added richness of perception. I was keenly aware of secret movements in the trees. A small striped squirrel climbed, spiral fashion in the way of squirrels, poking into crevices in the bark, bright eyes and rounded ears alert. A great velvet black bumblebee visited tiny purple flowers, the end section of his abdomen glowing rich orange red each time he flew through one of the patches of sunlight that dappled the forest. It is all but impossible to describe the new awareness that comes when words are abandoned. One is transported back, perhaps, to the world of early childhood when everything is fresh and so much of it is wonderful. Words can enhance experience, but they can also take so much away. We see an insect and at once we abstract certain characteristics and classify it—a fly. And in that very cognitive exercise, part of the wonder is gone. Once we have labeled the things around us we do not bother to look at them so carefully. Words are part of our rational selves, and to abandon them for a while is to give freer reign to our intuitive selves.

A sudden shower of twigs and the thud of an overripe fig close to my head shattered the magic. David was swinging down through the branches. Slowly I sat up, reluctant to return to the everyday world. David reached the ground, moved a few paces toward me, and sat. For a while he groomed himself, then lay back, one hand under his head, utterly relaxed, and gazed up toward the green ceiling above our heads. The gentle breeze rustled the leaves so that the shining stars of light gleamed and winked. And as I sat there, keeping vigil, I thought, as I have thought so often since, what an amazing privilege it was—to be utterly accepted thus by a wild, free animal. It is a privilege I shall never take for granted.

What happened next remains as vivid in my memory now, nearly forty years later, as it was at the time. When David Greybeard moved off along a well-marked trail, I followed. When he left the trail and moved through some dense undergrowth near a stream, I was sure I would lose him, for I became hopelessly entangled in the vines. But I found him sitting by the water, almost as if he were waiting for me. I looked into his large and lustrous eyes, set so wide apart; they seemed somehow to express his entire personality, his serene self-assurance, his inherent dignity. Most primates interpret a direct gaze as a threat; it is not so with chimpanzees. David had taught me that so long as I looked into his eyes without arrogance, without any request, he did not mind. And sometimes he gazed back at me as he did that afternoon. His eyes seemed almost like windows through which, if only I had the skill, I could look into his mind. How many times since that far-off day I have wished that I could, even if just for a few short moments, look out onto the world through the eyes, with the mind, of a chimpanzee. One such minute would be worth a lifetime of research. For we are human-bound, imprisoned within our human perspective, our human view of the world. Indeed, it is even hard for us to see the world from the perspective of cultures other than our own, or from the point of view of a member of the opposite sex.

As David and I sat there, I noticed a ripe red fruit from an oil nut palm lying on the ground. I held it toward him on the palm of my hand. David glanced at me and reached to take the nut. He dropped it, but gently held my hand. I needed no words to understand his message of reassurance: he didn't want the nut, but he understood my motivation, he knew I meant well. To this day I remember the soft pressure of his fingers. We had communicated in a language far more ancient than words, a language that we shared with our prehistoric ancestor, a language bridging our two worlds. And I was deeply moved. When David got up and walked away I let him go and stayed there quietly by the murmuring stream, holding on to the experience so that I could know it in my heart forever.

My rapidly growing understanding of David and his friends increased the deep respect I had always had for life-forms other than my own, and gave me a new appreciation not only of the chimpanzee's place in the scheme of things, but also of our own. Together the chimpanzees and the baboons and monkeys, the birds and insects, the teeming life of the vibrant forest, the stirrings of the never still waters of the great lake, and the uncountable stars and planets of the solar system formed one whole. All one, all part of the great mystery. And I was part of it too. A sense of calm came over me. More and more often I found myself thinking, "This is where I belong. This is what I came into this world to do." Gombe gave me similar feelings of peace to those that I had sometimes found in an ancient cathedral during those days when I lived in the bustling world of civilization.

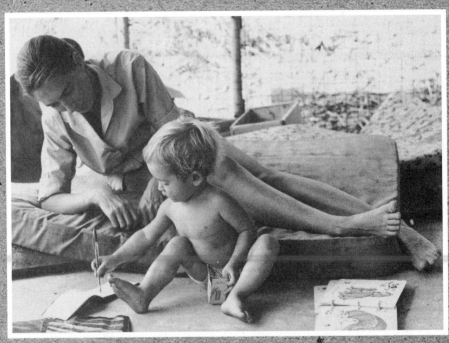

Time with Grub at Gombe, 1968

(Hugo van Lawick)

Chapter 6

A DECADE
OF CHANGE

THE DECADE FROM 1964 TO 1974 WAS BUSY and, in more ways than one, productive. I got my Ph.D. from Cambridge University and, eight years later, became an adjunct professor at Stanford University, teaching human biology to huge undergraduate classes for one quarter a year. I married Hugo van Lawick, the extraordinarily gifted filmmaker and photographer sent by the National Geographic Society to document the Gombe chimpanzee project. Together Hugo and I built up a research station. And we had a child, Hugo Eric Louis. Then, at the end of the decade, we divorced. Thus the ten-year period was filled with hard work—administration, teaching, analysis, and publication of data—and giant changes in my personal life. I discovered the joys and responsibilities of being a mother. I experienced, as have so many others, the bitterness of a close and joyful relationship with a spouse slowly changing and souring, and the intense emotional pain that this generates. And the sense of failure and guilt.

Hugo and I married in 1964. That was when Flo gave birth, and even as I meticulously recorded little Flint's development, so Hugo was able to document this progress with both 16 mm ciné and still cameras. Hugo had set up a banana-feeding station to help him get the footage he needed, and David Greybeard brought more and more members of his community to share the bounty. We then successfully applied for additional funding from the National Geographic Society to employ more students so that we could take advantage of the increased opportunity for collecting data. From these modest beginnings grew a research center that was to become one of the most dynamic interdisciplinary field stations for the study of animal behavior in the world.

During that ten-year period I spent varying amounts of time away from Gombe. I went on my first lecture tour in the United States, which I dreaded most terribly, but managed to survive, acquiring some experience while at the same time sharing some of my knowledge. Leaving Gombe was always a wrench, and the forest-covered slopes generally seemed slightly blurred when I looked back prior to rounding the headland on the way to Kigoma. It was lucky that I had the Birches and my family waiting more or less unchanged at the end of my first trip back to England, because everything else seemed different—harsh and almost alien. In fact, it was I who had changed. After months in Gombe I saw the "civilized" world that we have created with new eyes: the world of bricks and mortar, cities and buildings, roads and cars and machines. Nature was almost always so beautiful and so spiritually enriching; the man-made world seemed so often horribly ugly and spiritually impoverished. This contrast between the two worlds struck me, with increasing sadness, every time I arrived back in England from Gombe. Instead of the peace of the timeless forest and the simple, purposeful lives of its inhabitants I was plunged into the materialistic, wasteful—terribly, terribly wasteful—rat race of Western society. Instead of the soft rustling of the leaves, the gently sighing waves on the beach, the singing of the birds and crickets, my ears were assailed by the sounds of traffic, too-loud rock music, strident voices—and no silence. The fragrance of the white nighttime flowers, and the smell of dry earth after rain, were exchanged for the stink of gasoline or diesel fumes, other people's cooking, disinfectant overriding stale urine in public lavatories. When I was away from Gombe and plunged into the developed world I found it harder to sense the presence of God. I had not learned, then, to keep the peace of the forest within.

I also became aware, during the periods I spent in the Western world, of some of the damage that was being done to the environment. There was grave concern over the horrifying use of Agent Orange to defoliate enemy territory during the Vietnam War. There had been a major radioactive leak in one of the big British nuclear plants. Rachel Carson had published her landmark book *Silent Spring* in which she described how pesticides caused long-term hazards to birds, fish, and other wildlife, as well as domestic animals and humans, while providing only short-term gains in controlling the pests. President John F. Kennedy had formed a committee to investigate these allegations, which were confirmed: as a result DDT and some other pesticides had been banned by 1968 (but continued to be donated to developing countries in bulk, for many years). Another important book was *The Population Bomb* in which Paul Ehrlich expressed his concern about the frightening increases in human populations around the world.

Into that world, in 1967, our son, Hugo Eric Louis, was born. He became known as Grub, as he is still known affectionately today. Our African friends thought we should have called him Simba, because just before he was born, when Hugo and I were camping in the Ngorongoro Crater, our camp was visited in the night by three young male lions who ripped open the cook's tent and had to be gently herded away by our Land Rover. When we got back to the tent the gas ring we had lit (as part of our plan to wave flaming brands at the lions had they tried to get in) had set the tent flap on fire. And when we then sought refuge in a small wooden cabin nearby, there, on the veranda, was a huge black-maned lion digesting his meal while his lioness finished off their gazelle kill nearby.

Grub spent his early years either on the Serengeti, where Hugo was filming lions, hyenas, and wild dogs, or at Gombe, where he spent most of his time. We had to keep him away from the chimpanzees. After all, they are hunters and their favorite prey animals are other primates; to wild chimpanzees human infants are simply another kind of primate. There had been two reports of chimpanzees killing human infants for food in the Gombe area, and Hugo and I were taking no risks.

My life settled into a regular pattern. The glorious solitude of the first couple of years was gone forever, and I often thought back on that time with regret. Yet it was a purely selfish regret—I could never have gathered, on my own, even a tenth of the exciting information that we were learning from the efforts of the students and field staff. I spent the mornings in our house on the lakeshore writing scientific papers, reports, and proposals, and dealing with other administrative matters, while Grub played on the beach, always watched over by one of the staff. And at some point, for about an hour, I went up to the feeding station in the hope that some chimpanzees would show up. The afternoons I spent with Grub.

People have assumed that, because I stayed on at Gombe, having a child made little difference: "How lucky that you could raise a child and carry on with your work at the same time." It was not so. I stopped following the chimps—the students and field staff did that. I merely administered the research station. And spent time being a mother. There were times when I felt a deep sadness and sense of loss for those days when I roamed the forests, alone with the chimpanzees. Now, it seemed, there was a student keenly interested in every single individual chimpanzee as part of the particular aspect of behavior he or she was studying. Which was wonderful in a way, only it meant that I felt something of an interloper. However, I discovered every day anew that having my own child more than made up for that.

One thing I had learned from watching chimpanzees with their infants is that having a child should be *fun*. I spent every afternoon with Grub, and we spent a lot of the time playing, often in the lake, so that he was soon swimming like a fish. It was a marvelous time of learning for me. We all need, as adults, some experience to make us look at the world again through the eyes of a child. As I have mentioned, there was not much time for consciously *thinking* about the meaning of life, but every day I was *feeling* the meaning of life. Those years remain among the most significant in my experience to date. And I realize how fortunate I was. In our modern industrialized societies where economic success is seen as synonymous with happiness, there are many women who will never experience the pure joy of being a mother. Many *want* to work, to continue their careers, after having a child. Others *have* to work to bring their share of money into the household—either to keep up their standards, or simply in order to survive. And in the developing world, where there is so much abject crippling poverty along with large family size, neither motherhood nor childhood is likely to bring much joy. Grub and I were both lucky.

In addition to bringing a new love into my life, Grub's birth rekindled my interest in the nature versus nurture debate, which was at that time producing bitter arguments in scientific circles. Were we humans mainly the product of our genetic makeup or the product of our environment? In recent years, of course, these flames of controversy have died down, and it is now generally accepted that in all animals with reasonably complex brains, adult behavior is acquired through a mix of inherited traits and experience gained as the individual goes through life. In other words, our behavior is neither wholly determined by our genes nor wholly free from them. The more sophisticated an animal's brain, the greater the role that learning is likely to play in shaping its behavior, and the more variation we shall find between one individual and another. And the information acquired and lessons learned during infancy and childhood, when behavior is at its most flexible, are likely to have particular significance.

Of course, like all mothers, I wanted to give my son the best possible start in life. He was my first (and as it turned out, my only) child—and I had to choose between various sources of advice. There was my own mother, there was Dr. Spock—and there was Flo. My observations of chimpanzee mothers with their infants had, even back then, taught me that a secure childhood was likely to lead to self-reliance and independence in adulthood, while a disturbed early life might well result in an insecure adult. Most important, the chimpanzee observations suggested, was the character of the mother, the nature of her relationship with her infant and, to some extent, with other individuals in her community. Mothers who were, like Flo, playful, affectionate, tolerant, and above all supportive, seemed to raise offspring who, as adults, had good relaxed relationships with community members. Mothers who were more harsh, less caring, less playful, like Passion, raised individuals who, as adults, tended to be tense and ill at ease. This applied particularly to daughters, but there was evidence that sons were affected also. It seemed, too, that mothers who had relaxed relations with other adults and who were assertive and confident—again like Flo—provided their offspring with a better start in life than did timid, low-ranking females like Olly whose interactions with others were tense. All the information that we have gained since those early days has substantiated those early impressions.

We cannot assume that factors influencing the development of a chimpanzee infant will be significant also for a human child. But common sense and intuition told me that it was most likely the case. I wanted to make sure that there was a lot of fun in Grub's life. I had learned from Flo that distraction rather than punishment was the best way to teach a small infant. But I had also learned the importance of discipline and consistency. In the end I raised my own son on a mixture of wisdom gleaned from Vanne, Flo, Dr. Spock—and mother nature.

For the first three years of Grub's life we were not parted for even one night, and I devoted at least half of each day solely to him. His early schooling was done by correspondence course. I tried to teach him myself, but when that didn't work out, Hugo and I took on a series of young people who wanted a year's experience between high school and college. Their payment was time spent at Gombe. Then, when Grub was nine years old, he went to school in England, where he lived with Vanne at the Birches. I have always been horrified at the English custom of sending small children, from overseas, off to boarding schools "back home." But this was different. The Birches, with Danny, Vanne, Olly, and Audrey, was an extension of Grub's home. We spent all his holidays together: I went back to Bournemouth for Christmas and Easter, and he came to Tanzania for the summer. Some weekends during school vacations Grub visited Hugo, who was editing films in London at the time.

There is no doubt that my observation of the chimpanzees helped me to be a better mother, but I found also that the experience of being myself a mother helped me better understand chimpanzee maternal behavior: it is hard to empathize with or understand emotions we ourselves have not experienced. It was not until Grub came along, for example, that I began to understand the basic, powerful instincts of mother-love. If someone frightened Grub, or threatened his well-being in any way, I felt a surge of anger. How much more easily I could now understand the feelings of a chimpanzee mother who furiously waved her arms and barked out threats to any who approached her infant too closely, or at a playmate who inadvertently hurt her child.

In 1968 our little camp in the forest was shattered by tragedy: one of the American students fell over a hidden precipice while following chimpanzees and was killed. Ruth Davies was bright, attractive, and full of life. She loved Gombe and the chimpanzees. She was passionately interested in the dominance interactions of the adult males and spent hours observing Mike, Goliath, David Greybeard, the brothers Hugh and Charlie, and the rest. It was this, indirectly, that led to her death. At that time everyone recorded their ongoing observations on little tape recorders, and Ruth's was found close to her body. The tape provided a record of the last hours of her life, rather like the black box of a plane. She had been with Hugh, traveling far in the south, when the accident happened. The tape recorded her exhaustion, for she was struggling for breath at the end. And so, somehow, she had slipped and plunged over a cliff face that was, as we discovered afterward, almost completely concealed by overhanging vegetation.

Ruth's parents decided that their daughter should be buried in the Gombe hills that she had so loved in life. They flew out for the simple service and said that, despite their grief, they were glad to have seen, just the once, the place that had meant so much to Ruth. I too am glad she found her final resting place there; for a long time, I sensed her presence; a gentle, quiet presence, at peace in the forests where, she had often told me, she spent some of the happiest days of her life.

Grub was about one and a half years old when Ruth died. He had come to love her when she stayed with Hugo and me for a few weeks. Although we never tried to explain her death to him, he clearly gathered what was going on in the way that small children do. Grub and I were idly going through a photo album when we suddenly came to a picture of Ruth playing with him in the garden. He pointed: "Ruth!" and then, sadly, "Ruth all broken now."

After Ruth's death it was decided that every student should be accompanied by a local Tanzanian. The doctor who carried out the postmortem on Ruth's body had been able to reassure us that she had not suffered, that she had been killed instantaneously. But during the five-day search we had agonized that she might be lying in great pain, unable to attract attention. If only she had not been on her own—a companion could at least have returned to tell us where she was. And so Hilali Matama,

Eslom Mpongo, Hamisi Mkono, Yahaya Alamasi, and many others joined our field staff. It quickly became apparent that these men, from the little villages around the park, were potentially first-class field researchers. We spent a lot of time training them and soon they became an indispensable part of our research team.

Unfortunately, while I believe I did reasonably well as a mother to my son, things did not work out between my husband and me. We began spending more time apart as Hugo made a film in West Africa and I traveled to America to lecture. And there were basic areas of incompatibility as well. Of course, we had known about these differences in outlook before we married—but as is the case with most young people, we each believed that our chosen partner would change. And when this didn't happen, and the quarreling and bickering got worse, we decided, in 1974, to divorce. Hugo and I remained friends, but it was all very sad, especially for Grub, for he, of course, loved us both.

It was during this emotionally trying period that I had the opportunity to visit Notre Dame, when I went to Paris for a UNESCO conference on aggression. I had wanted to go inside the famous cathedral ever since reading Victor Hugo's *The Hunchback of Notre Dame*. Little did I know just how important that visit would be —for that was when, as described in the introduction, I had an experience of ecstasy—or so it seemed to me; and that revived my old preoccupation with the philosophy and meaning of life. Was there a guiding force in the universe, a creator of matter and thus of life itself? Was there a purpose to life on planet earth? And if so, what role were we humans supposed to play in the overall picture? In particular, what was my role to be?

There are really only two ways, it seems to me, in which we can think about our existence here on earth.

We either agree with Macbeth that life is nothing more than a "tale told by an idiot," a purposeless emergence of life-forms including the clever, greedy, selfish, and unfortunately destructive species that we call *Homo sapiens*—the "evolutionary goof." Or we believe that, as Pierre Teilhard de Chardin put it, "There is something afoot in the universe, something that looks like gestation and birth." In other words, a plan, a purpose to it all.

As I thought about these ultimate questions during the trying time of my divorce, I realized that my experience in the forest, my understanding of the chimpanzees, had given me a new perspective. I personally was utterly convinced that there was a great spiritual power that we call God, Allah, or Brahma, although I knew, equally certainly, that my finite mind could never comprehend its form or nature. But even if there was no God, even if human beings had no soul, it would still be true that evolution had created a remarkable animal— the human animal—during its millions of years of labor. So very like our closest biological relatives, the chimpanzees, yet so different. For our study of the chimpanzees had helped to pinpoint not only the similarities between them and us, but also those ways in which we are most different. Admittedly we are not the only beings with personalities, reasoning powers, altruism, and emotions like joy and sorrow; nor are we the only beings capable of mental as well as physical suffering. But our intellect has grown mightily in complexity since the first true men branched off from the ape-man stock some two million years ago. And we, and only we, have developed a sophisticated spoken language. For the first time in evolution, a species evolved that was able to teach its young about objects and events not present, to pass on wisdom gleaned from the successes—and the mistakes—of the past, to make plans for the distant future, to discuss ideas so that they could grow, sometimes out of all recognition, through the combined wisdom of the group.

With language we can ask, as can no other living being, those questions about who we are and why we are here. And this highly developed intellect means, surely, that we have a responsibility toward the other life-forms of our planet whose continued existence is threatened by the thoughtless behavior of our own human species— *quite regardless of whether or not we believe in God.* Indeed, those who acknowledge no God, but are convinced that we are in this world as an evolutionary accident, may well be more active in environmental responsibility—for if there is no God, then, obviously, it is entirely up to us to put things right. On the other hand, I have encountered a number of people with a strong faith in God who shrug off their own human responsibilities, believing that everything is safely "in God's hands." I was brought up to believe that "God helps those who help themselves." We should all take responsibility, all play our part in helping to clean up and heal the planet that, in so many ways, we have desecrated.

I think that perhaps my experience in Notre Dame was a sort of call to action. I think I heard, in a form suitable for mortal ears, the voice of God—although, at the time, I did not think of it like that. And I did not hear any words, only the sound. Words or not, the experience was powerful, and served to jolt me back into the world into which I had been born, the twentieth century with all its problems. It helped me to realize that the spiritual power that I felt so strongly in the wild and beautiful world of the forest was one and the same with that which I had known in my childhood, in the days of Trevor, in the days when I used to spend long hours in ancient cathedrals.

Indeed, as I look back, my visit to Notre Dame was a milestone along my path. Eventually, when the time was right, I would remember that glorious experience and the words would be revealed. But that would not be for some time to come. In the meantime events were stirring that would test my resilience, and my belief in God, as never before.

(Gay Stryler)

With Derek, 1976

Chapter 7

PARADISE LOST

IT WAS JUST BEFORE MY WORLD TURNED upside-down
that I met the man who would, for a few short years, be
my new partner—in love and in endeavor—Derek
Bryceson. He was director of Tanzania's national parks
and a member of parliament in Dar es Salaam. He had a
passionate love for and loyalty to his adoptive country
and for many years was the only freely elected white in
black Africa. If I had not met him, I'm convinced that the
kidnapping incident that occurred in Gombe in May
1975 would have brought the research there to an end.
He had a strong and forceful character; he was honest to
the point of brutality; and he had a wonderful sense of
humor. He was also an idealist with the will and energy
to work for positive change.

During World War II Derek had been a fighter pilot in
the RAF, but after only a few months of active service he
had been shot down. He damaged his spine in the crash
and was told he would never walk again. He was just

nineteen years old. Determined to prove the doctors wrong, he had, through sheer determination, taught himself to walk with the help of one cane. He had just enough muscle in one leg to move it forward; the other had to be swung forward from the hip. He learned to drive, too, even though he had to lift his left leg with one hand in order to transfer the foot from the clutch to the brake.

Once able to walk, Derek went to Cambridge, where he earned a bachelor's degree in agriculture. He turned down a "cushy armchair" farming job in England which, he told me, had been "suitable for an invalid." Instead he went to Kenya, where he farmed for two years. Then he applied, successfully, to the British government for one of the wheat farms on the foothills of Mount Kilimanjaro; and there, after two years, he met the charismatic political leader Julius Nyerere and became committed to working for Tanzanian independence. For the remainder of his life Derek was a key player in the politics of Tanzania, holding several cabinet posts, including agriculture and health.

President Nyerere had appointed Derek director of parks shortly before I met him. He visited the parks regularly, and sometimes Grub and I joined him in his little four-seater Cessna. It was during one of those trips that we had a brush with death—and somehow, perhaps sensing the impermanence of life on earth, it led to our decision to get married. We had been flying for almost an hour when a small plume of smoke, similar to that made by a cigarette not quite stubbed out in an ashtray, suddenly appeared from under the instrument panel. We were headed for the Ruaha National Park, another forty-five minutes' flying ahead of us. Below, the terrain was rugged, rocky, and covered with trees. Derek checked the instruments; apart from the smoke all seemed okay.

Apart from the smoke! Clearly, in the best of all worlds, one would prefer that there was no smoke. However, there was nothing to be done—except hope for the best, and pray. We all tried to ignore it, but I found it almost impossible to keep my eyes away from the little gray wisp. Fortunately it got no bigger, but those forty-five minutes seemed to go on forever.

At last we reached the national park. The ranger camp and rest house came into view, and we could see the little bush airstrip by the great Ruaha River. And still no flames. Then as we came down to land a herd of zebras decided to cross the runway. Our pilot pulled the plane's nose up. And then, quite suddenly, he lost his nerve. After all that time flying in the company of a wisp of smoke this last-minute delay temporarily unhinged his mind and instead of circling round and coming back to the airstrip, he came down for an emergency landing among the trees on the far side of the river. I was fussing with Grub's seat belt when I heard Derek say, urgently, "You're not trying to land here, are you? Don't!" The last word was a shout—but it was too late.

The plane, flying at twice its normal landing speed, hit the ground. By the grace of God one of the wings smashed into a tree so that the plane swung round—else nothing could have stopped us from flipping over and almost certainly bursting into flames. For what seemed a long time the plane continued to crash on through the bush, totally out of control. Finally, we came to a stop.

The pilot opened up his door and yelled, "Get out quickly—she's going up in flames," and then was gone, not only abandoning his passengers but also leaving the engine running.

"Get out, Grub!" I said to him. "Follow that man." Grub was wonderful. He did exactly as I told him, then, from a safe distance, turned and watched.

But Derek could not jump out. The door on his side of the plane would only open a couple of inches. The wheel of the plane on that side had buckled so badly that the plane sat at a crazy angle, with the opposite wing high up in the air. He could not even push his seat back so as to get more room to maneuver, for all our luggage that had been piled in the back of the plane had fallen onto the floor behind the front seats. Frantically I started hurling it out of the way.

"Have you lost your purse or something?" Derek said, an impish smile on his face. I stared at him. "Don't worry. She won't blaze up now," he reassured me. Oh that marvelous, dry, British sense of humor.

By the time Derek had managed to pull himself up and out through the other door the park staff had arrived. They were relieved to see us alive and unhurt, for they had watched the plane go down and thought they would find us all dead. We had to decide whether to wait for them to send a Land Rover around, over the little hand-operated ferry upstream, which would take about thirty minutes, or risk wading across the Ruaha River—despite the rather large crocodiles that were often seen there. Grub decided for us: if God had saved us when the plane crashed, He surely wouldn't let us be eaten by crocodiles? Desperately needing a cup of tea, for my legs had become weak now that we were safe, I agreed with him. And, whether by divine intervention or, more likely, because all the rangers splashed about in the water on each side of us, the crossing was crocodile-less.

At the park rest house we put on dry clothes and relaxed. Now that we were safe, we realized how very lucky we had been and the shock of it all began to sink in. As I sat there with Derek and Grub, drinking tea, I thought about the crash. I had been sure, as the plane slammed into the ground and careered among the trees, that we were about to die. I remember thinking to myself, "This plane is going to crash and burst into flames." Yet I had felt no fear whatsoever during the crash itself. None at all. I think the reflective part of my mind went numb. I just said to myself, "This is it!" You hear about people who, when facing death, see their life flash by in a series of vivid pictures. Nothing like that happened to me. It was disappointing really.

In the cool of evening we drove out into the park. We found a small herd of elephants drinking. The sun was low in the sky, orange-red behind the fever trees. To us, in the flush of well-being after our reprieve, Africa was beautiful as never before. And I said yes when Derek asked me to marry him.

After our marriage I continued to live at Gombe, as administrator of the research center. By 1975 there were sometimes as many as twenty students living at Gombe, studying not only the chimpanzees, but the baboons as well. We had graduate students from universities in the United States and Europe representing a wide variety of disciplines, mainly anthropology, ethology, and psychology. The students slept in little aluminum huts, covered with grass, hidden away among the trees near the camp. They all gathered together for meals in a large building near the lake and often Grub and I joined them. Derek continued to live in Dar es Salaam but he came to Gombe quite often during his routine visits to all the parks. And he helped me enormously with the running of the center.

In May came the sudden night of terror. Forty armed men crossed Lake Tanganyika in a small boat from Zaire (now Congo) and raided our camp. Awakened by shouting, the park warden, Etha Lohay, went out to investigate. She was captured and, with a rifle to her head, ordered to lead her captors to the student houses. She refused. Fortunately for Etha, the raiders had already found four students—the number they were after (two huts, two mattresses in each, had been prepared on the other side of the lake). Down at the beach, Etha was released. Looking with horror at the victims, their hands tied tightly behind their backs, Etha ran to find our Tanzanian student, Addie Lyaru. Taking off their white nightdresses, blending into the dark night, they hurried round, warning the other students. My house was farther along the lakeshore, and I heard about the raid only after the boat had left. Once we were sure the raiders had left we gathered, in a stunned group, to try to decide what to do. Four of the students—three Americans and one Dutch—were missing. Someone reported hearing four gunshots out on the lake and we were afraid the kidnap victims had been killed. It would be several weeks before we knew what had happened to them.

All non-Tanzanians had to leave Gombe, so we moved to Dar es Salaam, squeezing into Derek's little guest house, and waited for news. It was a nightmare period, greatly relieved when one of the kidnapped students was returned to Kigoma about two weeks later with a ransom demand. At least we knew that the other three were alive. But the demands were excessive, as the rebel group not only wanted a large sum of money and shipments of arms, but had requests for the Tanzanian government, some of which Derek knew could not or would not be granted. Eventually the rebels sent two representatives to Dar es Salaam to negotiate with the American and Dutch embassies. These talks dragged on endlessly and resulted in strained relations all round. It was a period of anguish that I prefer not to think of, and if it was hell for those of us waiting in Dar es Salaam, how much worse it was for the victims themselves, waiting and always wondering if they would be rescued or if they would die in the forests on the other side of the lake from the Gombe paradise from which they had been snatched.

Finally the ransom was paid—money which, it now transpires, was to fund the revolutionary movement of Laurent Kabila, who, twenty years later, would defeat President Mobutu, take over Zaire, and rename it the Democratic Republic of the Congo. After the money was handed over, on the lake at night, the rebels reneged on part of the agreement—only the two young women of the remaining three hostages were released. I was in deep despair at that time, for I was sure that the rebels would kill their last hostage as an example. The high-powered team that had come from America to negotiate had already gone home. Thank God the rebels, for some reason, decided to give up and, after keeping their hostage another couple of weeks, sent him back over the lake to Kigoma. The relief was overwhelming.

Thus all four victims were returned unharmed—physically unharmed, that is. It was the mental torment that had been so terrible. Day after day they had been told: "You must hope that your friends will pay to rescue you because otherwise we shall have to kill you." I suspect that they will never be entirely free from the psychological torment of those days. The memory, surely, will always be lurking there, ready to surface from the depths of the subconscious as terrible nightmares in times of sickness, loneliness, or depression.

After the incident Gombe was considered a "sensitive" area for many months, and we required special government permission for every visit. Without Derek, and the high regard in which he was held by the Tanzanian government, the kidnapping would have spelled the end of the Gombe research. On my own I could not have coped with the new problems that abounded. Derek was able to help with the administration of the research center as well as that of the park. And, most important, he helped to reorganize the Tanzanian field staff, encouraging them to take an increasingly responsible role in the day-to-day organization of the research. Also, from Dar, we were able to keep in daily touch with what was going on by radio. I tried to put the whole nightmare of the kidnapping behind me.

Yet when I returned to America in October 1975 I discovered that the incident was far from over. I was still teaching at Stanford University for two weeks in the spring and the whole of the fall quarter. We had all believed that the money for the ransom had been raised prior to the students' release, but found that this was not the case. Instead, efforts were still being made to collect the money. I contributed what I could, which was not much. And then began what was, for me, a strange and unreal nightmare.

Rumors had been spread. It was suggested that I should leave Stanford, after just two weeks. It might be better that way, I was told, "until things die down." Most of the rumors were about Derek. It was true that he had hoped the students' release might be secured without payment—just because of the precedent that would be set. But the idea that their death would have been a preferable alternative was absurd. He had even been in negotiations to see if his friends in the SAS could rescue them. There were tales also about my lack of responsibility: Why hadn't I given myself up in place of the students that night? The fact that I had not even known what was going on until after the students had been kidnapped was not taken into consideration.

These rumors were circulating in several parts of America. One thing is certain: had I left Stanford then, as had been suggested, I could probably never have gone back to the United States. As it was, I rented a house, and was soon joined by Vanne and Grub, and eventually Derek. Then I set about confronting the rumors. My efforts during the weeks of that fall quarter taught me the meaning of the biblical expression "to gird the loins." I girded my loins again and again, as I set out to confront the various people who were avoiding me. Sometimes this meant weekend plane journeys which I could ill afford. And all this just to explain from my own perspective what had happened. Vanne, as usual, was a tower of strength. We used to discuss strategies far into the night while Grub slept peacefully after his days at the little school on campus. And then, as I tossed and turned, trying to sleep, Danny's text would comfort me too: "As thy days, so shall thy strength be." And, of course, it was.

In addition to feeling distressed by what was going on, I was also puzzled, until I was interviewed by a man who was investigating twelve major kidnappings that had recently taken place in different parts of the world, one of them the famous Patty Hearst case. I shall never forget what he said at the end of our meeting. "Jane, I know you think that your situation is unfair and shocking. Unfortunately in every case that I have investigated when large sums of money were handed over, there was a breakdown in relationships. Friendship and trust turned to hostility and bitterness. In every case."

What a horrible commentary on human nature. Just when people are hurting and vulnerable, trying to pick up the threads of their lives, friendships disintegrate into feelings of hostility and bitterness. But for me, those tough weeks eventually came to an end, leaving me somewhat battered and exhausted—but at least most of the rumors had been laid to rest. It also marked the end of my teaching position at Stanford: it was the end of an era.

It is all long ago now, and I seldom think of those days. I only mention it here because it was so devastating at the time, and because it taught me so much about human nature. Many people I had thought to be true friends turned out to be fair-weather friends. I learned who my *real* friends were. And what a wonderful support they were. Some of my ex-students came from long distances to spend time with me, boosting my morale to no end. There is no question but that I emerged a stronger and more self-confident person. The whole series of experiences had been so utterly unexpected, so bizarre, and so challenging. I remember praying for strength to do what I had to do. I believe, in retrospect, that overcoming those challenges strengthened my faith in God.

After the kidnapping there was no longer a Ph.D. resident at Gombe, so that our main funding source was unable to continue supporting the research—yet another challenge. Two wonderful friends, Prince Ranieri di san Faustino and his wife, Genevieve, or Genie, wanted to help. Ranieri felt it important that I should be able to build up a fund myself, so that I need not be utterly dependent on grants. And so he set to work to get legal status for a nonprofit institute bearing my name. Tragically he passed away before this came into being, but Genie carried on with the paperwork and in 1976 the Jane Goodall Institute was founded. Over the years many supportive, talented, and dedicated people would serve on the board, helping to ensure the future of the chimpanzees of Gombe, and helping also to expand our programs. And so, despite the kidnapping and its confusing aftermath, the research at Gombe continued, though in a slightly different form: the information would no longer be collected solely by a team of students from around the world, but mainly by an increasingly skillful team of Tanzanian field staff recruited from the villages around the park. Eventually they would be joined by a handful of foreign researchers and a Tanzanian Ph.D.

For a couple of years after the kidnapping, however, there were no foreign students at Gombe. Indeed, for the first few months, I was not allowed to visit myself for more than a couple of days at a time. Gradually, though, everything relaxed and I was permitted to stay for a week or two. And then it was almost like going back to the old days, for I had my house on the beach to myself and, once again, could follow any chimpanzee I wanted to without fear of upsetting one of the students, or interfering with their study. On one of those visits, about three years after the kidnapping, I was sitting on the lakeshore, watching the glorious sunset, and thinking. The sky, a delicate duck egg blue, was patterned with clouds that hung, glowing red and gold, over the hills on the far side of the lake. It seemed so utterly peaceful. Yet just across the calm, softly sighing water to the west, in eastern Zaire, and northward toward Burundi, was a monstrous lack of peace—there was fear, hatred, and violence. The villagers in Zaire were frequently terrorized by groups of rebels from the same group as the kidnappers. Just the night before I had watched, through my binoculars, hungry flames leaping toward the sky—village huts that were burning, punishment because the rebels had not been given as much food as they had demanded. Apparently that was commonplace. Occasionally canoes full of sad and hungry refugees pulled onto the Gombe beaches.

Zaire had always been troubled, I reflected. After all, when Vanne and I had first arrived in Kigoma in 1960 the little town had been overrun with the first waves of refugees fleeing from what was then the Belgian Congo. They were Belgian refugees fleeing from the revolution that drove the old colonial masters out of the Congo— and which would lead to the emergence of Zaire under the dictatorship of President Mobutu. Hundreds of Belgians had fled over the lake, some wounded, many without any possessions, and had been temporarily cared for in a huge warehouse in Kigoma port. Vanne and I, temporarily stranded ourselves, had helped the people of Kigoma prepare food for the refugees. I still remember being part of the team that made some two thousand Spam sandwiches, wrapped them in damp cloths, and delivered them in a series of tin trunks. Vanne's and my departure for Gombe had been delayed for a week or so, till the authorities were sure things would stay calm.

After that stormy beginning, things had been quiet and peaceful. And although, in November 1961, I had been asked (by the British authorities) to leave Kigoma at the time of Tanganyika's independence in case rioting broke out, the people remained peaceful. Indeed, Louis Leakey had, unknowingly, chosen the most politically stable of all the twenty-one African countries where chimpanzees are still found; during all my forty-odd years in Tanzania there has never been rioting or rebellion, thanks largely to *Baba ya Taifa*, the Father of the Nation, Julius Nyerere. But Gombe was only twenty-two miles from the border with Burundi in the north, and periodically we were aware of the tense situation in that little country as conflicts between the Tutsi and the Hutu peoples flared up, each time resulting in the brutal killing of thousands of innocent men, women, and children.

In 1972 that ongoing and ancient conflict had erupted into full-scale massacres. We had sometimes heard the guns when the wind blew from the north, and had even made plans to hide in the hills should the situation worsen. But, apart from a marked increase in the number of French-speaking Africans walking southward along the beach, and in the streets of Kigoma, nothing—for us—had seemed to change.

I thought about all the violence as I sat watching the sun sink into the peaceful-looking mountains on the far side of the lake. Mountains where people, even as I looked, were hiding and in fear of their lives, planning how best to escape from their tormentors. And I thought how sad it was that, for all our sophisticated intellect, for all our noble aspirations, our aggressive behavior was not just similar in many ways to that of the chimpanzees—it was even worse. Worse because human beings have the potential to rise above their baser instincts, whereas chimpanzees probably do not. Certainly, I thought, the years of study at Gombe, the gradual unveiling of the dark side of chimpanzee nature, had thrown new light on how and why we humans behave as we do.

Faben

(Hugo van Lawick)

Chapter 8

THE ROOTS OF EVIL

LOUIS LEAKEY SENT ME TO GOMBE with the hope that a better understanding of chimpanzee behavior might provide us with a window on our past. Farsighted genius that he was, he told me he thought my work would take at least ten years to complete, and this at a time when studies of just *one* year were almost unheard of. Of course, when I set out I had no plan to remain at Gombe for ten years. It seemed a whole lifetime when I was twenty-six years old. Yet had I stopped after only ten years, I should have continued to believe that chimpanzees, though very like us in behavior, were rather *nicer.* Then came a series of shocking and horrific events.

In 1971 one of our researchers, David Bygott, observed a brutal attack on a female of a neighboring community. She was set upon by a group of "our" males who hit her and stamped on her, one after the other. During the course of this assault, which lasted more than five minutes, her infant of about eighteen months was seized, killed, and partially eaten. The mother managed to escape, but she was bleeding heavily and was so badly wounded that she probably died later. When David came back and described what he had seen we were stunned. We discussed it far into the night, eventually deciding that it must have been a once-only incident, a bizarre aberration. After all, the ringleader was the alpha male Humphrey, whom most of us considered something of a psychopath at the best of times, with a history of vicious attacks on females of his own community. Humphrey, we felt, must have encouraged the others to behave in such an uncharacteristic way.

Sadly, the "noble ape" was as mythical as the "noble savage"; we would witness many more incidents of brutal intercommunity aggression, several of which led to infant killing. Sometimes the interactions between "our" chimpanzees and the "stranger" females from other communities took a bizarre form. One of these unfortunate females was caught by a group of adult males as they patrolled their southern boundary. They climbed into the tree where she was feeding, her infant clinging to her belly. She made desperate attempts to appease the adult males who surrounded her, approaching with submissive grunts, crouching close to the branch. For a while it seemed that this was working. Some of them even began to feed. When one male passed close by, she reached out to touch him with a typical submissive gesture at which he jerked away, stared at the arm she had touched, seized a handful of leaves, and vigorously rubbed at his defiled hairs. And then, a few minutes later, all the males joined in a brutal gang attack. Her infant died, and her wounds were so severe that, although we had no proof of her death, it had seemed almost impossible that she could recover.

In 1975 we recorded the first of the observed cannibalistic attacks made by the high-ranking female Passion, and her young adult daughter, Pom, on newborn babies of females *of their own community*. I was in Dar es Salaam when I heard about this. Passion and Pom had killed and eaten Gilka's baby. That's what the message sounded like on the two-way radio. I hoped we'd got it wrong—how could such a thing happen? Unfortunately it was only too true.

Derek and I flew to Gombe and heard the story in gruesome detail. Gilka had been sitting cradling her infant when Passion had appeared, stared for a moment, then charged with bristling hair. Gilka had fled, screaming loudly. But she was lame; one wrist had been partially paralyzed during an epidemic of polio in 1966. Crippled, and with a baby to support, she hadn't stood a chance. Passion had seized the infant, killed him with one strong bite to the forehead, then settled down to share the grisly feast with her daughter and juvenile son.

Why had this happened? There was no shortage of food at Gombe at the time—Passion had not needed the infant's flesh for her survival. And Gilka wasn't from a neighboring chimpanzee community; she and Passion had known one another all their lives. As we discussed the horrible incident, we began to wonder whether a similar fate had befallen Gilka's firstborn twelve months earlier; he also had vanished when he was a couple of weeks old. The final horror came one year later when Gilka again gave birth and again lost her infant to Passion. She put up a fierce fight, despite her physical disabilities—

but this time Pom joined in and it was easy for her to seize and kill the baby while the stronger Passion attacked Gilka, inflicting wounds that never properly healed. She had lost three infants in as many years, and I think her spirit was broken.

Some two years later I came upon her dead body close to the swift-flowing Kakombe stream. She was not quite twenty years old, and I had known her all her life, for she was a tiny infant in the early 1960s. As I stood there I reflected on the long series of misfortunes that had dogged her almost from the start so that her life, begun with such promise, had unfolded into a tale of sadness. She had been an enchanting infant, filled with fun and an irrepressible gaiety despite the rather staid and asocial character of her mother. As a youngster she had delighted in male society and, a born show-off, would twirl and pirouette and somersault in an ecstasy of joy. Then, as a juvenile, she had contracted polio. The disease had not only left her with a semiparalyzed wrist but had killed her infant brother with whom she had been so utterly absorbed. As a young adolescent her elfin, heart-shaped face had been deformed by a cruel fungus disease. It had caused grotesque swelling of her nose and brow ridge, so much so that there had been times when she had been almost blind, bumping into things as she struggled along the trails. After the death of her mother she had seemed very lonely. Her strongest bonds had been with her elder brother, and it was touching to see how he waited for his lame sister on those occasions when they traveled together. I had been so pleased when she gave birth to her first infant—he would be a companion for her. But he had vanished when he was a couple of weeks old. Three times, in all, her experience of motherhood had been cruelly snatched away. Very likely Passion had killed all three infants. And Gilka had been such an attentive, affectionate mother during the few weeks that she had the babies with her.

It was dim and green in the forest, dappled with shifting spots of light where the rays of the late afternoon sun fell through the rustling leaves of the canopy above. There was the murmuring of the stream and then, catching at the heart, the pure, hauntingly beautiful song of a robin chat. As I looked down on her, I knew a sudden sense of peace. Gilka, at last, had shed the body that had become nothing but a burden.

During the four-year period from 1974 to 1978, ten infants were born into our study community—only one survived. We know that five of them (including Gilka's two) were killed and eaten by Passion and Pom, and we suspect the other three were also. We began to talk seriously about ways to prevent further attacks but, fortunately, both Passion and Pom gave birth themselves and the cannibalism stopped.

This did not mean that all was well, for the once peaceful-seeming chimpanzees were heavily engaged in what amounted to a sort of primitive warfare. This had begun when the chimpanzee community, whose members I had come to know so well, began to divide. Seven adult males and three mothers and their offspring began spending longer and longer periods of time in the southern part of the range over which the whole community roamed. By 1972 it was obvious that these chimpanzees had formed an entirely new and separate community. This southern, Kahama, community had given up the northern part of the range, while the Kasakela community now found itself excluded from places in the south where it had previously roamed at will. When males of the two communities encountered one another in the overlapping zone between the two, they threatened one another; the group with fewer males gave up quickly and retreated to the heart of its home range. This was typical territorial behavior.

But by 1974 the aggression became more serious. The first deadly attack was seen by Hilali Matama, our headman. Six Kasakela males moved silently toward their southern border where they encountered one of the young Kahama males, Godi, feeding quietly by himself. When he saw them he tried to flee, but he was seized and held to the ground while the Kasakela thugs beat him up, stamping on him, hitting him, and biting him for ten minutes. Then they left him lying on the ground, screaming weakly. Slowly he got up, still screaming, and gazed after them. He must have died of his wounds, for he was never seen again.

That was the first attack in a series of brutal assaults perpetrated by the powerful Kasakela community on individuals of the breakaway community: the Four-Year War. And it was not only the adult males who were victimized, but the adult females also. All the attacks lasted between ten and twenty minutes and resulted in the subsequent death of the victim. All told, four of the seven breakaway males were seen to be attacked; one was found dead, his body mutilated in a way that indicated he also had been victimized by the Kasakela males, and the remaining two simply disappeared. The attack on one of the three adult females was seen; the other two vanished. In other words, during the war, the entire community that moved south was annihilated—with the exception of three young childless females. They were actively recruited by the victorious males.

The four years from 1974 through 1977 were the darkest in Gombe's history, and some of the most intellectually and emotionally challenging years of my life. Our peaceful and idyllic world, our little paradise, had been turned upside-down: The kidnapping and the ensuing shock and fear. The violence of the Four-Year War, along with other intercommunity attacks. The cannibalistic behavior of Passion and Pom. And on the personal side, there had been my divorce with all its heartache and remorse. And, worst of all, came news of Danny's death. In just four years so much of my world had been shattered.

The kidnapping and its aftermath of bitterness and misery affected all of us who were part of it. Yet all my life I had known about kidnapping and ransom; experiencing it firsthand did little to change my view of the dark side of humanity. However, the brutal killings observed among the chimpanzees were different: they changed forever my view of chimpanzee nature. During the first ten years of the study I had believed, as mentioned previously, that the Gombe chimpanzees were, for the most part, rather nicer than human beings. I had known aggression could flare up, sometimes for seemingly trivial reasons; chimpanzees are volatile by nature, yet for the most part aggression within the community is more bluster and threat than fierce fighting—a whole lot of "sound and fury signifying nothing." Then suddenly we found that chimpanzees could be brutal—that they, like us, had a dark side to their nature.

For months I struggled to come to terms with this new knowledge. Often I awoke at night with horrific pictures of violence in my mind: Passion, looking up from the tiny dead body of Gilka's infant, blood smearing her lips; Satan cupping his hand to collect and drink the blood that ran from Sniff's wounded face; Faben twisting Godi's broken leg, round and round. And Madam Bee lying hidden under the vegetation, slowly dying of her terrible wounds, while her ten-year-old daughter tried to comfort her, gently grooming her and keeping the flies away.

When I published the first observations of intercommunity killing at Gombe I came in for a good deal of criticism from certain scientists. Some critics said that the observations were merely "anecdotal" and should therefore be disregarded. This was patently absurd. We had watched, at close range, not just one but five brutal attacks on the Kahama community, and recorded many assaults on stranger females from neighboring social groups. Then there were those scientists who were convinced that the Gombe chimpanzees were not normal because of our banana-feeding policy. This was a valid criticism. However, the intercommunity attacks on neighboring females all took place at the periphery of the Kasakela range, far from the feeding station. And the Kahama individuals had all left the banana-rich territory, voluntarily and apparently permanently. In no instance could it be said that the attacks occurred because they were trying to return. Even more significantly, other field researchers had observed similar aggressive territorial behavior in other parts of the chimpanzees' range across Africa.

Even among scientists who accepted the Gombe data, there were those who believed that it had been a mistake to publish the facts; they thought that I should play down the aggressiveness whenever possible. Why this strong resistance? It was my first experience with the politics of science, the pressure to publish or not to publish for political, religious, or social reasons. One colleague said, after I had told him about the violence among the chimps, "You should never publish this because it will give irresponsible scientists and writers the data they need to 'prove' that our human tendency to engage in conflict is innate, that war is, therefore, inevitable—an unfortunate and regrettable legacy from our brutal ape-like ancestors."

It was during the early 1970s that the subject of aggression became so highly political. This was hardly surprising, since questions about the nature of aggression were still linked with the horrors of the second world war that we had recently lived through. On one side of the debate were those who believed that aggression was innate, coded in our genes; on the other, those who held that a human infant came into the world like a blank sheet of paper upon which the events that occurred during its life would be etched and that this would determine the child's adult behavior.

The first conference on this nature versus nurture debate that I attended was organized by UNESCO in Paris. I was amazed to hear scientists whom I greatly respected solemnly declare that all aggression, in their opinion, was learned. Therefore, they argued, by dint of eliminating all experience of violence and aggression, all stories about it, all nationalism, all martial music, all competition, all punishment, and all sorts of other experiences that I forget now, from the lives of children, we should succeed in creating a utopian society without aggression. After all, ran the argument, those peoples untouched by "progress" like the Bushmen and the Eskimos were totally without aggression and warfare: clearly then the true nature of the human being was utterly peaceful. Already that had been proven untrue, but the "noble savage" concept was still one that many clung to. My comments at that conference about fighting for dominance and intercommunity conflict in the chimpanzees, along with other descriptions of aggressive behavior, were welcomed by half of those present, and hotly disputed by the other half.

There was one scientist in particular, whom I had always greatly admired, but who, to my surprise, came out strongly on the "blank slate" side of the controversy. I shall never forget asking him, over a cup of coffee: "Do you *really* believe that all aggression is learned? I don't see how you can, as an ethologist." "Jane," he replied, "I'd rather not talk about what I really believe." He went down in my estimation.

I shall always remember too the psychologist from the Soviet Union. We were, of course, at the height of the Cold War, and he had to go off and make a phone call to his boss before he dared to answer any question that had even a remotely political or controversial slant.

I had gone to Gombe neither to prove that the chimps were better or worse than humans, nor to provide myself with a platform for making sweeping pronouncements about the "true" nature of the human species. I had gone to learn, to observe, and to record what I observed; and I wanted to share my observations and reflections with others as honestly and clearly as I could. Certainly I felt strongly it was better to face up to the facts, however unsettling, than to live in a state of denial.

Once the details of the intercommunity conflicts at

Gombe were published, a number of writers did indeed use the data to argue that it proved, once and for all, that violence was deeply embedded in our genes, inherited from our ancient primate ancestors. We humans, they concluded, were bloodthirsty creatures: crime and warfare were therefore inevitable. This view gained additional credibility with the 1976 publication of Richard Dawkins's sociobiological study of human motivation, *The Selfish Gene*. Dawkins argued that our behavior is determined primarily by our genes. Since the "goal" of these specks of protein is to propagate themselves, most of what we do is shaped by the need for genetic survival, either through our own reproductive success or through that of our relatives because they share various proportions of our genes. This means that we are likely to help our kin, particularly those to whom we are the most closely related, such as brothers and sisters, in order to ensure the survival of our genes. And what if we help a nonrelative? This is not really because of any wellspring of human caring or love, but rather because we (or more accurately our genes) "expect" our good deed to be reciprocated. I rescue you from drowning today in the expectation that one day you will rescue me, or my relatives. And we are innately selfish—in that everything we do is for our own ultimate genetic survival. Moreover, as Dawkins commented in a subsequent paper, we should not expect any help from a God, for we live in a universe run by nothing "but blind, pitiless indifference."

Dawkins's book became a best-seller in part, I think, because for many people it provided an excuse for human selfishness and cruelty. It was just our genes. We couldn't help it. At the same time, medicine was revealing the physical causes underlying many psychological disturbances. It was comforting, perhaps, to disclaim responsibility for our bad behavior. I thought back to the stories of sadistic brutality and torture told by Holocaust survivors. Did Dawkins's theory help to explain how, in a supposedly cultured, civilized country, mass killings and genocide on such a scale could have taken place?

I concluded back then, and I still believe, that it is pointless to deny that we humans harbor innate aggressive and violent tendencies. My own instinctive surges of anger when my precious infant Grub seemed to be threatened are proof enough for me. And many scientific experiments have shown that aggressive patterns, at the very least, are easy to learn. In the early 1970s, when I was an associate professor at Stanford, the psychiatrist Robert Bindora was conducting an experiment to test how readily small children learned aggressive patterns. He produced a dummy human figure, set it in front of a group of kids between two and three years old, then proceeded to beat, pummel, punch, stamp on, and kick it. He repeated each of these actions several times, slowly and clearly. Then, at varying times afterward, he gave these same children access to the dummy and recorded their response. As might be expected, his little subjects eagerly attacked the figure, performing many of the same actions that he had demonstrated. A good argument against allowing small children to watch violence on television. (I begged for a similar experiment in which the dummy would be kissed, embraced, stroked, and so on. But it was never done.)

And so the behaviors of the Gombe chimpanzees provided fuel for much theorizing; and many scientists were eagerly arguing about them, using them—or not—to substantiate or refute their own pet theories on the nature of *human* aggression; whereas I, with my work at Gombe, was trying to understand a little better the nature of *chimpanzee* aggression. My question was: How far along our human path, which has led to hatred and evil and full-scale war, have chimpanzees traveled?

(David Bygott)

Chapter 9

PRECURSORS TO WAR

IT WAS BOTH FASCINATING AND APPALLING to learn that chimpanzees were capable of hostile and territorial behavior that was not unlike certain forms of primitive human warfare. War had always seemed to me to be a purely human behavior. Accounts of warlike behavior date back to the very first written records of human history; it seems to be an almost universal characteristic of human groups. Wars have been fought over a wide range of issues, including culturally and intellectually determined ideological ones. They have functioned, at least ecologically, to secure living space and adequate resources for the victors. To some extent too, they have served to reduce population levels, thus conserving natural resources.

Moreover, as Darwin pointed out, warfare in prehistoric times, since it involved conflict between groups, rather than between individuals, must have put considerable selective pressure on the development of increasingly sophisticated cooperation among group members. Communication skills would also have been crucial: the emergence of a complex spoken language would have given the greatest advantage of all. Qualities of intelligence, courage, and altruism would have been highly valued and the best warriors may well have had more women and fathered more offspring than cowardly and less skilled group members. This process would escalate, because the greater the intelligence, cooperation, and courage of one group, the greater the demands placed on its enemies. It has actually been suggested that warfare may have been the principal evolutionary pressure that created the huge gap between the human brain and that of our closest living relatives, the anthropoid apes. Whole groups of hominids with inferior brains could not win wars and were therefore exterminated.

Certainly the first true humans were unique by virtue of their large brains. It was because the human brain is so large when compared with that of a chimpanzee that paleontologists for years hunted for a half-ape, half-human skeleton that would provide a fossil link between the human and the ape. In fact, this so-called "missing link" is surely comprised of a series of vanished brains, each more complex than the one that came before it. These brains, alas, have forever been lost to science, save for a few faint imprints on fossil craniums.

When we think of war, we usually picture vast armies on the move, terrifying confrontations between men mounted on horses, marching on foot, driving armored jeeps and tanks, flying fighter planes or bombers and, in the worst scenario, pressing buttons that, in an instant, could destroy whole countries. Human wars are waged between countries; and between factions within countries—revolutions and civil wars have been among the most brutal of all.

The Four-Year War of the Gombe chimpanzees could not, of course, measure up to human warfare of this sort, yet it had become clear that the apes were on the very threshold of this otherwise uniquely human achievement. After all, in human history the large-scale deployments of men and weapons did not emerge, fully fledged, overnight. Like all our cultural advancements, war evolved gradually over the centuries from primitive chimplike aggression to the organized armed conflict of today. There are still living groups of indigenous peoples whose form of warfare is not so different from that of the Four-Year War of the Gombe chimpanzees—where raiding parties creep into the territory of the next village to kill and plunder.

Whilst warfare in its typical human form is a cultural development, certain preadaptations must have existed in our earliest ancestors to permit its emergence in the first place. The most crucial of these would have included cooperative group living and hunting skills, territoriality, use of weapons, and the ability to make cooperative plans. There would also need to have been an inherent fear or hatred of strangers, expressed by aggressive attack. The Gombe chimpanzees clearly possessed, to a greater or lesser degree, the above qualities.

Certainly chimpanzees were aggressively territorial. Not only did they protect their home range from incursion by "strangers"—that is, individuals of either sex (with the exception of adolescent females) from neighboring communities—but they also actively patrolled the boundaries of their home range at least once a week, monitoring the movements of their neighbors. And not only did they *defend* their territory, they also sometimes *enlarged* it at the expense of a weaker neighbor. The most likely cause of the Four-Year War at Gombe was the Kasakela males' frustration at being denied access to an area over which they had roamed until it was occupied by the breakaway community.

It was obvious, too, that some male chimpanzees, particularly the younger ones, found intercommunity conflict absolutely thrilling. Despite the risk, adolescent males had sometimes crept closer and closer to watch the "enemy" even when the rest of their "patrol" had retreated to its own home range. This fascination with danger would have been crucial to the emergence of warfare in early humans. The killing of adult conspecifics (members of the same species) is not common among mammals, as such conflicts can be dangerous for the aggressors. It has always been necessary to encourage human warriors by cultural methods: glorifying their role, condemning cowardice, offering high rewards for bravery and skill on the battlefield, and so on. But if human males were inherently disposed to find aggression attractive, particularly aggression directed against neighbors, this would make the training of soldiers much easier. And this does seem to be true. All the male members of my family, in both world wars, had rushed to join up the moment the clarion call went out. Derek had been underage; he toured every air force training center until he found one that was not too particular about red tape. We know, only too well, how human beings are fascinated by death and suffering. Public hangings were among the most popular of events in medieval England. Just today, as I was writing this chapter (August 1997), I read in the newspaper how ten thousand people gathered in western Teheran for the execution of a convicted rapist. They watched as he was lifted by a crane, a noose around his neck, high into the air above them. Gradually he kicked and jerked less vigorously as the air was choked out of him. The biggest crowds at motor races gather at the dangerous corners; the most popular jumps for the crowds at steeplechases are those known to fell the greatest number of horses. Miles-long traffic jams form when there has been a particularly bad accident—partly because everyone slows down to look. It is, of course, because these things are out of the ordinary, and many people who lead otherwise humdrum lives feel in need of stimulation. This is why violence, on television and in our newspapers and magazines, is deemed newsworthy.

One of the most significant facts established about human behavior, as it relates to warfare and other acts of violence against conspecifics, is the following: cultural evolution permits the development of *pseudospeciation*. Pseudospeciation, simply defined, means the transmission of individually acquired behavior from one generation to the next within a particular group. Over time this leads to the collective culture (the customs and traditions) of that group. Pseudospeciation (or cultural speciation as I prefer) in humans means, among other things, that the members of one group (the *in*-group) may not only see themselves as different from members of another group (the *out*-group), but also behave in different ways to group and nongroup individuals. In its extreme form, cultural speciation leads to the dehumanizing of out-group members, so that they may come to be regarded almost as members of a different species. This frees group members from the inhibitions and social sanctions that operate within the group, and enables them to direct acts toward "those others" which would not be tolerated within the group. Slavery and torture at one end of the scale, ridicule and ostracism at the other.

The Gombe chimpanzees quite clearly show the precursors to cultural speciation. Their sense of group identity is strong; they clearly differentiate between individuals who "belong" (to the community) and those who do not. Infants of females who are part of the group are protected while infants of females who do not belong may be killed. This sense of group identity is far more sophisticated than mere xenophobia. The members of the Kahama community had, before the split, enjoyed close and friendly relations with their aggressors; in some cases they had grown up with them and had traveled, fed, played, groomed, and slept together. By separating themselves, it was as though the Kahamans had forfeited their "right" to be treated as group members—instead, they were treated as strangers. And, just as civil wars in our own species can be the most shocking, so it was with the assaults on these onetime friends. All those attacks were brutal, but the worst, for me, was the attack on my old friend Goliath, who had, inexplicably, cast his lot with the southerners. He was so ancient, thin, and frail and utterly harmless. He was trying desperately to hide, crouching under some thick undergrowth, when they found him. He was dragged out, screaming. Five adult males, his former grooming partners, took part in this assault. And an adolescent seized every opportunity to rush in and contribute his own small blows, screaming in excitement. For eighteen minutes they attacked, hitting and biting and dragging, twisting one leg round and round. When they left, wild with excitement, the old male tried to sit up, but fell back, shivering. Although we searched for him every day for a week we never saw him again.

Time and again the Kasakela males, when attacking Kahama chimps, showed aggressive patterns not seen during fights with members of their own community yet seen regularly when chimpanzees are trying to incapacitate and dismember a large prey animal. So that in addition to being hit and kicked and pounded on, the unfortunate Kahama victims had their bones broken, strips of skin torn off, and, as we saw with Goliath, their limbs twisted round. They were dragged and flailed in the gang assaults. One aggressor even drank his victims' blood. The Kahama chimps were indeed treated as though they were prey animals—they were thoroughly "de-chimpized."

Unfortunately, cultural speciation has become very highly developed in human societies around the world. Our tendency to form select in-groups from which we exclude those who do not share our ethnic background, socioeconomic position, political persuasions, religious beliefs, and so on is one of the major causes of war, rioting, gang violence, and other kinds of conflict. We find examples of our human tendency to form in-groups from which we exclude others in our cities, towns, and villages, in schools and neighborhoods. Children very quickly form exclusive groups, sticking together, supporting each other, and distancing themselves from all others. Children who have formed such a group can be extremely cruel to "outsiders" and some children suffer intensely as a result. William Golding's *Lord of the Flies* is a terrifying novel because we know that children, given the right (or, rather, the wrong) environment, *can* behave barbarically. Today, cultural speciation is obvious in the terrifying evolution of the modern gangs. Gangs similar to Los Angeles's Crips and Bloods exist throughout the world with their identifying colors and graffiti and other cultural differentiations. They are just one example of the evils resulting from cultural speciation in our own species.

In the late 1970s, as I tried to understand the relationship between chimpanzee aggression and human violence, there was much evidence of the evils of in- and out-grouping among human peoples around the world. There were the ethnic, political, and religious hatreds in Rwanda, Burundi, Israel, Palestine, Cambodia, Northern Ireland, Angola, and Somalia. Genocide, or *ethnic cleansing*, had led to the killing of hundreds and thousands—nay, millions—of humans. The rise to power of one man in Germany had led to the Holocaust, the most obvious horror of our time because of the vastness of its scale and the calculated cold-bloodedness of its monstrous plan. Indeed, when the full horror of Hitler's extermination program had filtered through to the general public, the free world firmly believed that such an outrage against humanity could never be repeated. Alas! Stalin, in the communist Soviet Union, was clamping down on individual freedom and condemning thousands to death as dissidents and traitors; the purges of Mao were exterminating countless thousands of innocent people in China; Pol Pot in Cambodia went on to carry out his own savage genocide.

It was particularly shocking for me to reflect on the extent to which different religious groups had, from the beginning, tried to force their beliefs on others. The number of wars throughout history that had been fought over religious issues was staggering. The so-called holy wars—fighting over whose god was *the* God—had resulted in an incomprehensible amount of suffering inflicted on unbelievers by those who had the upper hand at the time. Stories of torture during the terrible days of the Roman Catholic Spanish Inquisition had been among the most horrifying in my school history books.

Yet it was true also that at the heart of the teachings of the great religious leaders was a plea to renounce violence, to gather in rather than exclude those of different faiths. Although I never studied religion formally, my reading of the Bible and the sermons I heard, particularly Trevor's, had suggested that Jesus of Nazareth had been very sensitive to the perils of in-grouping. Throughout his life he had attempted to expand the circle of his compassion to include people of all races, creeds, and social classes, even the generally hated Romans: "Love your enemies, bless them that curse you, do good to them that hate you, and pray for them which despitefully use you and persecute you." He also advised: "Judge not that ye be not judged." Similar expressions of tolerance and inclusiveness can also, of course, be found in Eastern scriptures.

Clearly, I reflected, cultural speciation had been crippling to human moral and spiritual growth. It had hindered freedom of thought, limited our thinking, imprisoned us in the cultures into which we had been born. And, provided we remained locked within these cultural mind prisons, all our fine ideas about the Family of Man, the Global Village, and the uniting of nations would be just rhetoric. Although, to be sure, there was some comfort in knowing that at least we realized how we *ought* to want to live, and the kinds of relationships we *ought* to want to have. But it was obvious that unless we "walked the talk," racism, bigotry, and fanaticism, as well as hatred, arrogance, and bullying, would continue to flourish. (As, indeed, they have.)

Cultural speciation was clearly a barrier to world peace. So long as we continued to attach more importance to our own narrow group membership than to the "global village" we would propagate prejudice and ignorance. There was absolutely no harm in being part of a small group—indeed, with our hunter-gatherer band mentality it gave comfort, provided us with an inner circle of friends who could be utterly trusted, who were absolutely reliable. It helped give us peace of mind.

The danger came only from drawing that sharp line, digging that ditch, laying that minefield, between our own group and any other group that thought differently.

By the end of the 1970s, then, I had come to accept that the dark and evil side of human nature was deeply rooted in our ancient past. We had strong predispositions to act aggressively in certain kinds of contexts; and they were the same contexts—jealousy, competition for food or sex or territory, fear, revenge, and so on—that triggered aggression in chimpanzees. Moreover, I had learned that the apes show similar postures and gestures to ours when they are angry—swaggering, scowling, hitting, punching, kicking, scratching, pulling out hair, chasing. They hurl rocks and sticks. Without a doubt, if chimpanzees had guns and knives and knew how to handle them, they would use them as humans do.

In some respects, however, human aggressive behavior was, indeed, unique. Thus while it seemed that chimpanzees had *some* awareness of the pain they inflicted on their victims, they were surely not capable of cruelty in the human sense. Only we humans inflict physical or mental pain on living creatures *deliberately* despite—even *because of*—our knowledge of the suffering involved. Only we, I concluded, are capable of evil. And in our evilness we have designed a variety of tortures that have, over the centuries, caused unbelievable agony to millions of living, breathing human beings. Thus I could see that human wickedness is immeasurably worse than the worst aggression of the chimpanzees.

But did that mean that we humans must be forever enslaved to our evil genes? Surely not. Surely we, more than any other creatures, are able, if we so wish, to control our biological nature? And are not the caring and altruistic aspects of human nature equally part of our primate heredity?

What, if anything, I wondered, could our study of chimpanzees tell us about the roots of love.

(Michael Neugebauer)

Fannie and Fax

Chapter 10

COMPASSION
AND LOVE

Fʀᴏᴍ ᴛʜᴇ ᴇᴀʀʟɪᴇsᴛ ʏᴇᴀʀs ᴀᴛ Gᴏᴍʙᴇ I had been fascinated and delighted by the friendly and nurturing behavior that I observed so often among the chimpanzees.
Peaceful interactions within a community are seen much
more often than aggressive ones. Indeed, for hours, even
days, one can follow a small group of chimps and see no
aggression at all. Of course, these chimpanzees are, as we
have seen, capable of violence and brutality. But fights
between members of the same community seldom last
more than a few seconds and rarely result in wounding.
For the most part, relationships between the members of
a community are relaxed and friendly, and we see frequent expressions of caring, helping, compassion, altruism, and most definitely a form of love.

Chimpanzees are intensely physical. When friends
meet, after a separation, they may embrace and kiss each
other. When they are fearful or suddenly terribly excited

they reach out to touch each other—sometimes they show a whole orgy of contact-seeking behaviors, embracing, pressing open mouths upon each other, patting each other, holding hands. Friendships are maintained and poor relationships improved by the most important of all friendly behaviors—social grooming. Grooming enables adult chimpanzees to spend long hours in friendly, relaxed physical contact. A session may last more than an hour as the participants work their way, with soothing movements of their fingers, over every inch of each other's bodies. Grooming is used to calm tense or nervous companions, and mothers often quiet restless or distressed infants in the same way. And when chimps play, there is a lot of body contact as they tickle each other, and roll over and over in bouts of rough-and-tumble wrestling matches. Loud chuckles of chimpanzee laughter accompany these joyous play sessions so that even fully adult group members are sometimes compelled to join in.

As the years passed at Gombe and we learned more about who was related to whom in the chimpanzees' complex society it became obvious that ties between family members were particularly strong and enduring, and not just between mothers and their offspring, but also between siblings. I learned a great deal from the hours I spent with old Flo and her family. I watched as she not only rushed to the defense of her juvenile offspring, Flint and Fifi, but also tried to help her adult sons, Figan and Faben. When Flint was born, Fifi soon became utterly preoccupied with the new baby. As soon as she was allowed, she played with him, groomed him, and carried him around. Indeed, she became a real help to her mother. Eventually I realized that all young chimpanzees are fascinated and delighted by new arrivals in their families, and that these sibling relationships persist over many years. Brothers become close friends as they mature and often then become allies, protecting each other in social conflicts or when under attack by other individuals.

These sibling bonds are adaptive in many ways. On one occasion, nine-year-old Pom, leading her family along a forest trail, suddenly saw a big snake coiled up. Uttering a soft call of concern she rushed up a tree. But little brother Prof, still a bit unsteady on his feet at three years old, ignored her warning. Perhaps he did not understand its meaning or simply did not hear it. As he got closer and closer to the snake Pom's hair bristled with alarm, and she grinned hugely in fear. Suddenly, as though she couldn't bear it anymore, she rushed down to Prof, gathered him up, and climbed back up her tree.

One most moving story is about orphan Mel and Spindle, his adolescent protector. Mel was three and a quarter years old when his mother died. He had no elder brother or sister to adopt him. To our amazement (for we had thought he would die), he was adopted by twelve-year-old Spindle. Although all members of the Gombe chimpanzee population have a few genes in common, Spindle was certainly not closely related to Mel. Nevertheless, as the weeks went by, the two became inseparable. Spindle waited for Mel during travel; he permitted the infant to ride on his back, even allowed him to cling beneath, as a mother carries her baby, when Mel was frightened or when it was raining. Most remarkably, if Mel got too close to the big males during social excitement when inhibitions are sometimes swept aside, Spindle would hurry to remove his small charge from danger even though this usually meant he was buffeted himself. For a whole year this close relationship endured, and there can be no doubt that Spindle saved Mel's life. Why did Spindle act that way, burdening himself with the care of a small, sickly youngster who was not even a close relative? Probably we shall never know, but it is interesting to reflect that during the epidemic that claimed Mel's mother, Spindle's ancient mother died also. A typical twelve-year-old male chimpanzee, though perfectly able to fend for himself, will continue to spend much time with his mother, especially if he has been through a stressful time with the adult males, or been hurt in a fight. Is it possible that Spindle's loss of his mother left an empty space in his life? And that the close contact with a small dependent youngster helped to fill that space? Or did Spindle experience an emotion similar to that which we call compassion? Perhaps he felt a mixture of both.

Chimpanzees in zoos are often kept in enclosures surrounded or partially surrounded by water-filled moats. Since they do not swim, death by drowning has been a sadly frequent mishap. But almost always one or more of the victim's companions have attempted to rescue the individual in difficulties. There are a number of accounts of heroic rescues, or rescue attempts. In one instance an adult male lost his life as he tried to rescue a drowning infant who was not his own.

Evolutionary biologists do not count the helping of family members as true altruism. Your kin all share, to a greater or lesser extent, some of the same genes as yourself. So your action, they argue, is just a way of ensuring that as many of those precious genes as possible are preserved. Even if you lose your life through some helping act, your mother or sibling or child who has been saved will ensure that your own genes are still represented in future generations. Thus your behavior can still be seen as fundamentally selfish. And what if you help an individual who is not related to you? This is explained as an example of "reciprocal altruism"—help your companion today in the expectation that he will help you tomorrow. This sociobiological theory, while helpful in understanding the basic mechanism of the evolutionary process, tends to be dangerously reductionist when used as the sole explanation of human—or chimpanzee—behavior. After all, whilst our biological nature and instincts can hardly be denied, we are, and have been for thousands of years, caught up in cultural evolution as well. We do things which are sometimes quite unrelated to any hope for genetic survival in the future. Even Richard Dawkins, in an interview in the *London Times Magazine*, said, "Most of us, if we see somebody in great distress, weeping—we will go and put an arm around them and try to console them. It's a thing I have an overwhelming impulse to do . . . and so we know that we can rise above our Darwinian past." When he was asked how this could be, he smiled and said he didn't know. But I gradually came to see that a simple explanation presents itself.

Patterns of caring and helping and reassurance evolved, over thousands of years, in the context of the mother-child and family relationships. In this context they are clearly beneficial to the well-being of the living individuals as well as in the evolutionary sense. So these behaviors have become ever more firmly embedded in the genetic endowment of chimpanzees (and other higher, social animals). And so we would expect an individual who is constantly interacting with other familiar companions—with whom he plays, grooms, travels, and feeds and with whom he forms close relationships—to treat them, at least sometimes, as honorary family members. Obviously, then, he is likely to respond to the distress or pleas of these honorary family members as well as those of his blood relations. In other words, a close but not related companion may be treated as if he or she were biological kin.

Compassion and self-sacrifice are highly valued qualities in many human cultures. If we know that another person, particularly a close personal friend or relative, is suffering, we become upset. Only by doing something, by helping (or trying to help) can we alleviate our own discomfort. We may also feel the need to help people we do not know at all. We send money, or clothing, or medical equipment to earthquake victims, refugees, or other suffering people in all corners of the globe, once their plight has been brought to our attention. Do we do these things so that others will applaud our virtuous behavior? Or because the sight of starving children or homeless refugees evokes in us feelings of pity which make us terribly uncomfortable, feelings of guilt because we know we have so much, and they so little?

If our motivation to perform charitable acts is simply to advance our social standing, or to lessen our inner discomfort, should we not conclude that our action, in the final analysis, is nothing more than selfish? Some might argue thus—and in some cases it could be true. But I believe it is wrong—dangerous even—to accept reductionistic arguments of this sort that denigrate all that is most truly noble in our species. History resounds with tales of extraordinarily inspirational acts of courage and self-sacrifice. Good heavens!—the very fact that we can feel distressed by the plight of people we have never met says it all for me. It is, surely, remarkable and heartwarming that we can empathize, and feel truly saddened, when we hear of a child brain-damaged in an accident; an elderly couple losing their life savings to a thief; a family dog stolen and sold to a medical research lab and traced too late to be saved.

So here we are, the human ape, half sinner, half saint, with two opposing tendencies inherited from our ancient past pulling us now toward violence, now toward compassion and love. Are we, forever, to be torn in two different directions, cruel in one instance, kind the next? Or do we have the ability to control these tendencies, choosing the direction we wish to go? During the early 1970s these were the questions that gripped me. Yet here again, my observations of the apes offered at least a glimmer of an answer.

Thus chimpanzees, I realized, although freer to act the way they feel than we are, are not entirely uninhibited. As they get older, they usually give up the frustrated tantrums of childhood, although they may let off steam by charging through the undergrowth, sometimes slapping a bystander who gets in the way. An outburst of swearing and table thumping can sometimes do the same for humans. Chimpanzees have excellent mechanisms for defusing tense situations. Thus the victim in a fight, even though he or she is clearly fearful, often approaches the aggressor, uttering screams or whimpers of fear, and makes some gesture or posture of submission, such as crouching low to the ground, or holding out a pleading hand as though begging for reassurance. And the aggressor will usually respond—touching, patting, or even kissing or embracing the supplicant. The victim visibly relaxes and social harmony is restored. Indeed, for the most part, the chimpanzees follow Danny's favorite text: they seldom let the sun go down on their wrath.

One female chimpanzee, living in a large captive group in a zoo in Holland, became amazingly skillful at restoring peaceful relations. Whenever two of the adult males were sitting tense after a conflict, avoiding each other's gaze, there would be noticeable agitation running throughout the entire group. This old female would then initiate a grooming session with one of the rivals, during which she gradually moved a little closer to the second male—followed by her grooming partner. Then she would leave him and repeat her maneuver with his rival. Eventually the two males were so close that both could groom her at the same time. When she was thus the only thing separating them she quietly moved away, and, calmed by the grooming, and neither having to be the first to break the deadlock, they started to groom each other.

Surely, I thought, if chimpanzees can control their aggressive tendencies, and diffuse the situation when things get out of hand, so can we. And herein, perhaps, was the hope for our future: we really do have the ability to override our genetic heritage. Like strict parents or schoolteachers, we can reprimand our aggressive tendencies, deny them expression, thwart those selfish genes (unless we are suffering from some physiological or psychological disorder, and major strides have been made in medication for such conditions). Our brains are sufficiently sophisticated; it's a question of whether or not we really *want* to control our instincts.

In point of fact most of us discipline those rebel genes on a day-to-day basis. As did Whitson, a twelve-year-old African-American boy, in a little incident which could have escalated into violence, but which was beautifully defused. Young Whitson was one of a group of kids gathered in Colorado for a youth summit. It had just snowed—and Whitson, from San Francisco, had not seen more than about twenty snowflakes in his life. He made a snowball that got bigger and bigger and bigger as he rolled it along the ground. Somehow he managed, with help, to get this large and very heavy mass of impacted snow onto his head. He wanted to see how far he could carry it on the planned hike. I was right close by when a girl from Virginia, white and middle-class, came up behind him and, I suppose as a joke, pushed the snowball off his head. It shattered into many pieces on the hard ground. I was close by when this happened, so I saw Whitson's face, and saw the shock, the horror—and then, unmistakably, the expression of fury. Indeed, he raised a hand as if to strike her, though he was much the smaller. And then she, horrified at what she had all unthinkingly started, cried out, "Oh I am so so sorry. I don't know what made me do that. I'm really, really sorry," and she knelt to try to repair the broken ball. For a moment Whitson went rigid. Slowly he lowered his arm, slowly the rage left his face. And then he too knelt. Together they repaired the snowball. He won out over his aggressive impulse—and I was proud of them both.

Indeed, it is fortunate that we are not *compelled* to obey our aggressive urges. If we did not inhibit feelings of aggression continually, society would be extremely unruly, as is the case when social norms break down during rioting and warfare—when the ugly face of anarchy grins out of the chaos.

And so, as the 1970s came to a close, I began to take heart. Our knowledge of chimpanzee behavior does, indeed, indicate that our aggressive tendencies are deeply embedded in our primate heritage. Yet so too are our caring and altruistic ones. And just as it appears that our wicked deeds can be far, far worse than the aggressive behavior of chimpanzees, so too our acts of altruism and self-sacrifice often involve greater heroism than those performed by apes. Chimpanzees, as we have seen, may respond to the immediate need of a companion in distress, even when this involves a risk to themselves. However I think it is only we humans, with our sophisticated intellect, who are capable of performing acts of self-sacrifice with full knowledge of the costs that we may have to bear, not only at the time, but also, perhaps, at some future date.

Whether or not chimpanzees would choose to die in order to save a companion if they *could* comprehend the stakes, I do not know. It seems highly unlikely that apes have any understanding of the concept of death, or their own mortality: in which case they could not make a *conscious* decision to give up their lives for a friend—although their helping actions might result in just that. But we humans certainly can make conscious decisions of this sort. We find examples of heroic self-sacrifice all the time if we read the newspapers or watch television. A recent example in England was when Pete Goss, who was winning a round-the-world yacht race, turned back, in the teeth of a terrific storm, when he heard the distress signal of a fellow competitor. Unhesitatingly he not only risked his life to rescue a French rival from his yacht that was breaking up in huge seas, but also sacrificed his chance of winning a prestigious award. Some of the most inspiring tales of heroism have come from the battlefields of war when, time and again, men and women have risked—and lost—their lives to help a wounded or endangered companion. The highest award for bravery in England, the Victoria Cross, only too often has to be awarded posthumously. Resistance fighters in occupied countries have, again and again, carried out secret missions against the enemy despite the very real risk of death and, worse, torture; sacrificing themselves and even their families for their beliefs or their country.

Acts of self-sacrifice in the hell of the death camps were frequent. There was a moving incident that took place at Auschwitz when a Pole, facing a death sentence, sobbed and begged that his life might be spared so that he could stay with his two children. At this moment, the great priest Saint Maximilian Kolbe stepped forward and offered his life instead. After surviving two weeks in the starvation bunker, Kolbe was then murdered by the Nazis but the story lived on, serving as an inspiration to surviving prisoners: a beacon of hope and love had been lit in the dark confines of the concentration camp.

Nor was it only in the death camps that such acts took place. The extraordinary and selfless deeds of Oskar Schindler, who employed and rescued countless Jews in Poland, have been immortalized in Steven Spielberg's *Schindler's List*. Less well known is the heroic effort of two consuls in Nazi-occupied Lithuania. Jan Zwartendijk, act-ing Dutch consul, without any authorization wrote out almost two thousand transfer permits for Lithuanian Jews who were trying to escape the approaching Nazi occupation. These documents gave them permission, from the Dutch government, to enter the Dutch colony of Curaçao. Zwartendijk was fortunate to escape himself. Japanese consul Chiune Sugihara, in direct defiance of his superiors in Tokyo, wrote out visas for several thousand Jews to pass through Russia on their way to Curaçao. He knew that this involved personal risk and being disgraced and fired. But he was a samurai who had been taught to help those in need. "I may have to disobey my government," he said, "but if I don't, I would be disobeying God." He was indeed later disgraced in Tokyo, and ended his life in financial ruin and without honor: yet some eight thousand Lithuanian Jews, who would otherwise have been killed in the death camps, escaped. It was the third largest rescue operation in the history of the Holocaust. An estimated forty thousand descendants of the Jewish refugees saved in 1940 are alive today because of the courageous actions of these two remarkable men.

The most significant event for Christians (along with the Resurrection) is that Jesus offered up His life, gave Himself into the hands of His persecutors, knowing only too well the agony He would endure. "Father . . . take this cup from me," he prayed, in the Garden of Gethsemane. "Nevertheless, not my will, but Thine be done." He sacrificed himself because He believed His act would redeem mankind.

It is these undeniable qualities of human love and compassion and self-sacrifice that give me hope for the future. We are, indeed, often cruel and evil. Nobody can deny this. We gang up on one another, we torture each other, with words as well as deeds, we fight, we kill. But we are also capable of the most noble, generous, and heroic behavior.

Derek at the feeding station in Gombe

Chapter 11

DEATH

THE ROOTS OF HUMAN COMPASSION, altruism, and love, as we have seen, lie deeply embedded in our ancient past. Love takes many forms and often we use the word too loosely. We love our friends, our family, our pets, our country. We love nature, storms, the sea. We love God. Whatever it is that we love, the greater our love, the greater our corresponding sense of grief if the loved person or thing is lost. It is the depth of our love that will determine the depth of our grieving—not the nature of the object of our loving. A lonely person, living with a beloved cat or dog, will grieve far more for the passing of the pet, and rightly so, than for the passing of a relative—even a parent—with whom no truly loving relationship was formed.

Because humans have a concept of death, we know intellectually that death follows life. We know that we ourselves will come to the end of our time on earth. Almost certainly we are the only living creatures who have this knowledge. Chimpanzees understand the difference between life and death. Olly's month-old infant became almost totally paralyzed during the polio epidemic—he could only breathe and cry. And it seemed that he felt pain, for every time his mother moved he screamed. It was touching to see how tenderly she cradled him, arranging the tiny, limp limbs carefully so as not to crush them. Then, during a long grooming session between Olly and daughter Gilka, the baby died. The difference in the way Olly treated him was dramatic. She continued to carry him for the next three days, but it was a *thing*, not a baby, that she took with her. Dragging him by one leg, throwing him over her back, dropping him, head first, to the ground. She had lost infants before. She knew. But when a young mother, Mandy, lost her first infant, she continued to treat the corpse as though it was alive for at least three days. Only when the dead body began to smell and attract flies did she become less caring. Experience is needed, it seems, before a chimp learns that death is irreversible. If her next infant became sick, would Mandy fear that death might follow? Would she remember how sickness gradually weakened her baby until no life was left? Perhaps. The chimpanzees continually surprise us, demonstrating ever more of those qualities that once we believed unique to ourselves. But I do not believe that they have a concept of death. And most surely they can have no concept of life after death.

I personally have never been afraid of death itself for I have never wavered in believing that a part of us, the spirit or the soul, continues on. It is the process of *dying* that I shy away from. I would imagine we all do, for it is so often associated with sickness and pain—and today with all the indignities of modern hospital treatment, where life is maintained with tubes and drips. A kind of death in life. All of us, I'm sure, would prefer a sudden death, would want to leave the world quickly when our time comes—and not only for our own sake, but also for the sake of those who love us. (And, of course, it saves a lot of money. Dying can be a horribly expensive business!)

In the Western world death is not much talked of. In our society a growing percentage of our population is over sixty-five, yet the emphasis is on youthfulness, staying young. Sick people are quickly sent away to be cared for by strangers—and often not just for their own good, but because relatives don't want to be involved in their sickness. We are uncomfortable in the presence of the seriously sick, partly because we do not know, emotionally, how to cope with their pain and suffering, and partly, I suspect, because it reminds us of our own vulnerability. Seldom, today, do people lay out the bodies of departed loved ones in the living room so that friends and relatives can pay their last respects. It is considered too upsetting, too morbid. While we live, death must be kept out of sight. So we have created a strange artificial world in which the only people familiar with dying are hospice workers, doctors, nurses, paramedics, and morticians.

In the old days, people died at home, with their families gathered round them. Danny watched her mother die. She and a nurse were together by the bedside, and they watched the old lady take her last breath. And I'll never forget Danny saying to me: "We both saw a silver wisp come out of her mouth, and hover for a moment, then vanish. We knew it was her soul leaving her body."

I was with Derek when he died but I did not see his

soul leaving. I did hear his last labored breath. And I was with him throughout his last three months. Every day. It was the hardest time, the cruelest time, of my life—watching someone I loved dying slowly, and in pain, from cancer. I had always believed that this was something I simply could not cope with, but when the time came, I had no choice. I had to watch him get weaker, and suffer, and die. Many who read this book will have known the same harrowing experience. Those who have not may well have the grim experience ahead of them.

It was in September 1979, after a series of severe stomach pains, that Derek made an appointment to see a doctor in Dar es Salaam. I don't know if he suspected that it was cancer. And I don't know why I felt so sure what the diagnosis was going to be. But the moment he left the house I started to cry. It was as though I were caught in some novel; I just threw myself onto our bed and cried and cried. "Please God don't let it be cancer. Please God don't let it be cancer." I said it over and over and over again. I cried until I was exhausted. In fact, I got most of my crying out of the way before he came back to tell me they had found an abdominal mass.

After that things moved quickly, and within a week we were flying to England, where an appointment had been made with one of the best consultant surgeons in the country. The doctor was encouraging. He made his examination, studied the X rays and the results of a variety of tests, and then gave his verdict.

"Yes, you've got a tumor," he said, "in the colon. But it's a simple operation. There is a very high percentage of patients who make a full recovery and I don't think you have anything much to worry about."

And so, I thought to myself, all my crying was for nothing. We had a wonderful few days in Bournemouth, at the Birches. We felt elated. It was all going to be all right.

But it wasn't all right, it wasn't all right at all. We returned to London and Derek was wheeled away for the operation. "Don't hang around here," I was told. "Come back in three hours."

I was tense, and I walked around the streets, waiting, for three hours. And then I went back and waited in the waiting room. And waited and waited. A kindly nurse put her head around the door: "It's taking longer than we thought," she told me. I continued to wait. If I had the time I would like to redesign hospital waiting rooms. How many thousands, in just the same situation as I was, have waited in those bleak impersonal rooms. Waited for news that will make or break their lives.

Finally Derek was wheeled out, looking ghastly as people do after a serious operation, and with all kinds of tubes sticking out of him. How I hated to see him looking like that, my much loved husband. Soon they injected him with more anesthetic and wheeled him away.

By then it was nearly nine P.M., and finally the surgeon came to see me. I'll never forget that interview for the rest of my life. He said he needed to speak with me alone and ushered me into an empty two-bed ward. I remember that it was dark, no lights on at all, and for some reason the doctor didn't switch them on. He simply turned to me in the dim light coming in through the half-open door and said, "Well, I'm afraid I was wrong. It's hopeless. He's got metastases all over, throughout his insides. He's got three months to live, if that. But we can't tell him yet because we don't like to hit people when they're down."

At this point I was in a state of shock. I think I just

stared at him. "I'd give you a lift if I was going in your direction, but you're strong. I know you'll be able to cope," the surgeon said. "Take a taxi, won't you." He patted my shoulder, walked out of the dark room, and was gone.

It was brutal. I went on sitting there for what seemed like hours. Until a kind nurse came in with a cup of tea, which I couldn't drink. I had just been told that Derek was soon to die, that there was no hope. The week before, this same surgeon, all smiles, had told us all would be well, and we should enjoy our weekend. I have never felt so alone in my life. I was numb, sick with apprehension. Above all, not wanting to think.

I was staying with Pam Bryceson, Derek's sister-in-law. Her house was about thirty minutes away by the underground. When I went outside it was after ten o'clock and it was raining. I didn't have the will to look for a taxi, and I didn't want to talk to anyone. I didn't want to admit the truth to anyone. I wanted to stay in this unreal midnight world forever. Like a sleepwalker I retraced my steps to the underground. I went back down the same steps which I had climbed with so much hope that morning. I stood on the almost empty platform and tried to believe that this was all happening to somebody else. Finally a train came and I got in, and sat there, just sat there. I didn't want the journey to end. Perhaps if I stayed quiet I'd find, after all, that it was just a dream. I didn't dare allow myself to think about what I had been told. And so, zombie-like, I was carried on by the tube to some distant station, the last on the line. And, zombie-like, I crossed over and took the next one going back to central London. The last one, I think. It was all unreal. And when I got out of the train I still had a long way to walk. I could be mugged, I thought; I wish I would be mugged; I can't face Derek. It was raining even harder. I might get pneumonia, I thought. Please God, let me get pneumonia.

Of course, I got neither mugged nor sick. There was no escaping the next weeks, the worst weeks of my life. So many, many people have to face the same terrible ordeal, and now I know just how agonizing it is. When Pam opened the door that night, anxious to hear how the operation had gone, she took one look at me, drenched and pale and dead-looking, put her arms around me, and made me take off my soaking clothes. Poor Pam, she had just lost her husband, Derek's brother, and was still in mourning. And now she had this new sadness. She poured me a large whiskey, sat me by the fire, forced me to eat something, then made me take a sleeping pill, which I never do. "You must sleep, so that you can cope tomorrow," she told me.

Certainly I could not have coped with the horror of the next few days without Pam and her sympathy and her sleeping pills. And also I would repeat to myself, every evening before I slept, Danny's favorite text: "As thy days, so shall thy strength be." I spent all of each day with Derek, then returned to Pam's warm house to sleep. I didn't tell anyone else, because the only way I could keep it from Derek was if no one else knew. I wouldn't have told Pam if she hadn't been there when I got back that night. Soon, though, when I felt stronger, I called the family, and told them the awful news.

As always, Vanne was a tower of strength. She came up to London, and we made a plan. We would try other kinds of healing. And so, as Derek gradually recovered strength after the operation and we all maintained the pretense that he would soon be well, I made appointments with a number of homeopaths and healers all over

London. But none of them offered any hope. Finally, through a mutual friend, Vanne heard that Hepzibah Menuhin, the pianist, and sister of the great violinist Yehudi Menuhin, was being treated for cancer at a clinic in Germany, near Hanover. She was back in London for a couple of weeks, and I went to see her. Together we called her doctor and arranged for Derek to be admitted to his hospital. Then, when all had been organized, I told Derek the truth. It was easier telling him now that I had new hope—and easier for him to hear. We left the hospital, and the next day he and I flew to Germany.

Looking back, knowing what I know now—that the surgeon was right, that there was nothing that would stop the spread of the cancer—I still think it was the right decision. The worst part of it was that we were isolated from the rest of the world: very few people other than Hepzibah, her husband, Richard, and the doctor spoke English. Derek and I became very close in this strange new world, together almost every hour of every day. And for the first two of the three months that he would live, we truly believed that he would get well. We believed it absolutely. People have said "How terrible, that you had that false hope." I don't agree. For those two months Derek was filled with mental energy. He began working on an autobiography and I typed it for him. We listened to a lot of classical music together. His friends from the U.K. and Tanzania called, many from England flew over. The then Tanzanian ambassador to Germany was a frequent visitor. And we had many talks with Richard and Hepzibah. We talked for hours, every day.

Those talks were tremendously significant. Richard and Hepzibah believed in life after death, and in reincarnation. We discussed these things in such a matter-of-fact way that Derek began to accept that they were true. But this did not help us much when his health began to deteriorate, when his pain increased so that he could no longer bear to be without morphine, and when I realized but did not want to admit that the British surgeon had been right. Each day became a nightmare. Of course Derek must have known too, but he absolutely did not want to face up to it, or at least he did not want to talk about it. And Richard and Hepzibah were in very much the same situation.

As Derek's health deteriorated I found it increasingly difficult to face each new day and almost impossible to sleep at night. Again and again I had to reassure myself "As thy days, so *shall* thy strength be." The time came when I could not leave in the evening. One of the nurses found me slumped in a chair, and brought in a little bed. But I could not sleep even when Derek, heavily sedated, fell into the drugged, comatose state during which he got through the night. I was haunted by the last words he spoke: "I didn't know such pain was possible." In the end I pleaded with his doctor. "Please, please don't keep him alive this way. Please don't let him suffer anymore." The last day he did not regain consciousness, and in the night, as I lay, wakeful, listening to his rasping breathing, I heard the death rattle and knew he was, at last, free of pain and at peace. I climbed into his bed, and held him close, for the last time. That is how the nurse found us.

During Derek's cruel suffering my faith in God wavered. Indeed, for a while I believed that it was extinguished altogether. From the very start of our time in Germany, Derek and I prayed together, sometimes for an hour at a time, willing, with all the strength our minds were capable of, that the cancer cells would be destroyed. And I would go back to the little room I had rented and have a cup of tea and a chat with my very lovely, sympathetic, and helpful landlady, and sometimes her daughter and grandson would come round as well. And then I would go up to my room and pray some more. But it seemed that nobody heard. "My God! My God! why hast thou forsaken me?" It was, of course, a stage of emotional exhaustion. I was hurting for Derek and I was grieving. I wrote it all down, after he died, to try to exorcise the memory of pain. I wrote: "The gradual increase of pain, the injections at night instead of the pills. Oh the horror, the horror of it. Hell on earth. Suffering for the suffering of one I loved ever more deeply with each passing day. The misery, the anguish. The hoping, praying, desperately seeking a way to cope, damning myself for failure, praying."

You see: *damning myself for failure*. Illogical, but we are not logical in situations such as this. And of course I wanted to blame someone. I was angry with myself: I had tried everything, and failed. An Egyptian faith healer. An Indian spiritualist who possessed some curative dust, if only I could get hold of some. I got hold of it. Washing the body in cold tea. The doctors were dealing with the pills and chemotherapy and a variety of techniques that offered some promise. And nothing, nothing was helping. Instead it was getting worse. I was grieving, suffering— and angry. Angry at God, at fate—the unjustness of it all. And so, for a while after Derek's death, I rejected God, and the world seemed a bleak place. Made even bleaker by the fact that death is a taboo subject. People are afraid of rousing emotions of raw grief if they speak of the dead to those who mourn. How would they cope if the bereaved began to cry? How could they bear it? I knew the feeling well, and now I understood how wrong it was, adding to the loneliness. I realized that it was I who had to reach out to my friends. In a bizarre reversal of roles it was I who had to comfort them, reassure them that to talk of Derek was helpful, not harmful, to my spiritual recovery.

After Derek died I went back to the sanctuary of the Birches for a short time, and then I returned to Tanzania. Derek had wanted to be cremated and to have his ashes sprinkled on the sea that he had so loved in life; on his favorite part of the Indian Ocean, where we had so often snorkeled and, together, marveled at the magic world of the coral reef. It was a harrowing time, especially when, at Heathrow, I was handed the casket that contained his ashes. All that was left of his mortal flesh in one small box. Even now, nearly twenty years after his death, I can vividly recall the utter horror I experienced when I took it into my hands. And so I threw those powdery gray ashes out into the wind. Flesh and bone, the remains of my much loved husband, purified by the intense white heat of fire. It was raining and cold and almost unbearable as the handful of dust settled onto the sea, soon to be absorbed into the teeming life of the coral reef below.

A week later I went to Gombe. It was months since I had been there, and the field staff were really upset at the news about Derek, and understandably concerned for their own future. I was hoping to find healing and strength in the ancient forest. Hoping that contact with the chimpanzees, so accepting of what life brings them, would ease my grief.

The first two days were desperately sad, especially in the evening when I was all alone in the house where

Derek and Grub and I had known so much happiness. Which was peopled, now, by ghosts. And then on the third morning something happened. After my lonely cup of coffee, during which I sat in melancholy sadness and watched the changing colors of the lake, I set off to find the chimps. And as I climbed the steep slope to the feeding station, suddenly I found I was smiling. I was on the part of the trail that Derek, with his paralyzed legs, had found so difficult and tiring. But now it was I, the earthbound one, who was struggling in the heat—he was light and free. He was teasing me so that I laughed out loud.

That night something even more extraordinary happened. I was lying in the bed we had shared, listening to the sound of the waves on the shore, the crickets, all the familiar night sounds. I did not expect to sleep, yet sleep came quickly. And then, sometime during the night, I woke. Did I wake? Anyway, Derek was there. He was smiling and very, very much alive. He spoke to me. It seemed then that he spoke for a long time. He told me important things, things I should know, things I should do. And even as he spoke, my body, all at once, went rigid, and the blood rushed and pounded in my ears. Roaring, roaring. Roaring throughout my rigid body. Slowly I relaxed. "Well anyway," I said, when I could, perhaps aloud, "at least I know you're really here." And almost at once it all came back. My body went rigid again, and was filled again with roaring. I remember thinking "I must be dying" but I was not at all frightened. And when it stopped I remembered nothing at all—only that Derek had been there, that he had a message for me, that it was joyful. Nothing more. None of the wisdom. And almost immediately I fell into a deep sleep.

Later, back in Bournemouth, I wrote to a clairvoyant who had, in the past, been very helpful to Danny. She had retired and she was grieving the death of her own husband. But she agreed to speak with me on the phone. When I described what had happened there was a silence. Then she said, "That is what happened to me after my husband died. Whatever you do, if it happens again, don't try to get out of bed."

I told her I didn't think I could have, even if I'd wanted to. She explained that she had so desperately wanted to write down what she heard that she had forced herself to go and fetch a pencil and paper. As soon as she got out of bed she fainted, and came to lying on the floor, barely able to move. So, I wanted to know, what did she think had been going on? She told me it was an out-of-body experience. I had been, she said, on another plane of consciousness—the plane where Derek was. The roaring sound was caused by the spirit returning to the everyday plane of human consciousness. By moving she had, she believed, risked her life or her sanity.

Well, that was just her opinion. But whatever it was that happened, I knew the next morning that it had not been a normal dream. I was utterly exhausted when I got up—but happier, more able to cope. I had always believed that there is a state of being-ness that does not end with physical death; I had always known that mind could communicate with mind across distance; what happened after Derek's death made me suspect that mind can communicate with mind across time. I do not feel the need to prove this to anyone: there are many who feel the same but we are ill-equipped by Western education for the task of convincing unbelievers of the reality of the spirit. Science demands objective factual evidence—proof;

spiritual experience is subjective and leads to faith. It is enough, for me, that my faith gives me an inner peace and brings meaning to my own life. Yet I do want to share my experiences with those who want to hear. So let me relate two more incidents, both of which occurred on the night of Derek's death. Both involve children, my own son, Grub, who was in England at the time, and Lulu, a little girl who lived in Dar es Salaam.

At the time of Derek's illness, Grub, thirteen years old, was a boarder (his choice) at a little preparatory school near Bournemouth. He did not know that Derek was close to death. Well, the night that Derek was dying, Grub was awakened from his sleep by a vivid dream. In his dream Olly arrived at the school and spoke to him. "Grub, I have something very sad to tell you. Derek died last night." He went to sleep again, but once more was awakened by the dream, and Olly again repeated her message. When it happened a third time he became distressed, and could not sleep. He actually went to the school matron to tell her he was having terrible nightmares, though he did not tell her what they were.

In the morning Olly arrived at the school. Vanne was in Germany with me, having arrived the day before after an urgent feeling that she needed to see Derek. Olly took Grub outside into the garden and told him she had some sad news. "I know," he said. "Derek is dead, isn't he." Olly was stunned—until he told his dream.

Lulu, the same age as Grub at the time, suffered from Down's syndrome. Derek and I had been great friends with her parents and visited their house frequently. Indeed, when first I went back to Dar es Salaam after Derek's death I stayed with them, unable to bear my own empty house. Derek was good with children, and Lulu loved him. The night he died, sometime in the small hours, she woke up and she ran along to where Mary, her nanny, was sleeping.

"Mary," she said, urgently. "Please wake up. That man has come, and he likes me. He is smiling." Mary, half roused, told Lulu she had been dreaming, and to go back to bed. But Lulu persisted. "Please come, Mary. I want to show you. He is smiling." In the end Mary sat up, resigned.

"Lulu, tell me who you mean. Who is this man who is smiling at you?"

"I don't remember his name," said Lulu. "But he comes with Jane, and he walks with a stick. And he likes me. He really likes me."

Two children, in two parts of the world. Two children whom Derek had loved. It is so easy in a skeptical, reductionist scientific world to explain away these sorts of things as coincidental dreams, hallucinations, or psychological reactions triggered by the onset of pain, stress, or loss. But I have never been able to discount such experiences so easily—there have been too many events in my life, and in the lives of my friends, which have defied any kind of scientific explanation. Science does not have appropriate tools for the dissection of the spirit.

Years of war, when those who are loved are dying every day, are filled with powerful psychic experiences, and Vanne, who has always been psychic (though she never talks about it), certainly had her share. I have already told of her premonition of danger that saved our lives when the German plane dropped its bombs on our holiday village. The other incident occurred earlier in the war. She was taking a bath. Suddenly she called out, loudly and urgently: "Rex!" Rex was my father's younger brother.

She began to sob bitterly, tears pouring down her face. My father, on leave, rushed in to see what on earth was going on. "What ever is the matter?" he asked her. "I don't know, I don't know," she sobbed. "I only know it's Rex." Later she learned that she had cried out at the time Rex was shot down and killed in combat over Rhodesia. Hugo's mother had a similar experience when her husband's boat was torpedoed in the war. She was in England, and the ship sank thousands of miles away. It was at night and she woke up terrified, hearing the engines of a German plane overhead, and the sounds of heavy gunfire. She began to cry, knowing her husband was in danger. Gradually she realized that everything was quiet. There was no plane, no gunshots. Not even an air-raid warning. But that was the night her husband died at sea.

My grandmother, Danny, had an awareness of her own imminent departure. She'd always said that she never wanted to be a burden to her family, and toward the end of her life, at the age of ninety-seven, she struggled with bronchial pneumonia. For a time, she couldn't get out of bed by herself, and she hated it. Slowly, she got a little better, but she was not happy that her family had to spend so much time taking care of her. One evening when Vanne went up to say good night she found Danny reading all my grandfather's letters, which she kept by her bed. Danny leaned back on her pillows, carefully tying the ribbon back around Boxer's precious letters (she always called him Boxer, but we never knew why). A little smile came to her face.

"Well, darling, I think you'd better plan my obituary tonight."

She said goodbye to Olly too. And in the morning her

body had been abandoned, still with the little smile on its face. She had gone to join her beloved Boxer. And there was a note on the letters, asking that they be sent with her on her long journey.

During the first six months or so after Derek's death I often felt his presence. I had a strong conviction that in his spirit state he could not see or hear—or perhaps it was that he could not *feel* the things he had loved in earthly life—the sea, the pounding waves, ballet, the graceful hand-over-hand swinging of the young chimpanzees playing in the trees. And I felt very strongly that if I looked and listened with great concentration, and paid attention to every detail, he would be able to enjoy, for a little longer, the things he had loved—through my eyes, through my ears. Perhaps it was fancy, but it comforted me, the thought that he was there, that I could do something for him. And then, after a while, as though he knew that I was all right, that my days had, indeed, brought sufficient strength, I felt his presence less and less often. I knew it was time for him to move on and I did not try to call him back.

(Michael Neugebauer)

It was in the forest that I found "the peace that passeth understanding"

Chapter 12

HEALING

IT WAS IN THE FORESTS OF GOMBE that I sought healing after Derek's death. Gradually, during my visits, my bruised and battered spirit found solace. Time spent in the forests, following and watching and simply being with the chimpanzees, has always sustained the inner core of my being. And it did not fail me then. In the forest, death is not hidden—or only accidentally, by the fallen leaves. It is all around you all the time, a part of the endless cycle of life. Chimpanzees are born, they grow older, they get sick, and they die. And always there are the young ones to carry on the life of the species. These things brought a sense of perspective back into my life, and with it peace. Gradually, my sense of loss was purged of bitterness, and the futile railing against fate was stilled.

One day, among all the days, I remember most of all. It was May 1981 and I had finally made it to Gombe after a six-week tour in America—six weeks of nonstop lectures, fund-raising dinners, conferences, meetings, and lobbying for various chimpanzee issues. Six weeks in and out of hotels, living out of a suitcase, packing and unpacking. I was exhausted and I longed for the peace of the forest. I wanted nothing more than to be with the chimpanzees, renewing my acquaintance with my old friends, getting my climbing legs back, relishing the sights, sounds, and smells of the forest. I was glad to be away from Dar es Salaam, with all its sad associations—the house that Derek and I had shared, the palm trees we had bought and planted together, the rooms we had lived in together, the Indian Ocean in which Derek, so handicapped on land, had found freedom swimming among his beloved coral reefs.

Back in Gombe. It was early in the morning and I sat on the steps of my house by the lakeshore. It was very still. Suspended over the horizon, where the mountains of the Congo fringed Lake Tanganyika, was the last quarter of the waning moon and her path danced and sparkled toward me across the gently moving water. After enjoying a banana and a cup of coffee, I was off, climbing up the steep slopes behind my house, carrying only my little binoculars, a notebook, a pencil, and a handful of raisins for lunch. I never feel the need for food, and seldom for water, when I am roaming the forests. How good it felt to be alone at last, reveling in the simple life that had nourished my spirit for so long.

In the faint light from the moon reflected by the dew-laden grass, it was not difficult to find my way up the mountain. All around, the trees were shrouded with the last mysteries of the night's dreaming. It was quiet, utterly peaceful. The only sounds were the occasional chirp of a cricket, and the soft murmur where the waves caressed the stones on the beach below. Suddenly there was a burst of song, the duet of a pair of robin chats, hauntingly beautiful. I realized that the intensity of the light had changed; dawn had crept upon me unawares. The coming brightness of the sun had all but vanquished the silvery, indefinite illumination of its own radiance reflected by the moon.

Five minutes later I heard the rustlings of leaves overhead. I looked up and saw the branches moving against the lightening sky. The chimps had awakened. It was Fifi and her offspring, Freud, Frodo, and little Fanni. I followed when they moved off up the slope, Fanni riding on her mother's back like a diminutive jockey. Presently they climbed into a tall fig tree and began to feed. I heard the occasional soft thuds as skins and seeds of figs fell to the ground.

For several hours we moved leisurely from one food tree to the next, gradually climbing higher and higher. On an open grassy ridge the chimps climbed into a massive mbula tree, where Fifi, replete from the morning's feasting, made a large comfortable nest high above me. She dozed through a midday siesta, little Fanni asleep in her arms, Frodo and Freud playing nearby. How healing it was to be back at Gombe again, and by myself with the chimpanzees and their forest. I had left the busy, materialistic world so full of greed and selfishness and, for a little while, could feel myself, as in the early days, a part of nature. I felt very much in tune with the chimpanzees, for I was spending time with them not to observe, but simply because I needed their company, undemanding and free of pity. From where I sat I could look out over the Kasakela Valley. Just below me to the west was the Peak. A surge of memories flooded through me: from that vantage point I had learned so much in the early days, sitting and watching while, gradually, the chimpanzees had lost their fear of the strange white ape who had invaded their world. I recaptured some of my long-ago feelings as

I sat there, reflecting. The old excitement of discovery, of seeing things quite unknown to Western eyes. And the serenity that had come from living, day after day, as a part of the natural world. A world that dwarfs yet somehow enhances human emotions.

As I reflected on these things I had been only partly conscious of the approach of a storm. Suddenly, I realized that it was no longer growling in the distance but was right above. The sky was dark, almost black, and the rain clouds had obliterated the higher peaks. With the growing darkness came the stillness, the hush, that so often precedes a tropical downpour. Only the rumbling of the thunder, moving closer and closer, broke this stillness; the thunder and the rustling movements of the chimpanzees. All at once came a blinding flash of lightning, followed, a split second later, by an incredibly loud clap of thunder, that seemed almost to shake the solid rock before it rumbled on, bouncing from peak to peak. Then the dark and heavy clouds let loose such torrential rain that sky and earth seemed joined by moving water. I sat under a palm whose fronds, for a while, provided some shelter. Fifi sat hunched over, protecting her infant; Frodo pressed close against them in the nest; Freud sat with rounded back on a nearby branch. As the rain poured endlessly down, my palm fronds no longer provided shelter and I got wetter and wetter. I began to feel first chilly and then, as a cold wind sprang up, freezing; soon, turned in on myself, I lost all track of time. I and the chimpanzees formed a unit of silent, patient, and uncomplaining endurance.

It must have been an hour or more before the rain began to ease as the heart of the storm swept away to the south. At four-thirty the chimps climbed down, and we moved off through the soaked, dripping vegetation, back down the mountainside. Presently we arrived on a grassy ridge overlooking the lake. A pale, watery sun had appeared and its light caught the raindrops so that the world seemed hung with diamonds, sparkling on every leaf, every blade of grass. I crouched low to avoid destroying a jeweled spider's web that stretched, exquisite and fragile, across the trail.

I heard sounds of greeting as Fifi and her family joined Melissa and hers. They all climbed into a low tree to feed on fresh young leaves. I moved to a place where I could stand and watch as they enjoyed their last meal of the day. Down below, the lake was still dark and angry with white flecks where the waves broke, and rain clouds remained black in the south. To the north the sky was clear with only wisps of gray clouds still lingering. The scene was breathtaking in its beauty. In the soft sunlight, the chimpanzees' black coats were shot with coppery brown, the branches on which they sat were wet and dark as ebony, the young leaves a pale but brilliant green. And behind was the dramatic backcloth of the indigo sky where lightning flickered and distant thunder growled and rumbled.

Lost in awe at the beauty around me, I must have slipped into a state of heightened awareness. It is hard—impossible, really—to put into words the moment of truth that suddenly came upon me then. Even the mystics are unable to describe their brief flashes of spiritual ecstasy. It seemed to me, as I struggled afterward to recall the experience, that *self* was utterly absent: I and the chimpanzees, the earth and trees and air, seemed to merge, to become one with the spirit power of life itself. The air was filled with a feathered symphony, the evensong of birds. I heard new frequencies in their music and also in the singing insects' voices—notes so high and sweet I was amazed. Never had I been so intensely aware of the shape, the color of the individual leaves, the varied patterns of the veins that made each one unique. Scents were clear as well, easily identifiable: fermenting, over-ripe fruit; waterlogged earth; cold, wet bark; the damp odor of chimpanzee hair and, yes, my own too. And the aromatic scent of young, crushed leaves was almost over-powering. I sensed a new presence, then saw a bushbuck, quietly browsing upwind, his spiraled horns gleaming and his chestnut coat dark with rain.

Suddenly a distant chorus of pant-hoots elicited a reply from Fifi. As though wakening from some vivid dream I was back in the everyday world, cold, yet intensely alive. When the chimpanzees left, I stayed in that place—it seemed a most sacred place—scribbling some notes, try-ing to describe what, so briefly, I had experienced. I had not been visited by the angels or other heavenly beings that characterize the visions of the great mystics or the saints, yet for all that I believe it truly was a mystical ex-perience.

Time passed. Eventually I wandered back along the forest trail and scrambled down behind my house to the beach. The sun was a huge red orb just vanishing behind the Congo hills and I sat on the beach watching the ever-changing sunset as it painted the sky red and gold and dark purple. The surface of the lake, calm after the storm, glinted with gold and violet and red ripples below the flaming sky.

Later, as I sat by my little fire, cooking my dinner of beans, tomatoes, and an egg, I was still lost in the wonder of my experience. Yes, I thought, there are many win-dows through which we humans, searching for meaning, can look out into the world around us. There are those carved out by Western science, their panes polished by a succession of brilliant minds. Through them we can see ever farther, ever more clearly, into areas which until re-cently were beyond human knowledge. Through such a scientific window I had been taught to observe the chimpanzees. For more than twenty-five years I had sought, through careful recording and critical analysis, to piece together their complex social behavior, to understand the workings of their minds. And this had not only helped us to better understand their place in nature but also helped us to understand a little better some aspects of our own human behavior, our own place in the natural world.

Yet there are other windows through which we humans can look out into the world around us, windows through which the mystics and the holy men of the East, and the founders of the great world religions, have gazed as they searched for the meaning and purpose of our life on earth, not only in the wondrous beauty of the world, but also in its darkness and ugliness. And those Masters contemplated the truths that they saw, not with their minds only but with their hearts and souls too. From those revelations came the spiritual essence of the great scriptures, the holy books, and the most beautiful mystic poems and writings. That afternoon, it had been as though an unseen hand had drawn back a curtain and, for the briefest moment, I had seen through such a window. In a flash of "outsight" I had known timelessness and quiet ecstasy, sensed a truth of which mainstream science is merely a small fraction. And I knew that the revelation would be with me for the rest of my life, imperfectly remembered yet always within. A source of strength on which I could draw when life seemed harsh or cruel or desperate.

How sad that so many people seem to think that science and religion are mutually exclusive. Science has used modern technology and modern techniques to uncover so much about the formation and the development of life-forms on Planet Earth and about the solar system of which our little world is but a minute part. In recent times astronomers have charted the atmosphere of planets and identified new solar systems; neurologists have learned astounding truths about the workings of our brains; physicists have divided the atom into smaller and smaller particles; a sheep has been cloned; a little robot has been sent to wander about on the surface of Mars; the whole miraculous world of cyberspace has been opened up. Truly the human intellect is awesome. Alas, all of these amazing discoveries have led to a belief that every wonder of the natural world and of the universe—indeed, of infinity and time—can, in the end, be understood through the logic and the reasoning of a finite mind. And so, for many, science has taken the place of religion. It was not some intangible God who created the universe, they argue, it was the Big Bang. Physics, chemistry, and evolutionary biology can explain the start of the universe and the appearance and progress of life on earth, they say. To believe in God, in the human soul, and in life after death is simply a desperate and foolish attempt to give meaning to our lives.

But not all scientists believe thus. There are quantum physicists who have concluded that the concept of God is not, after all, merely wishful thinking. Physicist John C. Eccles, although he felt that questions regarding the human soul were matters beyond science, warned scientists that they should not give definite negative answers when asked about the continuity of the conscious self after death. There are those exploring the human brain who feel that no matter how much they discover about this extraordinary structure it will never add up to a complete understanding of the human mind—that the whole is, after all, greater than the sum of the parts. The Big Bang theory is yet another example of the incredible, the awe-inspiring ability of the human mind to learn about seemingly unknowable phenomena in the beginning of time. Time as we know it, or think we know it. But what about before time? And what about beyond space? I remembered so well how those questions had driven me to distraction when I was a child.

I lay flat on my back and looked up into the darkening sky. How sad it would be, I thought, if we humans ultimately were to lose all sense of mystery, all sense of awe. If our left brains were utterly to dominate the right so that logic and reason triumphed over intuition and alienated us absolutely from our innermost being, from our hearts, our souls. I watched as, one by one, the stars appeared, the brightest first and then, as the sun's light faded, more and more until the sky was studded with brilliant, flashing points of light. Albert Einstein, undeniably one of the greatest scientists and thinkers of our time, had sustained a mystical outlook on life that was, he said, constantly renewed from the wonder and humility that filled him when he gazed at the stars.

From at least Neanderthal times, and probably before, humans everywhere have worshipped their gods. And religious, spiritual beliefs have been among the strongest and most persistent of all human convictions, sometimes enduring through half a century or so of intense persecution. The tortures endured by the great Christian martyrs had haunted my imagination as a child. The indigenous peoples in many parts of the world had maintained their belief in the Creator, the Great Spirit, and continued to practice their religion secretly despite the risk of horrid punishments if found out. Belief in God had survived forty-five years of the communist regime in Eastern Europe.

As I continued to lie gazing at the star-studded sky, reluctant to move inside, I thought about the young man I had met during the six-week tour I had just finished. He had a holiday job, working as a bellhop in the big hotel where I was staying in Dallas, Texas. It was prom night, and I wandered down to watch the young girls in their beautiful evening gowns, their escorts elegant in their tuxedos. They seemed so happy, so carefree, their lives ahead of them. As I stood there, thinking about the future—theirs, mine, the world's—I heard a diffident voice:

"Excuse me, Doctor—aren't you Jane Goodall?" The bellhop was very young, very fresh-faced. But he looked worried. Partly because he felt that he should not be disturbing me, but partly, it transpired, because his mind was indeed troubled. He had a question to ask me. So we went and sat on some back stairs, away from the glittering groups and hand-holding couples, and talked about God and creation.

He had watched all my documentaries, read my books. He was fascinated, and he thought that what I did was great. But I talked about evolution. Was I religious? Did I believe in God? If so, how did that square with evolution? Had we really descended from chimpanzees? All these questions, asked with frank sincerity and genuine concern.

And so I tried to answer him as truthfully as I could, to explain my own beliefs. I told him that no one thought humans had descended from chimpanzees. I explained that I did believe in Darwinian evolution and told him of my time at Olduvai, when I had held the remains of extinct creatures in my hands. That I had traced, in the museum, the various stages of the evolution of, say, a horse: from a rabbit-sized creature that gradually, over thousands of years, changed, became better and better adapted to its environment and eventually was transformed into the modern horse. I told him I believed that millions of years ago there had been a primitive, apelike, humanlike creature, one branch of which had gone on to become the chimpanzee, another branch of which had eventually led to us.

"But that doesn't mean I don't believe in God," I said. And I told him something of my beliefs, and those of my family. How my grandfather had been a Congregational minister. I told him that I had always thought that the description of God creating the world in seven days might well have been an attempt to explain evolution in a parable. In that case, each of the days would have been several million years.

"And then, perhaps, God saw that a living being had evolved that was suitable for His purpose. *Homo sapiens* had the brain, the mind, the potential. Perhaps," I said, "that was when God breathed the Spirit into the first Man and the first Woman and filled them with the Holy Ghost."

The bellhop was looking considerably less worried. "Yes, I see," he said. "That could be right. That does seem to make sense."

I ended by telling him that it honestly didn't matter how we humans got to be the way we are, whether evolution or special creation was responsible. What mattered and mattered desperately was our future development. Were we going to go on destroying God's creation, fighting each other, hurting the other creatures of His planet? Or were we going to find ways to live in greater harmony with each other and with the natural world? That, I told him, was what was important. Not only for the future of the human species, but also for him, personally. He would have to make his own decision. When we finally parted his eyes were clear and untroubled, and he was smiling.

Thinking about that brief encounter, I smiled too, there on the beach at Gombe, thousands of miles from Texas. It had, I thought, been a useful half hour.

A wind sprang up and it grew chilly. I left the bright stars and went inside to bed. But not to sleep. My mind was still too full of the events of the day and I lay, suspended between sleep and waking, the circling thoughts going around and around. To try to still them, I imagined myself back in the forest. And, all unbidden, came images. Vividly I saw Danny, as she had been when Grub was small, sitting on the seat in the garden at the Birches, drinking a cup of tea. Then Uncle Eric after his last heart attack, old and shrunken, lying in the bed in the nursing home around the corner from our house, sent away only because Vanne and Olly were not strong enough to lift him. And I remembered how, on the night of his death, I had heard the haunting call of a barn owl, the bird that summons the souls of the dead. I did not mention it at the time, for no barn owls had been heard in Bournemouth for fifteen years or more. But months later I mentioned it to Vanne, and she looked utterly amazed, and said she had heard it too. I thought about Audrey, who had fallen while out on a walk with our dog, Cida, and cracked her skull. She got better, and lived for over a year. And then, one night, when Vanne went in with a last cup of tea, Audrey told her that Cida, who never went in her bedroom, had been sitting beside her bed and staring at her for a long time. When Vanne looked in later, Cida was still there. In the morning Audrey fell— and died. I thought of the last days of Cida's life, and how we all believed she was getting better—but it had been wishful thinking. And of Rusty's death, the passing of my childhood companion. Ginger, Baggins, Rippal, and Spider, my canine friends in Dar es Salaam. How sad I had been to lose them. And then I thought of Flo, and how I had sat with her body near the stream, remembering all that she had been, all that I had learned from her. And then, vividly, I remembered Derek, and how he had struggled up the hills to the feeding station, eager to watch the chimpanzees. I found I was crying and I cried for a long time, weeping away the anger, the sorrow—and the self-pity—of the previous year. I cried myself to sleep. But tears can be healing, and I woke knowing that while I would always grieve Derek's passing, and the manner of it, I could cope with my grieving. The forest, and the spiritual power that was so real in it, had given me the "peace that passeth understanding."

(Courtesy of Mohammad Yunus)

Mohammad Yunus, founder of the Grameen Bank,
who has brought hope to those living in dire poverty.

Chapter 13

MORAL EVOLUTION

Those few weeks in Gombe were extraordinarily meaningful. I found a renewal of strength, bodily and mentally, and with it a new sense of commitment. When I went back to Dar es Salaam, though I continued to sorrow for that which was lost, the memories of all that Derek and I had shared during our short marriage were now bittersweet—not bitter only, as before. Most of the time I was on my own in the big house with my two dogs, Seranda and Cinderella, two strays who had adopted me. Dogs can be such a comfort, and ever since Rusty helped to shape my attitude toward animals— and science—they have played a major part in my life. As I thought abut my healing time at Gombe, a poem began to take shape in my mind: "The Little Angels of the Trees and Flowers."

JANE GOODALL

I don't remember when first I heard
Them calling, with their silvery voices,
The little Angels of the trees and flowers.

They offered to unlock my mind
And take my soul away, to clean.
And oh! I welcomed them, and lay
Stretched out upon the fragrant
Grass, light as an empty husk.

Then they, with rueful smiles, did oil
The rusty hinges of my mind, and swept
Away the cobwebs, and hung my soul
Upon a topmost bough, to air,
Close to the purifying sun. And I was lucky
For as it fluttered there, a robin chat's sweet
Song rose through the trees till every fiber
Of my soul was bathed in harmony.

When all was clean and new they fetched
My soul and slipped it back and, smiling,
Danced away. And I—well, for a day or two—
I looked upon the world with all the
Innocence and wonder of a newborn babe.

And now, if I am sad, or filled
With sudden rage, I find some quiet place
With grass and leaves and earth, and sit there
Silently, and hope that they will come
And call me, with their silvery voices,
And make me clean again, those
Little Angels of the trees and flowers.

It was all very quiet without Derek to discuss what was
going on in the world, so I used the extra time that would

have been devoted to wifely things to immerse myself in the scientific analysis and writing up of the first two decades of research at Gombe. In addition, I kept abreast of current affairs: Derek and I had always read the *Economist* and *Newsweek*, and I continued to do so. And I discussed Tanzanian politics with my friends, many of whom were in the diplomatic community. Tanzania was suffering from the aftermath of the war in neighboring Uganda. It was because the Tanzanian army had moved in to strengthen the forces of ousted president Milton Obote that the bloody dictatorship of Idi Amin was finally brought to an end. Tanzanians paid dearly for this—the economy fell to its lowest ebb, food shortages continued, and the poverty of the poor increased.

At the war's end Tanzania was overrun with soldiers—returning heroes with no jobs who had, or found it easy to get hold of, guns and ammunition. There was a massive increase in armed robberies throughout the country. I still walked along the beach with the dogs, but with a new sense of apprehension. Once I was relieved of my watch by a thief who pressed an evil-looking screwdriver to my throat—I should have known better than to wear a watch.

However, despite the increase in crime, Tanzania was peaceful compared with many African countries. From Burundi, only a few miles north of the Gombe National Park, and its neighbor, Rwanda, there were rumblings that would, yet again, erupt into massive bloodshed as the Hutu rose up against the Tutsi minorities. Refugees were still arriving spasmodically from troubled eastern Zaire, just across the lake from Gombe. There was a coup in Ghana. There was trouble in Chad. On the larger world map the Cold War still simmered. Political and economic interests fueled the widespread sale of arms and land mines to the developing countries that served as playing fields for the economic games of the superpowers; games that had already left thousands of innocent people homeless, maimed, or dead. That was the year President Sadat was assassinated; attempts were made on the lives of Pope John Paul II and U.S. President Ronald Reagan; the IRA began its campaign of violence in the U.K.; and there was unrest and violence in Sri Lanka, El Salvador, India, Afghanistan, Lebanon. Within the next few years, Britain would invade the Falkland Islands, Mrs. Gandhi would be assassinated, the United States would bomb Libya, and—utterly shocking—we would learn that Iraq was using massive amounts of chemical weapons in its war with Iran, as well as on its own population. There were horrifying accounts of this from the victims who survived, mostly Kurd civilians.

Everywhere, it seemed, there were people suffering. There were the starving, sick, and homeless, not only in the developing world, but in the inner-city areas of even the most prosperous of countries in the Western world. Britain suffered the first serious riots among the black youth in one such area (Brixton). And over and above all that, the very air and earth and water of our precious planet were being poisoned, the natural world—our only world—was being destroyed.

Was there, I asked myself, hope for the future? It seemed that our selfish greed—our lust for power and land and wealth—was winning out over our longing for peace. The euphoria that I had felt following the defeat of Nazi Germany by the free world had long since worn away. I found myself wondering if Hugo and I had been justified in bringing a child into such a hopelessly wicked place.

About that time an old friend of mine, Hugh Caldwell, gave me a book, *Human Destiny*, written in 1937 by the French doctor-turned-philosopher LeCompte DuNuoy. He believed that we humans, having slowly and against all odds arrived and survived on planet earth, were in the process of acquiring the moral attributes that would enable us to become increasingly less aggressive and warlike and more caring and compassionate. This, he felt, was our ultimate destiny, the raison d'être for the human species. What an intriguing idea! The evolution of our physical structure was something with which I was quite familiar. After all, I had worked for Louis Leakey, a man who had dedicated most of his life to searching out the fossilized remains of our earliest forebears. And my years at Gombe had caused me to think carefully about cultural evolution, a development which was not, as many argued, peculiar to our species alone; the chimpanzees clearly demonstrated that they too had started along that road. And now DuNuoy was writing about moral evolution. I was fascinated and, as I considered his arguments, I found that many of them struck a responsive chord. I began to think about our seemingly hopeless situation in a new way.

In the tropical climate in which mankind probably evolved, food and warmth were all around. That early world would not have been a paradise, of course—from the start humans would have known periodic hunger and the pain of sickness and injuries. Just like the chimps. The first apelike humanlike hominids would have been surrounded by all manner of fearsome predators with sharp claws and teeth, many of whom could run faster or climb better than our ancestors. Nevertheless, hominids, with their ever increasing brain size, had held their own. And as they had increased in numbers, so it must have been necessary for some of them to move from the most optimal habitats into those where it was much harder to survive. Those with the biggest and best brains would have had an advantage over those who were less intelligent. And so the smart ones would have lived to pass on their genes. Gradually they had developed ever more sophisticated tools and been able, increasingly, to bend nature to their will. And then, somewhere along the way, our ancestors had acquired spoken language, a true milestone along the road to human uniqueness.

It was language that, for the first time, enabled our ancestors to teach others, including their children, about objects and events that were not actually present. There are other intelligent animals living today with complex brains and elaborate communication systems, but they cannot, so far as we know, do that. Chimpanzees and other apes can be taught many of the signs of American Sign Language, ASL. They have acquired three hundred or more, and can use them in new contexts and with each other as well as their trainers. But they did not, during their evolution, develop the uniquely human ability to talk about that which is not present, share events of the distant past, plan for the far-off future, and, most important, discuss ideas, bouncing them back and forth to share the accumulated wisdom of an entire group. This spoken language would have enabled our ancestors to articulate feelings of awe, feelings that would lead to religious belief, then to organized worship.

The chimpanzees, I believe, know feelings akin to awe. In the Kakombe valley is a magnificent waterfall.

There is a great roar as the water cascades down through the soft green air from the stream bed some eighty feet above. Over countless aeons the water has worn a perpendicular groove in the sheer rock. Ferns move ceaselessly in the wind created by the falling water, and vines hang down on either side. For me, it is a magical place, and a spiritual one. And sometimes, as they approach, the chimpanzees display in slow, rhythmic motion along the river bed. They pick up and throw great rocks and branches. They leap to seize the hanging vines, and swing out over the stream in the spray-drenched wind until it seems the slender stems must snap or be torn from their lofty moorings.

For ten minutes or more they may perform this magnificent "dance." Why? Is it not possible that the chimpanzees are responding to some feeling like awe? A feeling generated by the mystery of water; water that seems alive, always rushing past yet never going, always the same yet ever different. Was it perhaps similar feelings of awe that gave rise to the first animistic religions, the worship of the elements and the mysteries of nature over which there was no control? Only when our prehistoric ancestors developed language would it have been possible to discuss such internal feelings and create a shared religion.

Spoken language would also have enabled our stone age ancestors to develop a shared moral code of behavior. Chimpanzees show behaviors that seem likely precursors to human morality—as when a high-ranking individual breaks up a fight to save a weaker companion—but for the most part, in their society, "might" is "right," and the subordinates have to be submissive whether or not they are in the wrong. Humans, however, developed sophisticated moral, ethical codes of behavior. And they did so in all parts of the world in all cultures, even though good and bad were not always interpreted in the same way by all peoples.

DuNuoy suggested that we try to view our moral progress in the time frame of human evolution. Our physical form has evolved slowly over the aeons. From the first living specks of protoplasm it took billions of years before the first mammals appeared during Paleolithic times. *Homo sapiens*, modern man, has walked the planet for only a couple of million years. And so, although there always has been and still is a great deal that is clearly unethical and often downright evil in human practices everywhere, a growing number of people around the globe are more aware than ever before of what is wrong, what needs to change.

As I contemplated DuNuoy's arguments, our moral behavior—or the lack of it—could be seen in a new light. It was indeed tragic that our selfish instincts so often dominated our loving and altruistic ones, but, nevertheless, we had come a long way in a very short time—by evolutionary standards, that is. Less than a hundred years ago, for example, in my own country of England (and in other Western countries too), conditions for the poor were unspeakably terrible. Women and children—and ponies— were sent down into the mines to work in the near dark, in horrific conditions and for incredibly long periods, with very little rest between shifts, and but little food. Children, as well as adults, shivered in the winter with bare feet and few clothes in the unspeakable slums. Diseases such as tuberculosis and rickets were commonplace. Slavery was an accepted form of labor. Some of the recent books written about growing up in the slums of

Catholic Ireland paint such a shocking picture that we wonder how any child survived.

How different things had become in the U.K. by the 1980s, I reflected. Theoretically everyone had access to welfare. Conditions were still bad in some inner-city areas, but local governments and social workers were at least trying to improve them. The welfare state, for all its drawbacks, had sprung from ethical concerns for those who were unable to care for themselves and their families. Many charitable organizations were working to improve the condition of minority groups. Slavery had been banished, and when it became known that industry was making use of cheap slave labor in developing countries, there was massive public condemnation, which at least sometimes led to improved conditions for the workers.

Similar kinds of reforms had taken place in other democracies around the globe. Moreover, changes in thinking were taking place that would lead, thanks to the leadership of Mikhail Gorbachev, to the breakdown of the repressive communist dictatorship of the Soviet bloc and eventually to the collapse of communist regimes in other parts of the world. Human dignity and human rights were increasingly topics of concern, and even animal rights movements around the world were gaining more recognition and support. The violence, cruelty, oppression, and suppression that still plagued our world had, in and of themselves, led to international organizations such as the United Nations. And although this had not lived up to the expectations of its founders in such matters as preserving world peace and preventing genocide, the very fact that it had been formed was a major step in the right direction. Gradually, it seemed to me, human beings were reaching out and trying to help beyond the borders of their own nations. We had a long, long road ahead of us, but we were slowly moving in the right direction.

As I was pondering these things, Mohammad Yunus, an economics professor in Bangladesh, was not merely pondering the unjust fate of the beggars in the streets around him, but actively doing something to alleviate their plight. It had begun, for him, in 1974 when Bangladesh fell into the grip of a terrible famine. The streets of Dacca became increasingly crowded with those who had used their last strength to walk to the capital in search of food. They sat or lay in the streets, "skeletons covered by rags." They died by the score. It was a life-changing experience for Mohammad Yunus, who was, at the time, teaching economics at the university there. Suddenly, he says, he wanted to run away from academic life, the theories of economics, and find out what was going on in the streets around him, why people were dying, slowly and horribly, of hunger. He visited a nearby village and talked to a twenty-one-year-old woman, Sufia Degum, who was making bamboo stools. Her story was the story of thousands of women like her. She bought the bamboo for the equivalent of 22 U.S. cents that she borrowed from a *paikarw*, or middleman. To repay her loan, she had to sell him the stools at the end of each day. Her profit was the equivalent of 2 cents—on a good day. She could not borrow from a moneylender, as the interest rate was far too high. There was no way, no way at all, that she could ever break, for herself or her children, the vicious cycle of hunger and poverty: she had no way of getting hold of the 22 cents that could start her on her way to independence.

There were forty-two people in the village who were

in the same position as Sufia. The total amount of money that they needed to borrow to start their businesses was something less than $27. Mohammad Yunus, with $27 from his pocket, made those loans. He tried to persuade Bangladeshi banks to start a program of providing credit to people living in poverty. But the answer was always the same: "The poor are not creditworthy"—even when it was shown that they did, indeed, pay back their tiny loans.

And so Mohammad Yunus himself started a bank that would eventually bring new hope and a new life to millions of the poorest of the poor. The Grameen Bank, officially launched in 1983, expanded into other countries and would, within the next fifteen years, make loans, all very small, in excess of $2 billion. Years later I would meet Mohammad Yunus and hear him speak at a forum of world leaders. A quiet man, self-effacing, with the greatness like an aura shining around him and a mind sharp as a rapier. Truly, he is a genius among us. And, for me, a saint.

Stories like that illustrate the human potential for good, and DuNuoy's book helped to explain why we had not yet moved farther, faster, in our ponderous progress along the road to a more moral future. But was there going to be time, I wondered, for us to complete the journey? No thinking, rational person could feel anything but dismay at the rate at which humanity was destroying nature—destroying that which had, for millions of years, nurtured our birth and development as a species. In recent times, as modern beliefs and modern technology had swept away ancient beliefs and traditions and as human populations had increased in number, needing more and ever more land, countless people, particularly in the Western world, had lost, or were rapidly losing, all sense of our rightful place in the great scheme of things. My own spirit had been nourished and strengthened by nature and I had developed a very real understanding of and respect for the fascinating diversity of life-forms on earth, and their interdependence. And now forests, woodlands, grasslands, prairies, wetlands—all wild habitats—were disappearing at a terrifying rate. So too were many species of animals and plants—each unique, each slowly evolved over the millennia. Even in the last wilderness strongholds, such as the North and South Poles, there were signs of our human poisons and debris.

Most of this destruction was due to the greedy, wasteful societies of the affluent world, which, in order to maintain their absurd, materialistic, luxurious standards of living, were, to all intents and purposes, stealing food from the mouths of the poor in the developing world. The poor became poorer and both infant mortality and birth rates soared. The developing world struggled to cultivate the eroded soils of the spreading deserts, to get water from the ever lower water tables, while Western societies covered thousands of square miles of rich agricultural land with concrete, cut down thousands of square miles of rain forest to create grazing or grow grain for cattle in order to feed meat to their overweight citizens, and paid (scandalously inadequately) Third World farmers to grow cash crops such as coffee and tea, so that there was even less land available for subsistence farming.

But there were, I knew, signs of changing attitudes. Governments were starting to pay heed to environmentalists who stressed the desperate need to stop polluting and destroying the natural world before it was too late. Indeed, during the 1980s environmental issues soared to the top of the political agenda of many nations for a variety of reasons: the sobering nuclear catastrophe at Chernobyl; news of the unexpected and horrifying long-term effects of DDT, which had, already, infiltrated ecosystems throughout the world; early warnings of the cumulative effects of the so-called greenhouse gases, and the depletion of the ozone layer.

But it had taken a long time for this kind of information to become widely known by the general public. And so, even as Western democratic governments struggled to address human rights in the sphere of individual freedom, their citizens were being, all unknowingly, exposed to an increasing variety of horrific poisons—from pesticides, from agricultural waste, from toxic waste in rubbish dumps, from synthetic chemicals in pharmaceutical products, from irresponsible misuse of antibiotics, including in intensively farmed animals. (The grave threat of genetically engineered foods had not yet burst upon the unsuspecting public, nor the risk of viruses and retroviruses crossing the species barrier from other animals, especially from monkeys and apes, to humans as a result of eating them or using them for medical research in the laboratory.) While none of these harmful by-products of science and technology had been deliberately planned, but had crept up on us unawares, it was, nevertheless, a long time before the alarming facts were shared by government and industry with the general public; change costs money. Inevitably, however, the truth had begun to leak out and more and more people had become increasingly concerned about the dangers that surrounded them. The lone voice of Rachel Carson, when she wrote *Silent Spring,* was joined by an ever increasing chorus of alarm and anger in support of her findings.

But back then, in the 1980s, the most important concern of all—the terrifying rate of human population growth—was seldom mentioned. Paul Ehrlich's book *The Population Bomb* was largely ignored. The topic was held to be "politically sensitive," since any criticism of family size could be construed as interfering with an individual's right to self-determination. There had been a significant gathering of religious leaders to discuss the dreadful things that were happening to our environment, and all had agreed to include messages of warning to their flocks. But there had been no mention of population issues lest it anger some of the participants. So the problem that seemed to me, along with Western overconsumption, to be the most serious was deliberately ignored. What folly! The natural resources of the world were not inexhaustible; the world's human population was increasing inexorably; therefore the time was approaching when there would be more humans than the planet could feed and shelter, wilderness areas and most other species would be gone, the complex web of life, the biodiversity of the world's ecosystems, would be destroyed. The inevitable outcome would be human extinction.

The only ray of hope, I thought, was that as more and more of these issues moved out into the public domain, more and more people were able to see that we had made and were continuing to make horrible mistakes; and this new understanding was a first step along a path that could, eventually, bring about massive change. The trouble was, I reflected, that people in the developed countries had come to believe that a high standard of living was their right. I thought, as I have thought throughout my life, how lucky I had been in my own childhood. Because I had grown up during World War II, the luxuries now taken for granted by middle-class Westerners were, quite simply, unavailable—except at exorbitant prices on the black market. I had learned the true value of food, clothing, shelter—and life itself. Along with my contemporaries I had moved into a postwar world in which self-reliance was a necessary quality. We did not feel it was our right to have a bicycle, a television, a dishwasher, and so on; those were things you saved up for, and were proud of because they were earned by the sweat of your brow.

Of course, I understood why those who had lived through war or economic disasters, and who had built for themselves a good life and a high standard of living, were rightly proud to be able to provide for their children those things which they themselves had not had. And why their children, inevitably, took those things for granted. It meant that new values and new expectations had crept into our societies along with the new standards of living. Hence the materialistic and often greedy and selfish lifestyle of so many young people in the Western world, especially in the United States.

But, I wondered, were they content with such a lifestyle? Often their behavior suggested that they felt something was missing from their world. Was it, perhaps, a craving for meaning in life which had led to the emergence of the hippies, the flower children of the late 1960s and early 1970s? Was that why so many young people of wealthy parents had left their families to seek new experiences? They had tried living in communes, they had been fascinated by newly emerging cults, they had experimented with the effects of drugs, they had traveled to India in search of gurus. Desperately, or so it seemed to me, they had sought to escape from the soul-numbing materialistic hedonism of their time. And of course, they had rejected formal religion just as they had rejected everything that pertained to "the Establishment" and what they perceived as the old-fashioned, outmoded values of their conservative, middle-class parents.

I thought about the quickening of interest in the lifestyles and spiritual values of the indigenous peoples of the world, especially in North America. What a perfect solution for the environmental crisis if we could go back to the ways of the American Indians—the Native Americans or First Nation peoples—who, for hundreds of years, had lived in harmony with nature, taking only what they needed to live, and giving thanks, and giving back. I knew that there were Elders who still lived by the old values, the old sense of reverence for the Great Spirit, the Creator. But while it sounded attractive, very few Westerners, I thought, could tolerate such a way of life— for it would mean having to forgo the luxuries which we had come to think of as necessities. It would be hard to endure the vagaries of mother nature without the soft protective cocoon that was wrapped around us—at least the economically privileged among us—at birth. I thought, half sadly, half with amusement, of the archaeologist of the future who would analyze the physical makeup of these cocoons: cars—many of them, since the custom is to trade one in every few years; a series of apartments and/or houses, as families grew or moved around the country; washing machines; household effects; dishwashers; hi-fis, CD players, countless TVs and computers and cell phones; zillions of gadgets varying with the interests and occupations of the inhabitants of the cocoons; enough clothing and footwear to keep an

African village clad for years; endless fast food packages. We could extend this list, on and on. And let us not forget the little plastic cards that paid for it all. The pile of material stuff used and cast aside, or accumulated, during a lifetime. The measure of *outward* success. And if some priest or monk was to sift through the *inner* lives of those same people, and lay out the spiritual acquisitions, the measure of success of the soul, how, I wondered, would the two tallies compare, material versus spiritual acquisitions?

I contemplated my own record, somewhat ruefully. I didn't like a lot of what I found. I had always been puzzled by the admonition to "love thy neighbor as thyself." How could I love myself, when so often I failed to live up to the standards that I set? But suddenly it seemed clearer, and I thought I understood. The "self" that we had to love was not our ego, not the everyday person who went around behaving thoughtlessly, selfishly, sometimes unkindly, but the flame of pure spirit that is in each and every one of us, that is part of the Creator; what the Buddhists call *Kernal*. That which is loved, I realized, can grow. We had to learn to understand and love this Spirit within in order to find peace within. And only then could we reach out beyond the narrow prison of our own lives, seeking reunion with the Spiritual Power that we call God, or Allah, the Tao, Brahma, the Creator, or whatever our personal belief prescribes. Once we had attained that goal, our power to connect with others, so that together we could create a better world, would be immeasurably greater.

The ability to reach beyond their upbringing, their culture, and their immediate surroundings has always, I realized, been a characteristic of the greatest spiritual leaders and the saints. Our task, then, if we would hasten our moral evolution, progress a little more quickly toward our human destiny, is obvious—formidable, but in the long run not impossible. We will have to evolve, all of us, from ordinary, everyday human beings—into saints! Ordinary people, like you and me, will have to become saints, or at least mini-saints. The great saints and the Masters were not supernatural beings; they were mortals like us, made of flesh and blood. They, like us, needed air to breathe, and food and drink (though not in abundance). And they all believed in a Spiritual Power, in God. That enabled them to tap in to the great spiritual energy "in which we live and move and have our being." They lived on this energy, breathed it into their lungs so that it ran in the blood, giving them strength. We must strive, each of us, to join them. I imagine them standing as though on a bridge, suspended between God and earth, and it was this image that led to this poem:

ONLY THEY CAN WHISPER
SONGS OF HOPE

The world has need of them, those who stand upon the
    Bridge,
Who know the pain in the singing of a bird
And the beauty beyond a flower dying:
Who have heard the crystal harmony
Within the silence of a snow-peaked mountain—
For who but they can bring life's meaning
To the living dead?

Oh, the world needs those standing on the Bridge,
For they know how Eternity reaches to earth

REASON FOR HOPE

In the wind that brings music to the leaves
Of the forest: in the drops of rain that caress
The sleeping life of the desert: in the sunbeams
Of the first spring day in an alpine meadow.
Only they can blow the dust from the seeing eyes
Of those who are blind.

Yet pity them! those who stand on the Bridge.
For they, having known utter Peace,
Are moved by an ancient compassion
To reach back to those who cry out
From a world which has lost its meaning:
A world where the atom—the clay of the Sculptor—
Is torn apart, in the name of science,
For the destruction of Love.

And so they stand there on the Bridge
Torn by the anguish of free will:
Yearning with unshed tears
To go back—to return
To the starlight of their beginnings
To the utter peace
Of the unfleshed spirit.
Yet only they can whisper songs of hope
To those who struggle, helpless, towards light.

Oh, let them not desert us, those on the Bridge,
Those who have known Love in the freedom
Of the night sky and know the meaning
Of the moon's existence beyond
Man's fumbling footsteps into space.
For they know the Eternal Power
That encompasses life's beginnings
And gathers up its endings,
And lays them, like Joseph's coat,

On the never changing, always moving canvas
That stretches beyond the Universe
And is contained in the eye
Of a little frog.

And what about those, and there are many, who do not
believe in a God—those who are atheists? It does not
make any difference, I thought. A life lived in the service
of humanity, a love of and respect for all living things—
those attributes are the essence of saintlike behavior.

I thought about the power for good, the power for evil,
that exists in each one of us. What a difference a single
individual could make in our gradual progress toward a
moral world. Indeed, I mused, every one of us had a role
to play. Our contributions were different. Some made a
great splashing as they moved through the waters of life
and the ripples spread far and wide. Others seemed to
sink without a stir—but surely, it was not so, just that the
movement of their passage was deep down, creating
change that was out of sight. And some, buried silently in
contemporary mud, had been dug up afterward with a
great swirling of the waters. At all different levels the ripples and currents passed or mingled, and some merged
inextricably. With each merging a new force was created,
itself as unique as the two beings who forged it. What
joys the world would have lost if some of those forces had
never been created, and what pain in other instances
would it have been spared. Forces released not only by
the meeting of minds, but of bodies, too.

Billions of couplings led to the bodies and minds of
Beethoven, Saint Francis, Hitler. The blending and mix-
ing of billions of unique life strands can lead to one
person so strong, for good or evil, that he or she can in-

fluence the lives of billions of others and change the course of history. It was obvious that every human, every unique being, played some role in the shaping of progress, though only some got into the history books. Throughout every second of every day there was change abroad in the world, change due to the impact of mind on mind; teacher and pupil, parent and child, world leader and citizen, writer or actor and the general public. Yes, each one of us carried seeds for change. Seeds that needed nurturing to realize their potential.

I had no doubt that, given time, we humans were capable of creating a moral society. The trouble was, as I knew only too well, time was running out. I had observed the chimpanzees, I had held in my hands the bones of our ancient stone age ancestors. I knew from whence, over millions of weary years, we had come. And I knew the direction in which we were headed. But we did not have the luxury of millions of years for all humans to become true saints. Not if we continued destroying our environment at the present rate. So, I thought, we would simply have to try, each and every one of us, to become just a little bit more saintlike. That, surely, we could do.

(Courtesy of Linda Koebner)

Chapter 14

ON THE ROAD
TO DAMASCUS

In October 1986, the pattern of my life changed forever. This was the indirect result of the publication of *The Chimpanzees of Gombe* by Harvard University Press. In order to write that book I had struggled to master a great deal of information that biologists usually acquire as undergraduates—topics such as the influence of hormones on aggression, sociobiological theory, and so on. It was hard work but worthwhile. Before expanding my knowledge I had felt ill at ease when talking to "proper" scientists. Snide remarks in the 1960s and 1970s about the "*Geographic* cover girl" had, I suspect, rankled more than I had admitted, even to myself. But the book was well received when it was finally published, and my self-confidence had a terrific boost.

To celebrate the publication of this book, Dr. Paul Heltne, director of the Chicago Academy of Sciences, suggested holding a conference: Understanding Chimpanzees. All the field biologists studying chimpanzees in Africa were invited, as were some working, noninvasively, in captive settings. It was an amazing gathering; almost all the great names in chimpanzee research were there. The event lasted four days; its after-effects lasted far longer. It wrought in me a cataclysmic change, similar, perhaps, to that described by Paul of Tarsus as he traveled on the road to Damascus, the experience that changed him from gentile to the most fervent and tireless of Jesus' disciples. When I arrived in Chicago I was a research scientist, planning the second volume of *The Chimpanzees of Gombe*. When I left I was already, in my heart, committed to conservation and education. Somehow I knew that Volume 2 would probably never be written—certainly not while I was still active and filled with energy.

The content of the meeting was mainly scientific but there was a session on conservation. I think we were all shocked when we realized the extent to which the chimpanzees across Africa were vanishing. At the turn of the century there must have been as many as two million chimpanzees in twenty-five African nations, but during the last half of the twentieth century their number had been reduced to less than 150,000, and only five countries had significant populations of five thousand or more. And even in those remaining strongholds, chimpanzees were gradually and relentlessly losing ground to the needs of ever growing human populations. Trees were being razed for dwellings, firewood, charcoal, and cultivation; logging and mining activities had penetrated ever deeper into the virgin forests, and human infectious diseases to which chimpanzees are susceptible followed. People had settled along the roads, cutting down ever

(Hugo van Lawick)

The four generations—
Grub, me, Vanne, and
Danny—at the Birches,
1971.

With Flo and family,
1964.

(Hugo van Lawick)

Hilali Matama
and Goblin.

(Hugo van Lawick)

Flo.

Fifi, Ferdinand, Gremlin, and Gaia.

Fanni and Fax.

Freud.

Gimble.

Gremlin.

Fifi.

Faustino.

Galahad.

*All chimp photos, except Flo, by Michael Neugebauer.

Derek, Wagga, and I on the verandah of our house in Dar es Salaam.

With President Nyerere in Dar es Salaam.

With my father outside Buckingham Palace, after receiving the CBE (Commander, Order of the British Empire) from Her Majesty, Queen Elizabeth II.

(Steve Matthews)

In 1986, when I first met Whiskey on his two-foot chain in Burundi.

(PETA)

Two chimps imprisoned at SEMA in a tiny cage.

(PETA)

Two chimps rescued from SEMA, showing that we can make a difference.

(Mary Lewis)

Chief Leonard George,
a true spiritual leader,
in Vancouver, British
Columbia.

(Mary Lewis)

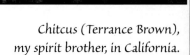

Chitcus (Terrance Brown),
my spirit brother, in California.

(Roger Kyler)

Gary Haun, the
"Amazing Haundini,"
who gave me my mascot,
Mr. H.

(Jack Blackshear, Conoco Inc.)

Children Can Make a Difference.

During Wildlife Awareness week in Angola.

An environmental dance put on by a Roots & Shoots group.

(David Grubbs)

My greatest source of inspiration:
Vanne, my mother, in 1995.

(Michael Neugebauer)

(Michael Neugebauer)

My family—all of us!—at the Birches, 1997.

(Michael Neugebauer)

With the orphaned Uruhara at Sweetwaters Sanctuary in Kenya.

more trees, growing their crops, setting their snares, hunting. Dwindling chimpanzee populations had become increasingly fragmented and many groups were so small that inbreeding was inevitable: there was no hope of their long-term survival. In some countries in West and Central Africa, chimpanzees were hunted for food. They always had been, but whereas in the old days the hunters shot only enough meat for their villages, now hunting had become commercial. Hunters from town traveled deep into the heart of the last remaining forests on logging trucks, shooting everything they could. Then they smoked or sun-dried the meat, loaded it onto the trucks, and took it to the towns. It was a commercial business— the bush meat trade. It catered to the cultural preference of many people for the flesh of wild animals. (Years later it would be shown that chimpanzees carry a variant of the human HIV virus. It is not impossible that the virus may have crossed over to humans as a result of hunters butchering chimpanzees for meat.)

Then there was the live animal trade. Even in places where chimps were not eaten, females were often killed so that their infants might be captured and sold, locally as pets, or for the international entertainment or medical research industries.

Another sobering session highlighted the conditions in which chimpanzees were kept in some medical research laboratories in the United States and other parts of the world. What I learned shocked me to my core, leaving me with a burning passion to do something.

For twenty-five years I had lived my dream. I had gloried in the solitude of the forest, learning from some of the most fascinating creatures of our times. Now, with my newfound professional confidence, the time had come for me to use the knowledge I had acquired to try to help the chimps in their time of need. Up until this point I had believed that there was nothing I could do that would make a difference. My credentials, I had thought, had not been sufficiently academic for me to stand up to those scientists engaged in medical research. And why on earth would politicians listen to anything I had to say? But now, after all the work I had put into writing *The Chimpanzees of Gombe*, I had the self-confidence to embark on visits to research laboratories where I had discussions with the scientists and the staff, official visits to the governments of various African countries, campaigns and lobbying efforts on behalf of chimpanzees in labs, circuses, and other degrading captive situations, and a nonstop series of lectures.

What if I had known, at that time, that my efforts would keep me more or less permanently on the road? That over the years ahead I would never remain in any one place for longer than three weeks, and that such "roosting periods" would only occur two or three times a year and would provide my only opportunities for serious writing? And that my precious time at Gombe would be whittled away until I was able to get there only a few times a year, for only one or two weeks at a time? Would I have been strong enough, committed enough, to start out along such a hard road? I was so utterly moved and shocked by what I had learned at the conference that I believe the answer would have been yes. I didn't have to make the choice, for my life, it almost seems, was taken over by a force far too strong to fight against. Like Saint Paul I found myself unable to "kick against the pricks."

My campaign to help the chimpanzees in Africa

would send me traveling to different chimp range countries with an exhibit called "Understanding Chimpanzees," which was the focal point of a Wildlife Awareness Week. I would meet (when possible) heads of state, environment and wildlife ministers and other government officials, and make contact with environmental organizations and anyone involved in chimpanzee research and/or conservation. I persuaded dedicated people within each country to organize these Wildlife Awareness Weeks. Every stop included school visits, public lectures, fund-raising events, and as many media appearances as possible. We managed to put on very successful events in Uganda, Burundi, Congo-Brazzaville, Angola, Sierra Leone, and Zambia. And, of course, several in Tanzania, in Kigoma as well as Dar es Salaam. Conservation projects were also initiated in Zaire, South Africa, and Kenya.

It was during those visits that I was brought face-to-face with the terrible plight of hundreds of orphan chimpanzees. They had been born into a Gombe-like world, but their mothers had been shot—for meat or simply to steal their infants for the live animal trade. My concern would lead to the development of sanctuaries for chimps confiscated by government officials—from the marketplace or from the roadside. And for others handed over to us by people who had bought them as pets. A chimpanzee is as strong as a man by the time he or she is six years old, and even for those who have lived as part of a human family, eating at the table, playing with the children, going on visits, the time eventually comes when they can no longer be kept safely in the house. They want to be chimps, and do chimp things: they resent discipline, they can inflict serious bites, they become potentially dangerous.

There were many who urged me not to get involved with orphan chimps. It would be costly, and we would have to care for them throughout their long lives (as long as sixty years), for they can almost never be returned to the wild. It would be better, I was told, to use the precious dollars to try to save the wild chimpanzees and their habitat. Others felt I should help the African people rather than "mere" animals. But for me there was no dilemma. I could not turn my back on the outstretched hands, the pleading eyes, the pathetic malnourished bodies of the orphans. And so our sanctuary programs began. Each one became a focal point for a conservation education program, especially for children. Moreover, as at Gombe, we tried to involve the local people, employing as many as we could, buying fruit and vegetables from them, boosting the local economy. The villagers, often for the first time, had an opportunity to observe the fascinating social interactions between chimpanzees. Tourists were fascinated too, and in Kenya and Uganda the sanctuaries eventually became self-supporting.

Whenever there were chimpanzees in local zoos I went to see how they were kept. Those visits were distressing; it was hardly surprising that the animals were starving, since the keepers themselves and their families often had very little to eat. We were able to make some improvements—at zoos in Congo-Brazzaville, Uganda, Angola—for small amounts of money and with the involvement of the local expatriate communities.

Visits to some of the medical research labs in America and Europe were worse, for although the chimps were well fed, their conditions were utterly bleak and sterile and filled with boredom. Moreover, there was no excuse: with government and industry putting billions of dollars into animal research, those responsible should have been able to provide a better environment. I shall never forget watching a videotape that had been secretly filmed by animal rights activists inside a federally funded laboratory, SEMA, Inc. It arrived, as had been promised, soon after the Chicago conference. I was in Bournemouth where I had just spent Christmas with my family. After watching this video we were all in tears, almost too shocked to speak. The footage showed young chimpanzees in tiny cages, far gone in depression and despair. I had, of course, known that chimps were used in medical research, but I had never dreamed of conditions as bleak as those at SEMA, conditions that were totally unacceptable, and clearly psychologically damaging to the chimps. I wanted to speak out against such cruelty but I knew that I could not do this on the evidence of a videotape—I had to see the conditions with my own eyes. Could it really be so bad? I asked for permission to visit the laboratory; to my surprise permission was granted, and a date was set in March 1987.

I absolutely, utterly dreaded that visit, and as the time came close I felt almost physically sick. It would be my first confrontation with the white-coated scientists who, rightly or wrongly, I regarded as the enemy. When the day came, I was glad to have, in my pocket, a little card on which Vanne, knowing how anxious I was, had written two of Winston Churchill's famous wartime morale-boosting quotes to the nation: "This is not a time for doubts or weakness—this is the supreme hour to which we are called," and "Arm yourselves, and be ye men of valor, and be in readiness for the conflict." SEMA, Inc.

was in Rockville, Maryland, and my route from downtown Washington took me past the British embassy—and lo! there was that marvelous bronze statue of Churchill standing outside, hand up in his famous V for victory sign. What a wonderful omen.

I needed every bit of courage I could muster to get through that visit. Even repeated viewing of the videotape had not prepared me for the stark reality. From the outside world of sunshine I was ushered through subterranean corridors into the dim basement world of the laboratory animal. We went into a room where infant chimpanzees, one or two years old, were crammed, two together, into tiny cages that measured (as I later learned) some twenty-two inches by twenty inches square, and twenty-four inches high. Each cage was inside an "isolette," which looked a bit like a microwave oven and permitted only filtered germ-free air to enter the chimps' prison. From the small window of each isolette two infants peered at us. Not yet part of any experiment, they had already spent four months of quarantine in their tiny cells. At least they had each other, but not for long. Once their quarantine was over they would be separated, I was told, and placed in single isolettes, then infected with hepatitis or HIV or some other viral disease.

A juvenile female rocked from side to side, sealed off from the outside world. We needed a flashlight to see her properly. A technician was told to open her cage, lift her out. She sat in his arms like a rag doll, listless, apathetic. He did not speak to her. She did not look at him or try to interact with him in any way. She was either drugged, or far gone in despair. Her name, they said, was Barbie.

I am still haunted by the memory of Barbie's eyes, and the eyes of the other chimps I saw that day. They were dull and blank, like the eyes of people who have lost all hope; like the eyes of children I have seen in Africa, refugees who have lost their parents and their homes. Chimpanzee children are so like human children, in so many ways. They use similar movements to express their feelings. And their emotional needs are the same—both need friendly contact and reassurance and fun and the opportunity to engage in wild bouts of play. And they need love.

When I emerged from the underground lab, shocked and sad, I was taken to sit at a table with SEMA and National Institutes of Health personnel. I realized that everyone was looking at me, questioningly. What on earth could I say? And then, as so often happens when my mind goes blank, words came.

"I think you all know what I felt in there," I said. "And since you are all decent, compassionate people, I assume you feel much the same." They could hardly contradict. I talked about the lives of chimpanzees in the wild, their close family ties, their long and carefree childhood. I described their use of tools, their love of comfort, the rich variety of their diet, and some of our recent insights into the workings of the chimpanzee mind. Then I broached the idea of a workshop, a meeting at which biomedical scientists and veterinarians and technicians from labs could discuss, with field scientists and ethologists and animal welfare advocates, what could be done to improve conditions for the lab chimpanzees.

The workshop took place, but the NIH dropped out and the document that outlined what we considered the absolute minimum requirement for lab chimps as regards cage size, social life, and mental stimulation was largely disregarded by the regulatory body, the U.S. Department of Agriculture. Nevertheless, over the years that document, refined during three other workshops, one in the Netherlands, has been useful in many ways in our fight for improvement in the lives of lab animals. Useful because it included the views of scientists and other people who worked in the labs themselves, and not just animal rights advocates.

I became convinced that it should be mandatory for all scientists who make use of the living bodies of animals, whatever the species, to learn something about the natural behavior of those animals, and to see for themselves how their research affects the individuals involved. Only then can they balance the benefit (or hoped-for benefit) to humanity against the cost in suffering to the animals.

Chimpanzees, differing from us in the structure of DNA by only just over 1 percent, also resemble us closely in the composition of the blood and immune systems. They can catch or be infected with all human contagious diseases. And this, of course, is why they have been used as "guinea pigs" to try to find out more about human diseases such as hepatitis and AIDS, and to search for vaccines and cures. But it is important to realize that the anatomy of the brain and central nervous system of the Great Apes is also remarkably similar to ours—more so than any other living creature. If physiological similarities between chimpanzee and man mean that a disease pattern is likely to follow a similar course in our two species and be affected by similar preventative or curative agents, is it not logical to infer that similarities in the central nervous systems of chimpanzees and ourselves may have led to corresponding similarities in cognitive abilities? And that chimpanzees may experience emotions similar to those of the human primate they so closely resemble? And have a similar capacity for suffering?

We cannot state, categorically, that chimpanzees experience mental states similar to those that we label, in ourselves, joy, sadness, fear, despair, and so on, but it seems likely. Certainly an infant chimpanzee has the same need for comfort and reassurance as an infant human. Chimpanzees do not shed tears, but those who understand the behavior of human children have little difficulty in correctly identifying the emotional state of a young chimpanzee. It is because I believe, so absolutely, that chimpanzees, like us, can suffer mentally as well as physically, can feel sad, depressed, and bored, that I find visits to research labs so chilling.

I first met JoJo, a fully adult male, in 1988. He had been in a standard lab cage, five feet by five feet square, seven feet high, for at least ten years. He was in a facility owned by New York University, the Laboratory for Experimental Medicine and Surgery in Primates—LEM-SIP. He and many others of the three hundred or so chimpanzees earned their keep: their bodies were rented to pharmaceutical companies for testing drugs or vaccines. In particular, chimpanzees were thought, at that time, to be good models for learning about AIDS. For although they do not get the symptoms of full-blown AIDS, the retrovirus stays alive in their blood. JoJo was destined to be given a new vaccine against HIV, then "challenged" by an injection of the retrovirus.

It was the first time I had visited *adult* chimpanzees in a lab. The veterinarian, Dr. Jim Mahoney, introduced me. "JoJo's very gentle," he said, as he walked away between the rows of cages, five on each side of the bleak, harshly lit underground room. I knelt down in front of

JoJo, and he reached as much of his hand as he could between the thick bars that formed a barrier between us. The bars were all around him, on every side, above and below. He had already been in this tiny prison for at least ten years; ten years of utter boredom interspersed with periods of fear and pain. There was nothing in his cage save an old motor tire for him to sit on. And he had no opportunity to contact others of his kind. I looked into his eyes. There was no hatred there, only a sort of gratitude because I had stopped to talk to him, helped to break the terrible grinding monotony of the day. Gently, he groomed the ridges where my nails pressed against the thin rubber of the gloves I had been given, along with mask and paper cap. I pushed my hand in between the bars and, lip smacking, he groomed the hairs on the back of my wrist, peeling the glove down.

JoJo's mother had been shot in Africa. Could he remember that life? I wondered. Did he sometimes dream of the great trees with the breeze rustling through the canopy, the birds singing, the comfort of his mother's arms? I thought of David Greybeard and the other chimpanzees of Gombe. I looked again at JoJo as he groomed me, and my vision blurred. Not for him the freedom to choose each day how he would spend his time and where and with whom. There was no comfort for him of soft forest floor or leafy nest, high in the treetops. And the sounds of nature were gone too, the tumbling of the streams, the roar of the waterfall through the dim greens and browns of the forest world, the wind rustling and sighing in the branches, the scuttlings of little creatures moving through the leaves, the chimpanzee calls rising, so clear, from the distant hills.

JoJo had lost his world long, long ago. Now he was in a

world of our choosing, a world that was hard and cold and bleak, concrete and steel, clanging doors, and the deafening volume of chimpanzee calls confined in underground rooms. Horrible sounds. A world where there were no windows, nothing to look at, nothing to play with. There was no comfort of gently grooming fingers, no friend to embrace and kiss in joyous morning greeting, no chance to impress with a magnificent display of malehood. JoJo had committed no crime, yet he was imprisoned, for life. The shame I felt was because I was human. Very gently JoJo reached out through the bars and touched my cheek where the tears ran down into my mask. He sniffed his finger, looked briefly into my eyes, went on grooming my wrist. I think Saint Francis stood beside us, and he too was weeping.

Anyone who tries to improve the lives of animals invariably comes in for criticism from those who believe that such efforts are misplaced in a world of suffering humanity. Certainly this was the opinion of a woman I met while on tour in America. It happened to be my birthday and I was enjoying a small surprise party. The sun was shining and the spring flowers brought a smile to one's heart. Suddenly my hostess came up, concerned, to point out a tight-faced woman who had just arrived. "She has a daughter with a heart problem," I was informed. "She's been told her daughter is only alive because of experimental work on dogs. She belongs to People for Animal Experimentation. I was familiar with that group and was glad I had been warned. I expected trouble and, indeed, the woman approached me soon afterward and proceeded to tear strips off me. If I had my way, her daughter would have died. People like me made her sick. It was quite a vicious verbal attack and the people around us drew back, embarrassed. When finally I could get a word in I told her my mother had a pig valve in her heart. It was from a commercially slaughtered hog, but the procedure had been worked out with pigs in a laboratory. "I happen to love pigs," I told her. "They are quite as intelligent as dogs—often more so. I just feel terribly grateful to the pig who saved my mother's life, and to the pigs who may have suffered to make the operation possible. So I want to do all I can to improve conditions for pigs—in the labs and on the farms. Don't you feel grateful to the dogs who saved your daughter? Wouldn't you like to support efforts to find alternatives so that no more dogs—or pigs—need be used in the future?"

The woman stared at me—she was speechless for a moment. Then she said: "No one ever put it like that before." The bitter, angry expression on her face had disappeared. "I shall pass on your message to my group," she said as she left.

The use of animals in experiments is a highly controversial issue. From the point of view of those who care about animals this is hardly surprising. In the name of science and with the various goals of improving human health, keeping dying people alive, ensuring human safety, testing researchers' hypotheses, and teaching students, animals are subjected to countless invasive, frightening, and sometimes very painful procedures. To test product safety and efficacy, animals such as rats and mice, guinea pigs, cats, dogs, and monkeys are injected with or forced to swallow, or have dripped into their eyes, a whole variety of substances. Surgical techniques are practiced by medical students on animals, and new surgical procedures are tested on animals. To try out experimental techniques for treating burns, vast areas of animals' bodies are subjected to first-degree burns. To discover more about the effect of smoking, taking drugs, eating too much fat, and so forth on human animals, other kinds of animals are forced to inhale huge quantities of smoke, take drugs, and overeat. To learn about biological systems, scientists stick electrodes into animals' brains, deafen, blind, kill, and dissect them. To learn about mental functions, researchers subject animals to a vast array of tests; mistakes are punished with electric shocks, food and water deprivation, and other cruelties. In short, what is done to animals in the name of science is often, from the animals' point of view, pure torture— and would be regarded as such if perpetrated by anyone who was not a scientist.

I have thought long and deeply about the ethical implications of animal research. Regardless of how much or how little these experiments benefit human health, should we exploit animals in this way? Human beings are animals. Experiments were made on human beings during the Nazi era in Europe. And in many other countries, at many other times, human beings, with or without their knowledge, have been used in potentially harmful experiments. The thought of deliberate experimentation on nonconsenting human beings horrifies us. And rightly so.

If a painful experiment is performed on another kind of animal being, other than a human being, our distress, presumably, will be more or less acute depending on the amount of suffering we believe that the animal endures. So it would be a good thing if we knew how much suffering various species of animals experience. Unfortunately we can never *know* this—after all, there is a huge difference even among humans regarding perception of pain: the same procedure can be agonizing for one person, and only mildly painful to another. However, there are certain things that we know cause pain to humans and animals alike, such as swallowing a poison that causes death due to its agonizing attack on the gut. Are we justified in causing agony of this sort in a healthy animal if, at some future time, humans may be spared such agony? This is a question that each of us must answer for ourselves. And our answers will vary depending on: 1) the species of animal involved; 2) our knowledge of the nature of that animal; and 3) our own experience of painful illness of this sort in ourselves or in loved ones.

Fortunately the growing animal welfare and animal rights movements have stimulated new efforts in the search for alternatives to the use of live animals in pharmaceutical and medical experimentation. It is unfortunate that, once such an alternative has been found, certified effective (by the Food and Drug Administration in the United States), there are no laws to prevent the further exploitation of animals for that particular purpose. It is unfortunate also that the hurdles that must be crossed before a new *nonanimal* procedure is approved are more numerous and harder to negotiate than is the case if a new *animal* procedure is proposed. There has been a good deal of research into the history of medicine tracing the contributions made by animal experimentation. This work shows clearly that animals have not been as critical to the advancement of medicine as is typically claimed by proponents of animal experimentation. Moreover, a great deal of animal research has been misleading, and resulted either in the withholding of drugs, sometimes for years, that were subsequently found to be highly beneficial to humans, or to the release and use of drugs that, though harmless to animals, have actually contributed to human suffering and death.

I believe one of the great challenges of the future—a challenge to young researchers in human and veterinary medicine—is to find alternatives to the use of live animals of all species in experimentation, with the goal of *eliminating them altogether.* We need a new mind-set: let us stop saying that, while it is unfortunate, *some* animals will always be needed, and, instead, admit that the practice is unethical and the sooner we stop doing it the better. Let science direct its collectively awesome intellect toward phasing out all animal research. Human history is full of inspiring stories of those who achieved the impossible.

Of course, while science is responsible for a great deal of animal suffering, including much that is unnecessary, it is not scientists alone who are guilty of animal abuse. Billions of animals are subjected to unspeakable pain, misery, and fear during intensive factory farming for food. From birth to death, in their pens or crates, on the sometimes interminable journeys to slaughter and, worst of all, in the abattoirs, they suffer. Wild animals are hunted, trapped, and poisoned. There is horrid exploitation of a huge variety of animal species in the live animal trade, and in training for entertainment, and in the pet industry. And there are countless "beasts of burden" whose treatment is nothing short of barbaric.

Over the past forty years animals have been increasingly subjected to intensive farming. This type of husbandry, which inflicts on sentient beings the assembly line method for maximum productivity, became widely adopted as small farms were forced out of business by giant corporations—agribusiness had arrived. I first became aware of this when I read Peter Singer's book *Ani-*

mal Liberation, in which he described, in graphic detail, what this entailed. Because laying hens were crammed, in some cases five birds into a cage only sixteen inches by eighteen inches, in "battery farms," they sometimes became cannibalistic. So they were "debeaked"—that is, they were strung upside down, in long lines, and conveyed past a machine that cut off their beaks. This procedure was painful; worse, the stumps would be sensitive for the rest of the hens' lives. Pigs, I read, were kept in small pens, barely able to move. Standing on slats that allowed dirt to be washed away, their feet became sore and deformed; their legs, weak from lack of exercise, often broke as the overweight pigs were forced toward their execution. Farrowing sows were pinned under hoops of steel so that they literally could not move—and accidentally squash a piglet. And one of the worst nightmares for pigs with their incredibly sensitive noses (remember the famous truffle hunters in France?) was that they could not escape the stench of their excrement, the ammonia of their urine—unbearable even for us with our poor human sense of smell. Veal calves, I discovered, were kept in crates so small that they could not turn around. And they were kept in the dark and deprived of light and iron so that their meat would be white. So intense was their craving for iron that they drank their urine.

I found that my whole attitude to eating flesh abruptly changed. When I looked at a piece of meat on my plate I saw it as part of a once living creature, killed for me, and it seemed to symbolize fear, pain, and death—not exactly appetizing. So I stopped eating meat. For me, one of the delightful side effects of becoming a vegetarian was the change in my own health. I felt lighter, more filled with clean energy. I was not wasting my body's time by asking it to sort out the good protein from all the waste products that the onetime living creature had also been trying to get rid of.

There are other issues relating to raising animals for food. Thousands of acres of rain forest are cleared to provide grazing for cows, or to grow crops for animal fodder. Not only are the indigenous peoples of the Amazon losing their forest heritage but also the whole process is extremely wasteful. It has been estimated that one acre of fertile land can produce between five hundred and six hundred pounds of vegetable protein from crops such as peas or beans. If the acre is used, instead, to grow a crop to feed animals, which we then kill and eat, we shall only get between forty and fifty-five pounds of animal protein from that acre.

At this point I want to make it quite clear that I do not condemn the eating of meat per se—only the practice of intensive farming. Let the meat eaters among us—most of my friends—try to partake of the flesh of animals who have enjoyed their lives and have been killed in the most painless way possible. And could we not offer up a prayer for the spirit of the once living creature that has died for us? In the olden days people did just that. Indigenous peoples still do. Any little thing that brings us back into communion with the natural world and the spiritual power that permeates all life will help us to move a little farther along the path of human moral and spiritual evolution.

If we accept that humans are not the only animals with personalities, not the only animals capable of rational thought and problem solving, not the only animals to experience joy and sadness and despair, and above all not the only animals to know psychological as well as physical suffering, we become (I hope) less arrogant, a little less sure that we have the inalienable right to make use of other life-forms in any way we please so long as there is a possible benefit for human animals. We are, of course, unique but we are not so different from the rest of the animal kingdom as we used to suppose. This knowledge leads to humility, to a new respect for the other amazing animal beings with whom we share this planet, especially those with complex brains and social behavior about whom we know the most, such as dogs and cats and pigs. Even if we only *suspect* that other living beings have feelings that may be similar to our own, or not too *dissimilar* to our own, we should have doubts about the ethics of treating those beings as mere "things" or "tools" for our own human purposes. Even if all animals used are bred especially for our use—in the laboratory, or for food, or for entertainment—does this make them, somehow, less pig? less monkey? less dog? Does this deprive them of feelings and the capacity to suffer? If we raised humans for medical experiments, would they be less human and suffer less and matter less than other humans? Were human slaves less able to feel pain, grief, and despair simply because they were born into slavery?

We need only to list some of those who have spoken out for kindness and compassion toward animals to realize how many of the truly great have been among their ranks. Albert Einstein begged us to widen the "circle of compassion to embrace all living creatures and the whole of nature in its beauty." Albert Schweitzer insisted, "We need a boundless ethic that includes animals too." Mahatma Gandhi believed, "You can tell about the people of a country by the way they treat their animals."

Throughout the ages, a number of eminent men have

been outspoken on the subject of meat-eating. Pythagorus wrote: "The earth affords a lavish supply of riches, of innocent food, and offers you banquets that involve no bloodshed or slaughter; only beasts satisfy their hunger with flesh." George Bernard Shaw, the British playwright, said: "We don't want to fight. And yet we gorge ourselves upon the dead." Benjamin Franklin declared that meat-eating was "unprovoked murder." And, most vehement of all, Leonardo da Vinci, surely one of the greatest minds of all time, considered the bodies of meat-eaters to be "burial places; graveyards for the animals they eat."

To me, cruelty is the worst of human sins. Once we accept that a living creature has feelings and suffers pain, then if we knowingly and deliberately inflict suffering on that creature we are equally guilty. Whether it be human or animal we brutalize *ourselves*.

It is not always an easy message to get across.

One of my favorite stories concerns a London taxi driver who, early one morning, took me to Heathrow Airport. I was tired, I had two weeks of lectures ahead of me, and I planned to doze in the car. But somehow the driver knew that I worked with chimpanzees and launched into a vindictive tirade against everyone who "wasted" money on animals. Especially his sister. He went on and on about his sister. She worked for a local animal protection group. There was so much human suffering, so many abused children. It made him sick to have a sister who cared about animals. There were far too many TV programs about animals. He always turned them off.

I was not in the mood for all that. I was just about to lean back in my seat and close my eyes when I realized that this was exactly the kind of irritating, blinkered person that so desperately needed to be made aware. He represented thousands who thought the same way. Ignorant of the issues, unable to discuss, only able to trot out the same old dogmatic statements that he had heard, and repeated, a hundred times. Quite clearly I had been meant to ride in that taxi.

So I sat uncomfortably sideways on the jump seat and talked to him all the way to Heathrow through the little open window behind him. I started off with stories about the chimps. He did listen, but it didn't seem to make any difference. I told him how chimps could learn sign language. I told him how some of them loved to paint. And how they felt emotions, and cared for each other, and even rescued each other. I recounted stories about dogs and other animals who had saved the lives of their owners. I suggested that we had a responsibility toward animals in captivity because we had deprived them of any ability to fend for themselves. And that there were already many people concerned about human problems, so surely it was okay for some to care about animals also.

But nothing seemed to make any difference. Caring about animals, he maintained stubbornly, was a waste of time. "But anyway, enjoy yourself in America," he said as I got out.

It was appropriate to give him a tip, regardless of his views, but I didn't have the right amount, and he had no change. So I told him to take a couple of pounds for himself, and give the rest to his sister, for her animal work. I never thought he would—but it appealed to my sense of humor.

When I got back to the U.K. after my tour one of the letters waiting for me was from the cab driver's sister.

"My brother gave me your donation," she wrote. "That was so very kind of you. But the most amazing thing is, something happened to my brother. What on earth did you do to him? He's so nice to me suddenly, and he's asking me all these questions about the animals. He's really interested in my work. He's changed. What did you do to him?"

My exhausting hour had paid off. Not only had he made his sister happy, but perhaps he had expounded his new understanding to some of his friends and converted one or more of *them*.

Today, attitudes are slowly changing. And they will continue to change as the general public becomes better informed, as more people with mass appeal spread the message—such as Sir Paul McCartney, who, after his wife's death, made the decision to become more involved with the animal issues that meant so much to her. Many of the major medical schools have dropped "dog lab" from their curriculum. Many veterinary schools in America are offering alternatives to the traditional way of learning by operating on healthy stray dogs and cats— healthy, that is, until the students begin cutting them up. The old SEMA lab, where I met Barbie, has a new name, reflecting a change in attitude. The isolettes are gone, the chimpanzees have quite large cages, and they remain in pairs for all experiments. JoJo, my sad acquaintance from LEMSIP, was retired to a sanctuary in California when the place closed down, and many other chimps from that lab were similarly placed in sanctuaries around North America.

We still have a long way to go. But we are moving in the right direction. If only we can overcome cruelty, to human and animal, with love and compassion we shall stand at the threshold of a new era in human moral and spiritual evolution—and realize, at last, our most unique quality: humanity.

There is a powerful force unleashed when young people
resolve to make a change

Chapter 15

HOPE

THE QUESTION I AM ASKED most often as I travel around the world springs from people's deepest fear: "Jane, do you think there is hope?" Is there hope for the rain forests of Africa? For the chimpanzees? For Africa's people? Is there hope for the planet, our beautiful planet that we are spoiling? Is there hope for us and for our children and grandchildren?

Sometimes it is hard to be optimistic. In Africa one can fly over mile after mile of country that was lush and green fifteen or twenty years ago which is now almost desert, where far more people and livestock are trying to live than the land can properly support. People, moreover, who are too poor to buy food from elsewhere. What lies ahead for them? And what of Gombe? When I first arrived there in 1960 the entire shoreline up and down the lake was forested. Gradually, over the years, the trees have been cut down by the local people for firewood, for

building poles, and to clear the land for cultivation.
Today the forests outside the boundary of the national
park have gone, leaving treeless slopes, where the precious topsoil is eroding away, washed down with each
rain into the lake, silting up the breeding grounds of the
fish. Even on the steepest slopes the forests are gone:
farmers have cleared them and are making pitiful attempts to grow crops of cassava and beans in the increasingly infertile soil that remains. Already, outside the
national park, the chimpanzees and most of the other animals have gone. And people are beginning to suffer; in
some places women must dig up the roots of trees long
since cut down to get the firewood they need for cooking.
And all this change is because the numbers of people
have increased dramatically—mainly due to the explo-
sive population growth, but also due to repeated influxes
of refugees from troubled Burundi in the north, and more
recently from eastern Congo. And this scenario is repeated again and again across the African continent and
other developing countries: increased population growth,
diminishing resources, and the destruction of nature, resulting in poverty and human suffering.

Yes, we are destroying our planet. The forests are
going, the soil is eroding, the water tables are drying, the
deserts are increasing. There is famine, disease, poverty,
and ignorance. There is human cruelty, greed, jealousy,
vindictiveness, and corruption. In our big cities there is
crime, drugs, gang violence; and thousands who are
homeless, their few belongings in prams or grocery carts
or on their backs, living, sleeping, and dying in doorways,
on gratings. There are ever growing numbers of street
children. There are ethnic conflicts, massacres, and broken peace treaties. Millions of innocent people have

been killed or maimed with bullets, machetes, and land mines. Millions more have become refugees. There is organized crime, sale of arms; and the new fear, as Russia's economy collapses, of an international black market in nuclear products from her vast and crumbling nuclear arsenal.

International terrorism has developed a new and more sinister face with the recent anti-American bombings in Africa. In Tanzania and Kenya the American embassies were targeted. The attack on a restaurant in Cape Town, simply because it was modeled on an American theme restaurant, is especially alarming. Throughout the world Americans will be looking over their shoulders, fearful not of their own shadows but of that thrown by their country. Terrorism, with its suicide bombings, is fueled by pure hate. By fanatical hate. In Palestine, I recently read, children, as young as seven years, are *taught* to hate in summer camp. A little girl of eight is shown on *Children's Club*, a popular TV series, announcing, "And when I shall wander into the entrance of Jerusalem I will turn into a suicide warrior." A little boy in his turn says, "We shall throw them into the sea. The day is near when we will settle our account with stones and bullets." This is the kind of blind hate that led to the recent and shocking bombing in Omagh in Northern Ireland, in the very teeth of the peace agreement. It led to Tutsi nuns killing Hutu nuns in the convent they shared during a recent uprising in Burundi; and to four grown Hutu men in a refugee camp trying to strangle a little seven-year-old Tutsi boy who had fled with his classmates after the death of his parents.

Nor is human violence all we have to fear. The billions of tons of synthetic chemicals that have been heedlessly released into the environment (particularly DDT and CFCs) have not only damaged the ecosystem and wildlife, but have also affected human endocrine systems, damaged infants in the womb, and reduced sperm counts. Women living within two miles of landfill sites in Britain apparently have a greater chance of developing cancer. And so long as we continue developing and using new synthetic chemicals, other catastrophes—which cannot be predicted—will occur. Belarus, terribly affected by the Chernobyl disaster, suffered radioactivity ninety times greater than Hiroshima; only 1 percent of the land remains entirely radiation-free. The babies look old, their faces wizened with sharp features. This list could go on and on—and on.

All this would seem to suggest a hope-less millennium ahead. Indeed, environmentalists have produced terrifying statistics that "prove" that life on planet earth is doomed, statistics computed from the rate at which the rain forests are being destroyed, the greenhouse gases building up, the human population growing, and so on. It is as though we were on a large ship. The lookout in the bow suddenly sees rocks ahead and alerts the crew. Yet it takes time for a big vessel to change course, so all attempts to avert disaster will fail. Of course, it will take time for the ship to disintegrate in the waves. Our world will end "not with a bang but a whimper." It is easy to imagine that such a fate awaits life, as we know it, on Spaceship Earth. Yet despite this, I do have hope for the future—for our future. But only if changes are made in the way we live—and made quickly. We do not, I think, have much time. And these changes must be made by us, you and me. If we go on leaving it to others, shipwreck is inevitable.

My reasons for hope are fourfold: (1) the human brain; (2) the resilience of nature; (3) the energy and enthusiasm that is found or can be kindled among young people worldwide; and (4) the indomitable human spirit.

First let us consider the human brain. So miraculous is this gray blob of matter that I sometimes wish I had a spare life in which to learn its marvels. It was this brain that enabled our earliest ancestors to survive in a harsh and primitive world and to colonize environments that were ever more challenging through cultural adaptations, rather than the slower physical changes that have enabled other animals, over time, to live in increasingly inhospitable places. Gradually, primitive tools such as those used by the chimpanzees became increasingly sophisticated and led to modern technology. This on the one hand has resulted in wonderful innovations that have hugely benefited people, and sometimes animals, in many parts of the world. My own mother would not be alive, nor would many other people I know, but for the marvels of modern medical science. Indeed, we have benefited in a thousand and one ways. And these technologies, along with the fantastic human brains that conceive of and make and use them, have helped us to learn more and more about the amazing world in which we live. On the other hand, tragically, technology has also created weapons of mass destruction and machinery that, even as it serves human needs (real or perceived), also destroys and pollutes the natural world. This dark side of technology is disastrous because of the huge and constantly increasing number of humans who rely on the finite resources of the planet and, especially, because of the greedy, selfish, materialistic Western lifestyle that has influenced almost all cultures around the globe. A lifestyle that drives people, in order to be successful, to join in the unbecoming scramble to acquire wealth, to acquire more and more and ever more "stuff."

The hope lies in the fact that, finally, we have begun to understand and face up to these problems. They are perceived, by growing numbers of the general public, not as figments of the imagination of a few crazy environmentalists (which was the case at one time), but as real concerns that threaten us and our children—and the survival of life on earth, as we know it. The Earth Summit at Rio de Janeiro was proof that, by 1992, these problems were acknowledged by governments from around the world. And even though the results of the conference were somewhat disappointing, the very fact that it was convened and so well attended was a massive first step. The same can be said for the 1998 Kyoto summit on clean air.

Many of the environmental problems were identified long ago. But they have become worse and begun to hurt. More people are concerned than ever before. Even in China, the government, which has for so long denied that it has any environmental problems, has been jolted into concern by the terrible floods of 1998. Today environmental concerns are freely discussed in the Chinese media. And so, although we have left it a bit late, I do believe that we can, collectively, avert total disaster. If we put our problem-solving abilities in high gear and join hands and brains and hearts around the world, surely we can find ways to live that are more in harmony with nature, and start to heal some of the wounds we have inflicted. After all, humans have accomplished "impossible" tasks before. Would anyone have believed you a hundred years ago if you had predicted there would soon be a man on the moon? a fax machine? a jumbo jet? People would have written you off as a nut case, for all those things would have been considered mere science fiction and quite impossible. Yet we have invented those technologies, done those things. And many, many more (most of which still seem like magic to me).

And there is more good news. Many companies have begun "greening" their operations. British Petroleum has committed millions of pounds to developing a whole line of products that utilize solar energy. Conoco, the multinational petroleum company that built our sanctuary for orphan chimpanzees in Congo-Brazzaville, carried out its African exploration, its seismic drilling, with real environmental responsibility. Its teams walked through the forest and equipment was dropped, every so often, by helicopter. There were no roads to mark their tracks. Far from the environmental watchdogs, in remote parts of Africa, Conoco nevertheless insisted on the same rigorous standards—with regard to personnel safety as well as the environment—that are enforced in the developed world. No African government will sit on "black gold," so it is important that the exploring, drilling, and pumping be done by the most responsible and ethical companies. And unless you and I support those companies, by purchasing their products, they will never survive in the competitive marketplace.

There are hundreds of similar examples of corporate environmental responsibility. And there are signs everywhere that illustrate a changing attitude. In the spring of 1997 I had my first ride in an electric car. It was quite an experience: driving at sixty miles an hour, emitting absolutely *no* polluting gases, in a vehicle that was 100 percent recyclable and designed to last fifty years. And there are even more environmentally friendly engines in the pipeline, such as the fuel cell that depends—to be flippant—on the passionate attraction of hydrogen for oxygen. (Or is it the other way around?) Anyway, their desire for fusion is so great that it generates the power to propel a car. And the by-product of the union which they eventually achieve—H_2O—can be used to quench the thirst of the driver! On a recent Continental Airlines flight to Japan, my menu stated that it was printed on recycled paper; my newspaper was collected so that it could be recycled; and my amenities bag was made of organic cotton. Then, as I transited at the airport in Bangkok, I picked up a local paper that had an article about a new law introduced to combat air pollution: motorists caught with idling engines would face heavy fines. When I got to Japan my attention was caught by a newspaper article about a big girls school in Tokyo that was providing all students with uniforms made from recycled plastic bottles—like the jacket I was wearing at the time. And my hotel had signs in the bathroom and also by the bed, giving me the option of using my towel and bed linen for more than one day; since I was staying several nights I took good care to fold the towel, as advised, and leave it on the rail. After all, I don't wash my towels and sheets every day at home. More and more hotels all over the world are putting up similar notices; the environment benefits, and so do the hotels, for it saves them money.

Gary Zeller has invented the "eco-brick." It is lighter and cheaper than the kind of brick you build houses with. It is made, by his special process, out of industrial waste, including toxic waste. So strong is its coating that it is expected to last at least three hundred years. The eco-bricks are helping to solve waste disposal problems in parts of Eastern Europe and various places in the developing world; at the same time they are being used to cheaply build schools, hospitals, and so on. I hope that many more factories for eco-bricks can be set up. In Europe it is suggested that women living within two miles of a waste disposal dump run the risk of giving birth to babies with serious birth defects such as spina bifida and hole in the heart. Clearly, we need eco-brick factories—and some of the other inventive ways of dealing with waste that are on the market—in place of dumps.

My second reason for hope lies in the amazing resilience of nature if we give her a chance—and, if necessary, a helping hand. There are many success stories. The lower reaches of the River Thames in London were once so poisoned that almost all life was dead; today, after a massive cleanup operation, fish are swimming, and many birds have returned to breed. A few years ago I visited Nagasaki, the site of the second atomic bomb that ended World War II. Scientists predicted that nothing would grow for at least thirty years. In fact, green things (though undoubtedly radioactive at first) appeared very quickly. And one little sapling didn't even die. It is a big tree today with a thick gnarled trunk that has great cracks and fissures, all black inside. But each spring that tree puts out new leaves. I carry one as a symbol of hope.

Two years ago I gave a lecture in Sudbury, in Canada. For a hundred years the toxic emissions from a nickel mine had polluted the environment for miles around. I saw photos of a countryside that looked as barren as a lunar landscape. Yet all around me it was lush and green. The citizens, finally realizing that their health as well as their environment were at risk, had decided to do something about it. The mine had reduced its emissions by 98 percent in about fifteen years. As a symbol of hope, they gave me a feather from one of the peregrine falcons that once again nested there—after being locally extinct for more than forty years.

Recently I had the privilege of spending a day with a most remarkable forester, Merv Wilkonson, and his wife, Ann. Since 1939 Merv has logged his 136-acre forest in British Columbia nine times: walk into it today and it is like walking into one of nature's cathedrals. The forest is beautiful, the old giant trees still standing, more animal species there than when he began—and no pesticides have been used. The surrounding people are happy— they have sustainable jobs. You see, it *can* be done.

When I first went to Gombe in 1960 the forest stretched for mile upon mile along the shores of Lake Tanganyika with just a few small villages, a few places cleared for growing crops. By 1995, as I have described, the only forest left was within the thirty square miles of the Gombe national park. How to preserve this precious oasis of trees when the people all around were struggling to survive? The Jane Goodall Institute, with funding from the European Union, began a program of reforestation, agroforestry, erosion control, and the introduction of contour farming, or terracing along with other forms of erosion control. Today, thanks to our extraordinary and inspired project manager, George Strunden, and his team of Tanzanians under Emmanuel Mtiti, there are tree nurseries in twenty-seven villages: fruit trees, shade trees, and fast-growing species for building poles mixed with indigenous varieties. Many woodlots have been established, much loved by the women who must otherwise travel farther and farther for firewood. There are conservation-education programs in the villages and in all the schools. There are micro-credit schemes for groups of women to start sustainable development projects that will improve the quality of their lives without destroying the environment. In cooperation with the regional medical authority, primary health care, family planning, and AIDS education programs are delivered to the villages. In cooperation with UNICEF and the International Rescue Committee, fresh water and new-style latrines will be introduced in thirty-three villages. Thousands of people now have hope for a new future—and they understand the need to protect the last small population of chimpanzees in their midst. They have bought into the program, taken ownership. It will live on after we pull out—and so will the chimpanzees.

There are animal species that have been brought back from the brink of extinction and reintroduced into the wild. I met Don Merten, who saved the black robin in New Zealand. When he began his breeding program there were only five of these little birds in existence—and of these it transpired that only one female and one male were fertile. Now there are 250 black robins. Of course, they are all genetically identical, but they have been placed on different islands so that the outbreak of some disease will not destroy them all. In Taiwan I met a herd of the beautiful spotted Formosan deer that were part of a release program. Gone from the wild for the past thirty years, but gradually bred up from the seventeen individuals remaining in various zoos, many of them are now free in the Ken Tung National Park. An antler shed by one of the first to be released is another of my symbols of hope.

There are, in fact, success stories everywhere. The trouble is, most of us don't get involved. Most of us don't realize the difference we could make. We love to shrug off our own responsibilities, to point fingers at others. "Surely," we say, "the pollution, waste, and other ills are not our fault. They are the fault of industry, business, science. They are the fault of the politicians." This leads to a destructive and potentially deadly apathy. Let us remember, always, that we are the consumers. By exercising free choice, by choosing what to buy, what *not* to buy, we have the power, collectively, to change the ethics of business, of industry. We have the potential to exert immense power for good—we each carry it with us, in our purses, checkbooks, and credit cards. No one will force us to buy genetically engineered food, or meat from factory farms, or furniture made from clear-cut forests. We can search for and buy organically grown food, free-range eggs, and so on. But, you say, it costs a little more. Yes, it does. But as more and more people buy these products the prices will drop. And anyway, are we, or are we not, prepared to pay a few extra pennies to buy the future for our children?

It's no good blaming politicians—at least those elected by democratic process. For where is the politician who will push for a tough environmental law, one that will require some degree of sacrifice, unless he or she knows that at least 50 percent of the electorate will be supportive. And we are the electorate. Our votes count. Your vote counts; so does mine.

The trouble is that we suffer—all of us—from *just me-ism.* "I am just one person. What I do, or don't do, can't possibly make any difference. So why should I bother?" Imagine: as more and more people around the world become aware of what is good and what is bad for the environment, and for society, this means there are thousands, then millions, then billions all thinking the same: "It

can't make any difference what I do—it's just me."
Think how it would be if we could turn that around—
thousands and millions and billions of people all knowing
that what they do *does* make a difference. What would
that area in town—the one that is such a disgrace—look
like if every passing person picked up one piece of litter?
Better still, if no one threw it in the first place. Think
how much water would be saved if *everyone* turned off the
tap while brushing their teeth and how much energy
would be saved if we *all* switched off the lights when we
left a room—any room. And if everyone biked or walked
when it was practical, shared a car, or took public transportation—the reduction in air pollution would be dramatic. Imagine if *no one* bought cosmetics or household
products that had been tested on animals? That would
bring about change far more effectively than the attempts by animal rights advocates to influence government regulations. If *everyone* demanded eggs from freely
roaming chickens, how quickly poultry farming would
change! There are more vegetarians than ever—imagine
the difference if *everyone* stopped eating meat—even for
a couple of days a week. Because, if the demand were
less, animals could be humanely farmed.

It can be argued that changes of this sort will lead to
major social injustices. Meat farmers, for example, would
need alternative livelihoods. The same is true for trap-
pers and miners and those in the animal laboratory industry, and so forth. I am not, for a single moment,
denying the complexity, the interrelatedness, the social
and political implications of these issues. But we cannot
condone forever the pursuit of unethical, cruel, and destructive behaviors simply because to end them will create problems: would anyone advocate the continuation of

concentration camps in order to ensure the jobs of those in charge?

My third reason for hope lies in the new understanding, commitment, and energy of young people around the world. As they find out about the environmental and social problems that are now part of their heritage, they want to fight to right the wrongs. Of course they do—they have a vested interest in this, for it will be their world tomorrow. They will be moving into leadership positions, into the workforce, becoming parents themselves. The sooner they start sorting out the mess, the better. Young people, when informed and empowered, when they realize that what they do truly makes a difference, can indeed change the world. They are changing it already.

Because I believe that nothing is more important, I am devoting much of my time to developing a program for youth—Roots & Shoots. This is a symbolic name: *roots* creep underground everywhere and make a firm foundation; *shoots* seem new and small, but to reach the light can break apart brick walls. Brick walls of overpopulation, deforestation, soil erosion, desertification, poverty, hunger, disease, pollution; and human greed, materialism, cruelty, crime, warfare—all the problems that we humans have inflicted on the planet. The message of Roots & Shoots is one of hope: hundreds and thousands of roots and shoots—young people—around the world *can* break through. The program stresses the value of the individual—every single one of us matters, has a role to play, makes a difference. We cannot live through a day without impacting the world around us—and we have a choice: What sort of impact do we want to make? And it is not only *humans* who matter as individuals—so too do animals.

The Roots & Shoots groups, from kindergarten to university, are involved in three kinds of hands-on projects: demonstrating care and concern for 1) the environment, 2) animals, and 3) the local community. Their tools are knowledge and understanding, persistence and hard work, love and compassion. What they actually do depends on where they are and on the nature of local problems, since the goal is to improve the world around them. In Tanzania they might plant trees, try to improve the conditions of livestock in the markets, visit children in hospital. In South Central Los Angeles, they might clear garbage, share information about pet care, help out a neighbor. And so on.

If members are interested—and they almost always are—they can be partnered with other Roots & Shoots groups in other neighborhoods and other countries. Partners share information about their problems and what they are doing to try to solve them, as well as about themselves and how they live. There is strong emphasis in the movement on breaking down barriers between ethnic, religious, and socioeconomic groups, between generations, between countries. And between humans and animals. As of April 1999 there are some two thousand groups in more than forty countries.

Encouraging and empowering young people, giving *them* hope, is my contribution to their future and, thus, the future of our planet. There is much I could say about the projects that these young people have already tackled, about the way in which the program has been spread, from school to school, city to city, by the young people themselves. But that is another book. Here I will simply say that I derive much of my energy from this program. From reading the reports that come in from groups around the world, illustrating all the different ways they are making a difference. From my visits to the schools, the shining eyes, the excitement, the commitment. And from the realization that children, already, are influencing their parents.

There is a powerful force unleashed when young people resolve to make a change. The convictions of one small child that her action would make a difference has touched the hearts of many. Amber Mary was five years old when she came up to me, with her mother, at the end of a lecture in Tampa, Florida. In one hand she clutched a small toy Snoopy dog, in the other a plastic bag with a few pennies inside. Her mother had found out only that morning why Amber Mary had been saving up her pocket money. She had seen one of the National Geographic Specials, *Among the Wild Chimpanzees*. In it, little Flint dies of grief after losing his mother, Flo. Amber Mary knew about grief—her own brother had died, just a year before, from leukemia. And he had always loved watching the chimpanzees at the zoo. Amber Mary also knew that I was looking after orphan chimpanzees. And so she saved up her allowance, week after week, until she could buy the toy—would I give it to one of the sad orphan chimps? Perhaps it would help him be less lonely at night. And with the few pennies of change, would I buy him some bananas? We all had wet eyes by the time the story was told.

Amber Mary is a wonderful illustration of my fourth reason for hope: all the amazing and wonderful people I meet or hear about as I travel around the world. There are those who have set out to accomplish almost impossible things, and because they never gave up, achieved their goals against seemingly hopeless odds, or blazed a path along which others could follow. There are those who suddenly rise to an occasion and perform heroic deeds that no one—even including themselves—believed them capable of. We all know of people who have overcome horrendous physical disabilities to lead lives that are truly inspirational—shining examples to us all. And then there is a whole gigantic, determined army of those who quietly give their lives in the service of others—human or animal. What is so inspiring, exciting, absolutely exhilarating, is that these wonderful people are all around us. We see them in world leaders and street children, scientists and waiters, artists and truck drivers. When people ask me, "Jane, where do you get your energy from? How can you cope with such a grueling schedule?" I always smile, and tell them, "Much of it comes from the spiritual power I feel around us. But an awful lot of it comes from the amazing people I meet." It is about the *only* advantage of continual travel to new places.

Mikhail Gorbachev had long been a hero of mine and I was thrilled to meet him. He dared to challenge the iron fist of the repressive communist regime of the Eastern bloc—the regime that, for the first time in human history, built a wall not to keep the enemy out, but to keep its own people in. And it was a privilege to meet Nelson Mandela. I had never thought that apartheid would end in my lifetime; and that when it did there would be a bloodbath. But thanks to Mandela's charismatic leadership, apartheid has ended, and there has been no bloodshed. Of course, in the former Soviet Union and in the new South Africa many political, economic, and social problems have surfaced. Always it seems that the change to democracy in countries where ethnic and tribal hatreds were held in check by the iron-fist dictator results initially in chaos and turbulence. Nevertheless, we cannot doubt that the actions of Gorbachev and Mandela represent giant steps toward human dignity and freedom.

And I meet so many other remarkable people, all over the world, who are devoting their lives to improving the lot of the disadvantaged among us. And of course there are many who are helping animals too. Jon Stocking, for example, when he had a job as cook on a tuna fishing boat, was horrified to see how dolphins became trapped and drowned. When he heard the crying of a baby dolphin and its mother gazed into his eyes, as though begging for help, he found himself leaping into water boiling with the thrashing of huge and terrified tuna, sharks, and dolphins. Jon, terrified himself, took the baby dolphin into his arms, felt it relax, and lifted it over the net. Somehow he got its mother over too. Then, with his knife, he cut the net and freed all the rest of them. Of course he lost his job. When he finally got home, Jon thought about the dolphin situation, and all the animals who were being driven toward extinction. What could he do? He had no degree. He was not wealthy. But he desperately wanted to make a difference. And he has. Now he makes chocolate bars—of the very best chocolate. Each Endangered Species Bar depicts an animal on the wrapper, and 11.7 percent of the profit—before the deduction of taxes—goes to an organization dedicated to fighting for the survival of that species. "Chocolate Jon," as we call him now, is another of my heroes. And there are increasing numbers of other businesses today that donate percentages of their profits to various good causes.

I have been privileged to meet some of the spiritual

leaders of the indigenous peoples of North America who, despite intense persecution and deliberate efforts to destroy their cultures, have held on to their original tribal customs, their belief in the Great Spirit or the Creator, and our interdependence with the planet, the animals, the plants, the rocks, water, sun, moon, and stars. Now they are preparing to strip off the blanket of apathy woven by a century of oppression and suppression. Chief Leonard George from Vancouver speaks to my very soul with his singing and the voice of his drum—the urgent, insistent, yet infinitely patient heartbeat of Mother Earth. He has been through much pain and trauma in his life and has emerged as a leader with the quiet and gentle simplicity of a truly spiritual person. And there is Chitcus (Terrence Brown), my spirit brother in California. His mother is the last true medicine woman of her tribe, and Chitcus is gradually moving toward his destined position of medicine man of the Karuk people. Every morning at dawn he makes smoke for me, with an Indian blessing, to give me extra strength as I travel around the world. Ed Ramone, the most decorated Native American of the Vietnam War, has even honored me with the name Tasheez Ween ina Maka, Sister of Mother Earth. And from Jonathan Lucero, an Apache, I received a small black carved bear for strength and courage which I hold in my hand during my lectures.

A few years ago I was given a simple wooden comb made by a Tanzanian leper who lost all his fingers and toes before the disease was checked. Yet with the stumps and his teeth he weaves patterns with strands of wool, decorating these combs so that he can sell them and live with dignity instead of begging.

A similar story concerns a Taiwanese musician. He lost

one hand and his eyesight when, at the age of twelve, he picked up a shiny metal ball on the beach; it was a land mine. He had always wanted to play the guitar and so his friends made him a metal band with a strong plastic pick, which he could strap to his stump. When I met him, he and his blind accordion-playing partner had just produced a CD that was a hit in Taipei. And when I was in Beijing there was a street musician playing a keyboard quite delightfully although he had no fingers or thumbs at all.

Most remarkable is the story of Paul Klein, who was injured, horribly injured, by an exploding stick of dynamite when he was six years old. Over the next two years he had to undergo a series of painful surgeries. The doctors had to repair his left eye. Then there were his two terribly mutilated hands. The left hand was the worst—the thumb and part of his wrist had been blown off. But his surgeon managed to reattach the remaining fingers. The thumb and last two fingers of his right hand were also reattached. During these ordeals he decided he wanted to become a surgeon himself—a goal that most people believed he could never achieve. But, as he said to me, "through positive thought and the help of many people" he actually qualified as a first-class orthopedic pediatric surgeon. He finds that people who undergo reconstructive surgery are often embarrassed for people to see their disfigurements. These people he helps by showing them his hands, and explaining how he overcame his own difficulties.

Then there is Gary Haun. He lost his eyesight when he was twenty-five years old in the U.S. Marines, yet managed to become an excellent magician—the Amazing Haundini. He performs for children, and they do not realize, until the end of the show, that he is blind. He talks to them about overcoming problems and getting on with life. He has also mastered scuba diving, cross-country skiing, sky diving, judo, and karate. Recently he climbed to the top of Mount Kilimanjaro. He is one of the most giving people I know. It was Gary who, in April 1994, gave me the toy monkey that would become my mascot. Gary thought he was giving me "yet another stuffed chimpanzee" until I made him feel that the creature had a tail—so it could not be a chimpanzee. I told him it looked like a sort of misshapen baboon, with upside-down ears and a tail only half the proper length. "Never mind," said Gary, unabashed. "Take him wherever you go and you will know I am with you in spirit." And so my mascot, Mr. H, as he was named (for Haun), has accompanied me to thirty countries (many of them several times) in the four and a half years I have had him. He is a great traveling companion; with his perpetual happy grin and banana that is always just about to be consumed, he somehow brings a smile to the most dour of faces. I tell people that they will never be quite the same again once they have touched him, for something of the indomitable spirit of Gary Haun will rub off on them. He has now been touched, patted, hugged, or kissed by well over 200,000 people—no wonder his once fluffy hair is matted, his once white face grubby-looking (despite repeated shampoos), and his body even more misshapen. But he has character. And as someone recently pointed out, the H of his name also stands for Hope.

Of course, I don't have to look very far to find inspiring people. Vanne had to go through open-heart surgery when she was seventy-five years old. Her clogged-up aortic valve was exchanged for the "bioplasticed" one from that commercially slaughtered pig. When I had finally persuaded her to have a proper checkup—because she looked ghastly—she was immediately scheduled for surgery. Which was, of course, successful. I spoke to the surgeon afterward, and he asked me what Vanne had been doing just before the operation. It had been Christmas so she'd been shopping and doing all the usual pre-Christmas things one does. "Well," he told me, "it may interest you to know that *physiologically* she was only capable of sitting up and lying down. Everything else she did you can attribute to willpower." He told me that in the ten years he had been doing that operation, hers was the most clogged-up valve he had encountered. So I am lucky—I have built-in inspiration, as it were. On the doorstep!

I shall conclude this chapter with a symbolic story. It is about an American, Rick Swope, a zoo visitor who rescued an adult male chimpanzee from drowning in the moat around his enclosure. And this despite the dire warning of a keeper and the threats of other adult male chimpanzees of the group. When asked what had made him risk his life he answered: "I looked into his eyes. It was like looking into the eyes of a man. And the message was: Won't *anybody* help me?"

That is the look that I've seen in the eyes of chimpanzees tied up in the African markets, from under the frills of the circus chimp, from behind the steel bars of the laboratory prisons. It's a look I've seen in the eyes of other suffering animals. And in the eyes of little children from Burundi who saw their parents slaughtered in the ethnic violence. In the eyes of the street children, and those that are caught up in the violence of our inner cities. Indeed, that appeal is all around us. Albert

Schweitzer wrote: "A man who possesses a veneration of life will not simply say his prayers. He will throw himself into the battle to preserve life, if for no other reason than that he is himself an extension of life around him."

I truly believe that more and more people are seeing the appeal in the eyes around them, feeling it in their hearts, and throwing themselves into the battle. Herein lies the real hope for our future; we are moving toward the ultimate destiny of our species—a state of compassion and love. Yes, I do have hope. I do believe we can look forward to a world in which our great-grandchildren and their children after them can live in peace. A world in which there will still be trees and chimpanzees swinging through them, and blue sky and birds singing, and the drumbeats of indigenous peoples reminding us powerfully of our link to Mother Earth and the Great Spirit—the God we worship. But, as I've stated repeatedly, we don't have much time. The planet's resources are running out. And so if we truly care about the future of our planet we must stop leaving it to "them" out there to solve all the problems. It is up to *us* to save the world for tomorrow: it's up to you and me.

(Courtesy of Henri Landwirth)

Henri Landwirth, who survived the horrors of the
Nazi death camps and eventually created Give Kids
the World, a place of joy for terminally ill children

Chapter 16

BEYOND
THE HOLOCAUST

Now I HAVE ONE LAST JOURNEY to share; a mind journey from evil to love. We are all horrified by the undeniable evidence of evil in humanity. When I was a child I learned to hate Germans, who were causing so much suffering. Even my sister, Judy, at three years old, was familiar with the names of some of the hated German enemies—Hitler, of course, and Himmler, Goebbels, and Göring. Danny used to "draw" their faces, or their whole bodies, in golden syrup on our teatime pieces of bread and margarine. I remember so, so vividly the satisfaction of biting into them, decapitating them, or amputating arms and legs. There was not much else we could do to show our hatred of these men. Even Danny was powerless to help me express my utter loathing of Hitler when the details of the Holocaust became known.

More than three decades passed after the end of the war before I visited one of the death camps. I knew I had to do this. And of them all, it had to be Auschwitz because that name symbolized for me the nightmare of the Holocaust. I did not think the visit would help me to understand; I did not think it would help to lay to rest the ghastly images. It was just something that my inner self told me I had to do. And so eventually I made the pilgrimage—with a German friend. Even more than I, perhaps, he needed to confront and come to terms with the past. Dietmar had been a child (the same age as I) in Berlin when the war started.

We first visited a museum in Berlin which has a collection of Holocaust photographs and documents. One letter I can never forget. It was part of an exchange of correspondence and orders, back and forth, as Hitler's henchmen made the arrangements to activate the machinery of his obscene "final solution." The gist of the letter was: It is to be expected that some of the guards will show empathy toward the prisoners; this must be stamped out immediately. With German thoroughness everything was thought of, every last detail worked out. It wasn't only the Jews and Gypsies, the mentally disabled and homosexuals, who suffered in Nazi Germany; so too did Germans who were not prepared to abandon the human value of compassion.

Dietmar and I took the train to Kraków and then another to Auschwitz. There are two camps there: Auschwitz I and Auschwitz II, or Birkenau, which was built to provide additional space for the Jews and Gypsies who flowed in on the transports from all around occupied Europe. We entered under the infamous archway with its cynical motto: *"Arbeit macht Frei."* Yes indeed—the freedom of death. Auschwitz I, today, is a giant museum. The walls of the brick buildings are lined with photographs of the prisoners in their ill-fitting striped "pajamas" having their heads measured (part of a gigantic, horrifying attempt to show biological ethnic differences). There are photographs of pogroms, of battles, of Nazi officials, of the führer. There is a great pile of the shoes that were removed from prisoners before they entered the gas ovens. A hut full of the suitcases taken from prisoners on arrival. A huge pile of hair, shaved from their heads. And a terrible collection of crutches, braces, artificial limbs, dental plates, and so on. There is a lamp shade made from human skin. There is the crematorium, with a detailed description of how it was fed. And the area where prisoners were publicly beaten and shot. There was too much horror to take in. The piles of possessions represented only those that had belonged to one or two of the thousands of transports; and Auschwitz was just one of the many death camps.

My mind was numbed. I did not feel anything, and was dismayed at what seemed like a lack of empathy. Suddenly I noticed a single child's shoe, set on its own in a little case and, close by, a treasured doll that must have been clutched on the nightmare train ride, then seized by callous, uncaring hands at the end of what had been one little girl's last journey. Those images penetrated devastatingly through the numbness; a wave of anger churned my insides, my heart raced. And then a huge sadness took over. I turned away, my vision blurred.

Birkenau was, I think, about two miles away. It was raining and cold but we walked; it seemed inappropriate to go by bus. Only six of the long wooden huts remain standing in the huge flat compound, now covered with grass. When it was occupied it was a sea of cold mud in winter and hard-baked naked earth in summer. Like a defoliated, symmetrical man-made forest, the corner supports, marking where the other huts had been, stood in row after endless, terrible row. The Gestapo had tried to destroy the camp, to conceal their crimes from the advancing Soviet troops, but had fled before finishing the job. The sentry towers stood, high above the camp, and the sentry bunkers, where guards stood with their eyes level with the ground. No one could escape. The comfortable mansion where the Gestapo had lived was on the outside of the cruel, unrelenting electric and barbed wire fence.

One of the six surviving huts was a latrine hut. Parallel rows of holes, back to back. Suddenly my mind was filled with all that I had read: I could almost hear the cries, smell the stench, feel the whips of the guards as they beat those who tried to sit, cramped with dysentery, for longer than the prescribed minute. And in the other huts, the bunks in tiers of three, lining both sides of the long, low, dark buildings. Slats of wood with gaps between them. The prisoners, skeletons, no warmth, huddled, stinking, scratching bedbugs. Cold. Horribly beaten—beaten for everything and for nothing at all. And always hungry. Hurting with the terrible pain of a hunger that we, who have not endured, cannot even imagine. The chilly day seemed suddenly freezing as I thought of the subzero frosty dawns, the wind racing across the flat land straight from Siberia, the lines of prisoners standing, naked, through the interminable roll calls. Every morning. Frozen, starving, sick. How had any of them survived? At Birkenau, where there was no museum, where there were no photos, and only one other couple visiting beside Dietmar and me, I felt the full horror of the Holocaust. The pain, the helplessness, the black despair, the apathy of the *Mussulmans,* the walking dead. How, in God's name, how could *any* have survived?

Three years later I would meet a man who not only survived, but who also overcame his bitterness, his hatred, and created a sanctuary of warmth, and light, and love for desperately sick children. Henri Landwirth is a truly amazing man. But before I share his story let me return for a moment to my own experience at Auschwitz. In the middle of one of the darkest of the six huts, pushing through the concrete under one of the bunks, a little plant had tentatively emerged. Its shoots reached toward the dim light from the minute overhead "skylights" (each about two inches by four inches of thick, cloudy glass); its hopeful buds were ready to burst open. It had broken through the legacy of the darkest and most calculatedly evil period of human history. Where would I ever find a more potent symbol for the impermanence of schemes hatched, surely, in hell? The hell that exists in twisted and warped human minds.

I had thought that the following day would be one for quiet reflection—sorting out impressions, coming to terms with the new experience. But it was not to be. For it just happened to be the Spring Children's Festival in Kraków. The church bells rang, the children were in their gay national costumes, there was singing and dancing in the streets. And the sun came out. It seemed to be another symbolic message, adding to the powerful impact of the Auschwitz visit.

And then, as though to complete this mind journey out of hate and brutality and unspeakable evil and into love and compassion, I met Henri Landwirth. He was just thirteen when war broke out. He was separated from his family and for the next five years was shifted from labor camps to concentration camps, one after the other—including Auschwitz-Birkenau. In his autobiography, *Gift of Life*, he describes those years during which he "saw, heard, and experienced man's inhumanity to man firsthand." And somehow he survived. But he was left "blinded by hatred . . . by a child's need to hurt others as I had been hurt." His final escape was miraculous—he and two other Jewish prisoners were marched out to be executed. But the war was nearly over, and the soldiers didn't want to kill them. They lined them up to be shot—as Henri's father had been shot—but then told them to run. They ran. And so Henri, desperately sick as he was, with his head smashed in by a rifle butt, his legs gangrenous from untreated sores, found his freedom.

Like so many other survivors he eventually, with the help of an aunt, made it to America. He arrived penniless, but through hard work, his charismatic personality, and shrewd business skills, Henri made a big success in hotel management. And then he changed direction, and turned his tremendous energy and implacable will to a new project—helping to grant the last wishes of children with terminal or life-threatening diseases. It all began when he realized that many children, whose last wish had been to visit Disney World in Florida and meet Mickey Mouse, had died before their wish could come true because the hotels were booked up so far ahead. So Henri set to work to change things. In 1988, with the help of many corporations, he built the children their own village. Give Kids the World is close to Disney World. For about a week, from the time they arrive at the Orlando airport, the families are given everything—accommodation (each family has its own chalet in The Village), food, transportation; and, thanks to Disney, everything at Disney World and the other theme parks is absolutely free. The Village is staffed by some two thousand volunteers. Henri took me around this amazing place. I saw the shining joy in the faces of desperately sick children who, for a few brief days, could forget the pain and fear of the hospital world. Their wishes had come true. And the brothers and sisters, who so often feel guilty or neglected or both, are made to feel special too. The parents—sometimes grandparents or aunts and uncles—are able to relax, to talk to others who understand, only too well, their anguish and their problems. There is a little chapel-like place of peace for those parents who want to pray, or simply to sit quietly and try to come to terms with what has happened. There is a book in which some have recorded their thoughts. I read an entry at random which said something like: Dear God, Christopher is such a good little boy, and he has been so brave. Soon he will be with you. Please look after him for us—we love him so very much. It was from his grandmother.

Henri has created a place of love. And it is real love—

I have watched him with the children, seen the light in his eyes—and theirs. And—the ultimate magic—Give Kids the World can lead to miracles. There are many parents who write to say that the pure joy and exhilaration of the experience gave their child a new lease on life. Some of them even recover completely.

In his book Henri writes that whilst at the death camps he lost touch with his spiritual side, "abandoning God, as I had felt abandoned." How did he recover his faith in God? How has he reconciled the unspeakable cruelties of the death camps and the suffering of innocent children, stricken with some terrible disease, with the existence of a just God, a caring God of love? Henri writes: "Where does a heart truly broken, a spirit hopelessly abandoned, find hope? What exists within a human being that allows for survival amidst such devastation? It must be God. . . . Who else could it be?"

For fifty years I have lived with the horror of the Holocaust, the images of torture and death imprinted on my child's mind never very far beneath the surface. The visit to Auschwitz and Birkenau helped to release some of the pain from my heart. Knowing Henri, marveling at his story of courage and success, has helped even more, for I have understood that I must come to terms with the past, break away from some of my own dark images. I learned, on that mind-journey, that there are things which I, with my finite mind, shall never be able to understand. And that, although I can never accept evil— deliberate, malicious cruelty to man or beast—and though I shall always fight it, I do not have to account for its presence among us. For now we can only see as "through a glass, darkly."

And so, for several reasons, that particular mind-journey was a vitally important part of my own spiritual pilgrimage through time and space. It helped my soul to grow.

With my great traveling companion, Mr. H.

(Michael Neugebauer)

Chapter 17

THE END AT THE BEGINNING

HＯＷ SHOULD I END A BOOK about a life that is not yet completed? Death is such a convenient end point, even if we believe, along with Chief Seattle, that "there is no death; only a changing of worlds." Nevertheless, I must bring this book to some sort of ending.

I am sitting in the Birches. Outside, in the much loved garden, are the selfsame trees that I looked at, and climbed, when I was a child, dreaming of Tarzan and Africa. And there are certain things and certain sounds that suddenly, with no warning, transport me back in time so that, for a few moments, I am a child again. Such as the song of a chaffinch or blackbird as I step out into the sun-filled garden; the old gray stone frog who still sits, as he sat sixty years ago, by the old gray stone bird-bath that is shaped like an ammonite; the heavy stone lawn roller, its wooden handle rotted, that Danny used to pull over the grass, vainly trying to flatten the unruly bumps and hollows; one of those old Sheffield-steel kitchen knives with a bone handle that Uncle Eric used to sharpen with a whetstone. What is it that links this woman, Jane Goodall, with that far-off child? Is it, as some suggest, simply a series of memories stored in a computer-like brain? Or is there something that we call a "soul" that has been with me from birth? Something apart from brain, apart even from mind. Something that links me with the spiritual power I sense around us? I think I have a soul. I have been told by very spiritual people that I have an *old* soul—in other words, a soul that has been through many incarnations. If there is such a thing as reincarnation—and I believe that there is—then those people are probably correct; it feels that way. I can never be certain, in this life. I can be certain, however, that memories are indeed stashed away by our amazing brains. This book has been written around memories that I plucked from the storehouse of my mind to share with anyone who cares to read it.

When I look back over my life, it seems that my time on earth has been divided into a series of clear-cut phases, all of which overlap. First, a time of *preparation*—preparation for life in general, and in particular for traveling to Africa and studying the chimpanzees. But I am still preparing—for whatever lies ahead. Second, the period that I remember with the most nostalgia: the *hunting and gathering* of information, the time I spent in the forest learning about and from the chimpanzees. We are still learning new things about these amazing beings. Third came *child raising* when I was a mother and a wife, a phase that overlapped with *analyzing and publishing* the chimpanzee data. The *sharing* of the knowledge I acquired was always important to me, but it did not become the driving force in my life until the "Damascus experience." This sharing aspect will continue for the rest of my days, and, through books, will continue, in some form, after I am dead. At least, I hope so.

My lecture tours are an important part of the sharing. They are exhausting but I am at the same time mentally and spiritually enriched as I travel through new parts of the world and am exposed, albeit too fleetingly, to new cultures. And, most important, I am inspired and energized by so many of the people I meet. After giving a lecture I usually sit at a table and sign books. Of course this helps us to sell merchandise, which is good for the Jane Goodall Institute's fund-raising, and for spreading information. But there is more to it than that. I sign programs and tickets and brochures, and books that people bought twenty years ago. For me this period of signing is important because it gives me a chance to make contact with those who were in the audience. And these people who line up, sometimes for two hours or more (the record was four hours, ten minutes), give me energy which I desperately need because during a talk I use up just about my whole supply, so that I am left feeling empty and cold. One volunteer who was helping me at one of these sessions put her finger on it when she said: "These people are feeding you, aren't they?" Yes, that is exactly what they are doing. I make a big effort to reach as many people in the room as possible in the hope that my message will enter their hearts as well as their minds. So that more and more of us can join hands and join hearts in our effort to make our world a better place for all life. And so when people come up afterward and say things that suggest that my message has indeed reached them and helped them—yes, they are feeding me.

I've found that people from all cultures, everywhere I've been, sometimes have tears in their eyes when they come up to me after a lecture. I used to be uneasy and embarrassed, but now I think I understand. I really believe that the essence of the message I share with them comes to me from outside; as if I am an eolian harp with strings vibrating to an invisible wind. Perhaps it came to me first through Trevor's sermons, all those years ago. Or was it through the music that so moved me in Notre Dame?

It is hard now, after twenty years, to recapture that moment of ecstasy in the cathedral—although the experience has never left me. It became incorporated into the warp and woof of my very being. If I hear Bach's fugue, no matter where I am, the result is the same: just as the chimes of Big Ben trigger an unconscious spasm of fear, so that music floods my whole being with love, joy, and a sort of spiritual exaltation. It was not important, I think, that the music was Bach, or that particular fugue. And I suspect the experience could have occurred in another cathedral, or a church, a mosque, a temple, a synagogue. It was the glorious reverberation of the organ in an ancient place of worship, sanctified over hundreds of years by the sincere prayers of so many thousands of people. The impact was so powerful I suppose because it came at a time when so much was changing in my life, when I was vulnerable. When I was, without knowing it, needing to be reconnected with the Spirit Power I call God—or perhaps I should say being reminded of my connection. The experience, whatever else it did, put me back on track; it forced me to rethink the meaning of my life on earth.

Only quite recently did I begin to wonder whether there had been some specific message for me, wordlessly conveyed by the powerful music, a message that I absorbed, but was not yet ready or able to interpret. And now, through experience and reflection, I believe that there was indeed a message. A very simple one: Each one of us matters, has a role to play, and makes a difference.

Each one of us must take responsibility for our own lives, and above all, show respect and love for living things around us, especially each other. Together we must reestablish our connections with the natural world and with the Spiritual Power that is around us. And then we can move, triumphantly, joyously, into the final stage of human evolution—spiritual evolution.

Is it arrogant, presumptuous, to think that I might have heard the Voice of God? Not at all. We all do—that "still, small voice" that we speak of, telling us what we ought to do. That, I think, is the Voice of God. Of course, it is usually called the voice of conscience, and if we feel more comfortable with that definition, that's fine. Whatever we call it, the important thing, I think, is to try to do what the voice tells us. My experience in the cathedral of Notre Dame was dramatic, awakening. It is the still, small voice that I hear now—and it bids me to share.

And that is what I try to do. I share that message in my lectures around the world, with all kinds of audiences and especially with children. And always I have this feeling—which may not be true at all—that I am being used as a messenger. There are times before a lecture when I have been absolutely exhausted, or actually sick, and terrified that I am going to utterly fail the audience. And those lectures are often among the best. Because, I think, I have been able to tap into the spiritual power that is always there, providing strength and courage if only we reach out: "Ask and it shall be given unto you; seek and ye shall find." That strength is available for us all. Of course, I also tap into the energy of the audience itself—the more enthusiastic and upbeat the crowd, the more lively the talk.

It would be dangerous to take any of this for granted. I was always taught: "God helps those who help themselves." I work hard to prepare my lectures, going through them in their entirety, including the slides, before every presentation, even if I have given more or less the identical talk many times before. I had the best role model: Uncle Eric. The night before each of his operating days he would lie in bed and review, in his mind, every case on the list. Even if it was something simple like an appendectomy he went through the entire procedure, trying to think of all the things that could go wrong and the appropriate response to each. That, I am sure, is why he was such a successful doctor—his meticulous attention to detail, and his huge compassion for each and every patient.

Another thing I am often asked: How can you seem so peaceful? People have asked that question, commented on it, at almost every lecture and all over the world. They want to know if I meditate. Not in a formal way, I tell them; but I do try to keep a finger hooked into the spiritual power as it were. And I do continually give thanks for all the amazing good fortune that has surrounded me for so much of my life. For all the wonderful people who have supported me, the feathers of my Eagle. And I give thanks for my good health. I feel grateful for that every day, because I know how incredibly lucky I am in this regard, and how fragile is the gift.

Also I have been privileged to know the peace of the forest. The forest—any forest—is, for me, the most spiritual place. So are the mountains, but I have not had much to do with mountains. It is my long days, months, and years in the forests of Gombe that help me to keep calm in the midst of chaos, for I carry the peace within me. Recently a powerful experience revitalized that spiritual peace. I was with a group of Roots & Shoots members, walking through a glorious old-growth forest on the slopes of Mount Hood in Oregon. Suddenly, from the trail, I saw an amazing tree. It had been burned, about a hundred years before, and only some forty feet of the trunk remained. It was completely hollow. I went into the tree through an opening almost like a small door, pointed at the top. The remaining outer shell of the tree, straight and tapering as the spire of a church, directed my eyes up and up, through the surrounding green of the forest, to the sky high above. I stood there, awed and humbled, and sent a prayer to God for the survival of the remaining forests in the world. The prayer seemed to be drawn up, and up—and surely it reached its destination? The members of my group joined me, five at a time, so that we could stand, holding hands, and pray for the forests. Chitcus, my Native American spirit brother, was there, and he made smoke from the sacred Kish'wuf root and chanted an Indian blessing. My inner peace was renewed and I was immeasurably strengthened.

And how marvelous memories can be! In the grim times I conjure them up, glorious moments from the past. As when I was sitting on the beach in Dar es Salaam early in the morning:

FIVE HERONS

Five herons flying past, low above the water,
Long necks tucked back: flying between the
    golden shimmering sea
And the gray and golden clouds of the sun's rising.
Behind, in sky of palest blue
Above the palm fronds,
The yellow moon sinks slowly to her rest.
Oh golden flying moment, snatched from time,
Valued above all price,
With loving care laid in the treasure house
Of memories and taken out, as now,
To feed my soul when all around is drear.

I have also learned to some extent to keep silly circling thoughts at bay. You work hard and do what you can to prepare for a dreaded meeting, or a particularly daunting lecture—and then let go. It is the same with a visit to the dentist. "This time tomorrow (or next week or whenever)," I say to myself, "and it will all be over." And, of course, there is Danny's favorite text: "As thy days, so shall thy strength be."

Another question I am asked repeatedly is: How can you keep calm when you go into an animal research lab? How can you stop yourself from yelling and shouting and accusing everyone of cruelty? The easy answer is that the aggressive approach simply doesn't work. In addition, while some people are, unfortunately, really sadistic, most people who are cruel to animals simply haven't understood their true nature. They don't believe that any animals, even those with complex brains, have minds and feelings and emotions similar to ours. It is my task to try to change their attitudes in this matter; they will not listen if I raise my voice and point an accusing finger. Instead they will become angry and hostile. And that will be the end of the dialogue. Real change will come only from within; laws and regulations are useful, but sadly easy to flout. So I keep the anger—which of course I feel—as hidden and controlled as possible. I try to reach gently into their hearts.

"How much longer can you keep up the pace," I am often asked. "When do you plan to retire?" Of course the time will come when I am physically unable to cope with so much travel. And that time may come sooner rather than later—we cannot tell what lies ahead. But certainly while I still have the strength and energy I shall just carry on. And I certainly hope I shall be granted a good many more years. After all, Danny did not leave us until she was ninety-seven, Olly is ninety-seven and still going strong, and Vanne and my father are ninety-four and ninety-three respectively. So I'm hoping for at least ten more really active years—and then some time for more peaceful reflection, time to do some of the things which my present lifestyle precludes.

I have many definite goals for the future. An important one is to build up an endowment so that our work in Africa—Gombe, the sanctuaries, and our programs to help the villagers—can continue in perpetuity. I want to put much effort into spreading Roots & Shoots around the globe, strengthening it, encouraging, motivating, and inspiring our youth. We have damaged their world so terribly and so many of them have become desperately—even suicidally—disillusioned. They need all the help they can get. I hope to write many more books on conservation for young people, especially for those in the developing world. To help them to understand why it is so important to save our natural resources, to respect life. One day I shall write a novel too! I have the plot all worked out, and when I can't sleep at night I lead my mind away from the day's problems to live in my world of fiction, becoming increasingly familiar with the characters. Another thing I would love to do is work some more on the Gombe chimpanzee data, specifically that relating to the long-term study of mothers and infants; to record infant development, to chart the changes throughout life in the Gombe chimpanzees, so that, one day, I can see publication of Volume 2 of *The Chimpanzees of Gombe*. But I sense I will probably not have time for this myself; I hope that one of the students will step in and do that. And I do want to spend a lot more time with my grandchildren, Merlin and Angel, who live in Dar es Salaam with Grub, and his wife, Maria.

Of course, as long as I live I shall continue to spread awareness about the true nature of animals, the extent of their suffering, and our responsibilities toward them. I shall go on speaking out against animal experimentation, intensive farming, fur farming, trapping, sport hunting, the exploitation of animals in entertainment, as beasts of burden, and as pets. Recently I had a marvelous opportunity to share my feelings about animals in a new setting, thanks to Alan Jones, dean of the beautiful Grace Cathedral in San Francisco. He asked me to deliver the sermon on Saint Francis's Day when the congregation take their animals—all manner of animals—to be blessed at the altar. What a fantastic experience. I took, as my text, Genesis Chapter 1, verse 26: "And God said, Let us make man in our image, after our likeness: and let them have dominion over the fish of the sea, and over the fowl of the air, and over the cattle, and over all the earth, and over every creeping thing that creepeth upon the earth." I explained that many Hebrew scholars believe the word "dominion" is a very poor translation of the original Hebrew word *v'yirdu*, which actually meant to *rule over*, as a wise king rules over his subjects, *with care and respect*. It implied a sense of responsibility and enlightened stewardship. Then I spoke of the humility I have learned from the chimpanzees—how we humans are not quite as different from the other animals as we used to think. I ended with one of Albert Schweitzer's moving prayers: "For animals that are overworked, underfed, and cruelly treated; for all wistful creatures in captivity that beat their wings against bars; for any that are hunted or lost or deserted or frightened or hungry; for all that must be put to death . . . and for those who deal with them we ask a heart of compassion and gentle hands and kindly words."

What does lie ahead? It cannot be denied that our human societies are cursed with war and crime and violence; it has been thus from the start of recorded history. It seems that every time some troubled part of the world solves its ideological, ethnic, or territorial problems, fighting flares up somewhere else. Perhaps things are meant to be this way, a sort of spiritual and moral obstacle course, with rewards in other worlds for those who triumph. Certainly it is when facing real danger that people appear in their true colors. Some go to pieces entirely; others survive but become bitter and cynical; and some emerge triumphant, stronger than before.

I had the good fortune to meet a truly inspirational group of young people who have survived the horrors of war. Among them were Miki Jacevik, who lived through the shelling of Sarajevo; Arn Chorn Pond, who was forced to be a boy soldier in the horrific campaigns of Pol Pot; and Hafsat Abiola, who escaped Nigeria after her mother was murdered, leaving her father in prison, in solitary confinement. They are so strong, like tempered steel, determined to join with other youth around the world to ensure a better future for their children. There are other young people who have not escaped from the horror. I met a ten-year-old Tutsi boy from a refugee camp in the Kigoma region. After looking into his eyes I was chilled. The incident inspired this bitter poem:

REFUGEE

She sits outside, on a stool, her face closed
And still with the hopelessness of tomorrow,
Drawn with remembered anguish
As this day, empty of hope like all the days
Since she arrived, draws to its end.

The setting sun gleams, reflected from the tin
Bowl on her lap, half filled with rice.
Slowly two tears from her closed eyes
Move down her cheeks. They glisten
In the end of the day's sun. She does not eat.

JANE GOODALL

What horrors, I wonder, has she seen?
Forced from her home, she and her family,
Fleeing from terror I can only guess at,
Bearing it with her yet as she sits there,
Motionless, a vehicle for grief.

Her suffering is outside my knowledge:
I have never been torn, like she, from
Living roots, herded, as cattle are herded,
By those who deal in numbers, not faces.
For they are good, the people of the camp—
They would break if they began to notice the faces.

All around her are alien people:
Alien voices speaking from an unknown
Culture with words she cannot understand.
Only the sun and moon and the stars in the night sky
Are the same—they were there yesterday. And God?

A child approaches. He is about ten, and thin.
He looks up at her closed face, and into the bowl
She holds in her still hands. She opens eyes that
Are dark with the pain of yesterday. But tomorrow—
Tomorrow is for the child. She gives him the rice
And he eats.

His eyes, reflecting the sun's last rays,
Smolder with dreams. Tomorrow he will be a man.
"Vengeance is Mine: I will repay" saith the Lord.
But the child does not hear God—his heart is full
With hatred. It is he—he who will repay.
This is his dream for tomorrow.

How tragic that so many children today are not brought
up to respect the fundamental values that were so important a part of my upbringing: honesty, self-discipline,
courage, respect for life, courtesy, compassion, and toler-

ance. Untold numbers of children in the affluent Western world, thrilled by the violence on their TV screens and thoroughly at home in the world of "virtual" reality, have lost all touch with "real" reality. Too often their parents are working and there is no one to provide the role models that could help them grow into responsible, caring adults. Instead they idolize pop stars and other unsuitable heroes of the screen, many of whom take drugs. No wonder they tend to become violent and uncaring themselves—long ago the chimps taught me of the enormous importance of early experience and good role models.

So what can we do? When I address groups of youth I tell them that there is a lot we can do, each and every one of us, just by trying to make the world around us a better place. It can be very simple: we can make a sad or lonely person smile; we can make a miserable dog wag his tail or a cat purr; we can give water to a little wilting plant. We cannot solve all the problems of the world, but we can often do something about the problems under our noses. We can't save all the starving children and beggars of Africa, of Asia, but what about the street children, the homeless, the aged in our own hometown?

It was the desperation of one struggling, desperate woman that motivated Mohammad Yunus, founder of the Grameen Bank in Bangladesh, to make his first tiny loan. He did not start out with a plan to spread his bank across the developing world. Similarly, it was the need of a single child that led Henri Landwirth to create Give Kids the World, which, today, brings joy and love into the lives of millions of sick children and their families.

If we ignore a cry for help we are likely to be plagued subsequently by guilt. I still remember how, when I was a child, I saw some boys pulling the legs off a live crab— and I cried but was afraid to say anything because they were bigger than me. Grub, when he was five, was punished by his teacher for getting into a fight with a much bigger boy who was terrifying a rabbit at school, squirting it with water from a hose. Good for Grub.

And so I have reached the end of my story. I have tried to answer the questions that people ask me, about my religious and spiritual beliefs, about my philosophy of life, about why I have hope for the future. I have answered as honestly and candidly as I can. Indeed, I have laid bare a lot of my mind, heart, and soul. But there is one story as yet untold. To me, with my love of symbolism (surely inherited from my superstitious Welsh forebears!), it seems that this story may explain why I have done much of what I have done, lived as I have lived. And why I must continue to the bitter—or perhaps glorious—end.

It happened when I was less than a year old—before I could talk. I was in my pram outside the grocery store, guarded by Peggy, our white bull terrier. Nanny was shopping inside. A dragonfly began swooping around me, and I screamed—so a well-intentioned passerby hit the dragonfly to the ground with his newspaper, and crushed it with his foot. I continued to scream all the way home. In fact I became so hysterical that they called the doctor, who prescribed a sedative to calm me down. I heard this story for the first time about five years ago. Vanne was writing about my early life and asked if I could remember the incident at all—why had I been so terrified?

As I read what she had written, the sixty intervening years fell away and I was transported back in time. I remembered lying in my nursery. There was a lot of green, I thought—and Vanne said yes, green curtains and green linoleum. And I remember watching a big blue dragonfly which had come in through the window. I protested when Nanny chased it out, but she said it might sting me, and that it had a sting as long as its "tail" (meaning, of course, its abdomen). That is a *long* sting! No wonder

I was scared when a dragonfly zoomed around my pram. But being afraid of something did not mean I wanted it killed. If I close my eyes I can see, with almost unbearable clarity, the glorious shimmering and still quivering wings, the blue "tail" gleaming in the sunlight, the head crushed on the sidewalk. Because of me it had died, perhaps in pain. I screamed in helpless outrage. And from a terrible sense of guilt.

Perhaps I have subconsciously lived my whole life trying to assuage that guilt. Perhaps the dragonfly was part of some plan, to bring a message to a little child, all those years ago. If so, all I can say, to my God, is: "Message received and understood." I have tried to assuage some of the guilt we all must feel, for our inhumanity to man and beast alike. And, with the support of all people of compassionate and loving heart, I shall go on trying until the end. And the end . . . will be the beginning?

Thomas D. Mangelsen

Epilogue (Spring 2003)

HOPE BEYOND 9/11

SINCE THE INITIAL PUBLICATION OF *Reason for Hope* in 1999 the world has changed. On the 11th of September, 2001, a massive terrorist attack destroyed the World Trade Center in New York and damaged the Pentagon; Osama bin Laden and his al Qa'eda network were thought to be responsible. In retaliation, the Bush administration, with the backing of the UN Security Council, bombed Afghanistan and, together with a coalition of Afghan warlords—the Northern Alliance—routed many of the Taliban forces and overturned the repressive Taliban regime. The fight against terrorism initially targeted bin Laden and his al Qa'eda network, which has cells across the globe. This proved extraordinarily difficult, since the enemy was so elusive, and no one really knew whether bin Laden was still alive. Therefore the face of Most Wanted Man was abruptly changed, from that of bin Laden to that of Saddam Hussein, despite a failure to link him or his country with the terrorist attacks of 9/11.

Saddam was accused of possessing large stores of illegal weapons of mass destruction. Despite the failure of the UN weapons inspectors to find any such large stores, the Bush administration, backed by British prime minister Tony Blair, decided that it was necessary to remove Saddam, overturn his regime, and build a new democracy that would, incidentally, be favorable to U.S. and British interests in Iraqi oil. This has plunged the world into an even more frightening state, and it seems likely to get a good deal worse. The fact that the Bush administration is routinely overturning legislation introduced to protect the environment is an additional cause for deep concern.

And so, everywhere I go, people are asking if I still have hope. "Surely, Jane, your optimism must have evaporated. What possible reason can you have for hope now?" In this short addendum to the new edition of *Reason for Hope* I shall try to show how I have maintained hope, although there have been a few very dark moments to be sure.

On September 9, 2001, two days before the attacks in New York and Washington, D.C., I was in Burlington, Vermont, taking part in a glorious celebration of the Earth Charter. It was a breathtakingly beautiful fall day. Early in the morning, a group of about a hundred people gathered, ready to set off on a silent walk, receptive to the natural world around us. We were led by Satish Kumar, advocate for peace and a follower of Mahatma Gandhi. Ahead of him was a huge and very handsome Clydesdale mare, Lucy. The early-morning sun brought a gloss to her polished black coat and warmed my back. My bare feet trod gently on vivid green grass, and above was a blue sky untouched by even the suggestion of a cloud. The only sounds as we walked toward an ancient barn, the largest in North America, was a gentle whickering from Lucy, the mooing of a cow in a nearby field, and the liquid notes of a few feathered songsters. Then, as we turned toward the barn where some two thousand people awaited our arrival, the glorious notes of a saxophone, played by Paul Winters, rose into the air. We passed through an avenue of trees, and it seemed that the dryads of Greek mythology had sprung to life, for the members of a dance group in white gowns with long white scarves were up in the branches. With graceful movements of upper body and arms they swayed to and fro, moving with the sound of the music. It was as though we had stepped into a little corner of heaven. The breeze blew a chill on my face, and I realized it was wet with tears. Yes, I thought, this is how it is meant to be. This is what it can, and one day must, be like on Earth. The beauty of nature and the artistry of mankind had blended: It was true harmony. The music was perfect, a haunting, powerful, and glorious voice; each note rose toward the great spiritual power that I felt among us, almost as a physical presence. And that was just the start of the joyous celebrations. All day there were talks and speeches and dances to honor Planet Earth and to encourage all attending to commit ourselves to new levels of stewardship.

Then came September 11, just two days later, and I was in New York. It would be hard to think of a greater contrast than that between the exhilarating and joyous day in Vermont and the horrific scenes that were played out around the World Trade Center. Flames, people screaming, leaping, and sobbing. Black smoke, clouds of toxic dust, bodies lying on the ground, glass, cement. Confusion. Panic. Shock. Horror. A sense of unreality and disbelief. These things, surely, were not really happening. But the images of evil, the destruction of man-made structures and God-made bodies on our television screens, were repeated, again and again and again, and outside there was a spreading haze of smoke and dust. Soon there was an eerie silence, punctuated only by the clanging bells of the ambulances and the police-car sirens. Out on the streets around our hotel, the Roger Smith, were small groups of people desperately trying to find out more. As the full enormity of the terrorist attack was revealed, there was growing anguish and fear. Almost everyone we met was worrying about a family member or friend.

My schedule had me in New York for just two days, but it was a week before I was able to leave. I kept wondering if there was some reason for my presence in the shattered city, for the timing was uncanny. If the attack had been one day earlier I would still have been in Vermont, and at first I wished so desperately that I was back in that beautiful place. I would close my eyes and think of the blue skies and sweet air and the clear water flowing in the river. Gradually, though, I began to realize that, for my own personal growth, it was important for me to be in the city of grief and anger and fear. The experience would help me to understand better, so that I could be more helpful as I talked with people around the country.

I have always found that the best way to cope in times of anxiety, distress, and fear is to try to get involved in something positive. I was in New York with Mary Lewis, my executive assistant, JGI vice president of outreach, and wonderful friend. We were joined by Nona Gandelman, JGI vice president of communication; she had flown in that morning on the last plane to land before LaGuardia was closed. She had actually seen the plane crash into the second of the Twin Towers, and she arrived in a state of shock. On the next day we forced ourselves to get back to work, for there was nothing we could do to help the rescue work. No one was allowed near Ground Zero.

As soon as it became apparent that the terrorists were Islamic fanatics inspired to acts of hatred by Osama bin Laden, it was clear that there would be a vicious backlash against Arabs and Muslims. There was so little understanding among the general public of differences between the moderate Muslims and the Taliban. We debated among ourselves as to what we could do. In the end we pulled together a wonderful group of youth, including Yasmin Delawari, a beautiful young Afghan American, who arranged for her father, Noor Delawari, to join us via speaker phone from Los Angeles. It was a wonderful meeting and led, among other things, to our Roots & Shoots Peace Initiative, which has since spread around the world. We were also able to join Satish Kumar, stranded as well in New York, for a small ceremony of prayer and healing that was very meaningful. A number of our Roots & Shoots members joined us.

At last the airport was open, and Mary and I were able to resume our interrupted tour. It took five hours to get from the cab to the airport and onto the plane. The New York skyline, now changed forever, fell away behind as we headed across the country, destination Portland. After we had been flying for about an hour, I started to feel distinctly odd, sort of sick in my stomach. It took a while to realize that it was fear that was gripping me. But fear of what? Certainly I wasn't afraid of being hijacked; it seemed to me that it was probably the safest time of all to be flying. Suddenly I knew. The next morning I had to face eight hundred high-school students and deliver a lecture titled "Reason for Hope". What could I say to those students? How could I talk about hope in the face of what I had just seen? As I struggled to come up with some kind of inspiring message, I stopped feeling afraid—I just felt utterly hopeless.

It was a long time before I fell asleep that night, as I

continued to wrestle with the problem of my talk. Finally my tired brain gave up. I reached out to the Great Spiritual Power and prayed for strength, prayed that I might find the right words in the morning, and slept. I woke up feeling quite calm—strangely calm, for I still had no idea what I would say to the students. I arrived in the auditorium and sat in the front row as the head of the school introduced me. And then it was upon me. I walked up to the podium and began to talk. The first part was easy: telling the students about the chimpanzees of Gombe, emphasizing how like us they are, giving updates on the lives of Goblin and Patti, Fifi and her family, Gremlin and the twins. I described the plight of all wild chimpanzees and their forests in Africa, and I pointed out how we have destroyed so much of the environment around the world. I talked about the social injustices that we find everywhere. And so: "Is there hope?" I asked rhetorically. I started out with my usual reasons for hope: the wonder of the human brain and the marvels of modern technology; the resilience of nature; the indomitable human spirit.

I couldn't leave it at that. They all knew I'd been in New York. And in that desperate moment, the message became clear. As though a dark cloud had blown away and I could see the sun again, I was able to talk about hope in spite of the threat of terrorism. And since that day it has become even clearer, and other insights, other reasons for hope in the face of evil and danger, have been revealed. The attack on Baghdad in the spring of 2003, fueling the hatred felt in so many parts of the world against America, and now against the UK also, will surely result in a terrifying escalation of terrorist attacks. But I am convinced that there is indeed hope beyond Baghdad.

On September 11 we had witnessed the ultimate evil:

the use of innocent people to kill innocent people. But on that same day there were acts of incredible heroism by the rescue workers, the police and firemen and many civilians also. Countless individuals had risked their lives, and many had lost their lives as a result. There were, incidentally, many heroic acts performed by the rescue dogs. And there was an outpouring of concern and generosity from around the city, around America and from many parts of the world. People donated money, food, medicine, and blood. People opened their homes to those who were homeless. And—for some months any-way—many people around the United States began to question their values, to wonder whether, perhaps, they should spend more time with family and loved ones and less time acquiring money and more money to acquire stuff and more stuff. And for a while in New York, there was a new sense of community. People were more polite, they smiled more and helped each other. In other parts of the country, too, people came up and told me that they were phoning their family more often after 9/11. And one woman, dabbing at her eyes, told me she'd been es-tranged from her son for fifteen years, but since 9/11 they had become reconciled and he was back, living in the house.

On that first day I told the students that I had lived through war, had firsthand experience of terrorism, bombs, and death. As I wrote in Chapter 1, even though I was only five years old when Britain declared war on Nazi Germany, my memory of that moment, when it was an-nounced on the wireless (we did not use the term "radio" back then), made a lasting impression. That Germany did not invade England was a miracle: Our only protec-tion in the south was a line of scaffolding and some barbed wire, as well as the heroism of so many young pilots in the Royal Air Force. They were shot down, horribly maimed, and killed, day after day. Yet still the young men joined up, flying on what seemed an impossible mission against the well-prepared might of the German Air Force. Indeed, as Churchill said, "Never in the history of mankind have so many owed so much to so few." To this day I remember the bombs, especially the few that fell near our seaside town. But although I did not experience the bombing of London, nor any of the big industrial towns that were the targets of the German raids, I heard about them, day after day. Uncle Eric, a surgeon in Whipps X hospital, used to come to Bournemouth for an occasional weekend, drawn and tired from his selfless work tending to those wounded in the air raids. I knew some of the people who were killed in World War II. It was a terrible war, during which thousands of innocent people were maimed and killed on all sides. And of course, Hitler's Third Reich also exterminated millions of Jews, Gypsies, and other non-Aryans in the concentration camps of the Holocaust.

I told the students how I had had personal experience of terrorist attacks. My closest shave with death was in London, when a rather large bomb was discovered in one of the meeting rooms at the Royal Overseas League. It had been taped inside the podium set up for a conference on IRA terrorism. My room in the club was just three floors above. Fortunately the hall porter noticed something odd when he was checking to see that everything was ready. We were all hurried out of the club at six o'clock that morning and not allowed back until five that afternoon, when it had been safely detonated. (I was glad to be an early riser, for many of my fellow club members were in nighties and curlers when they were bustled out into the chilly garden!) On three occasions in London I was evacuated from airports because of bomb scares, and twice from railway stations. For many years now people in different parts of the world have learned to live with the possibility of terrorist attacks. One simply gets on with life. After all, thousands of people die or are maimed in car accidents. It could happen to any of us at any time, and statistically, except in countries like Israel, we are more likely to be harmed by cars than bombs or snipers. Yet we don't go around in mortal fear of motorcars!

Soon after Mary and I got back on the road after 9/11, a woman left an envelope on the table during a book signing. When I subsequently opened it I found a quotation from Mahatma Gandhi: "If you look back through human history you find that every evil regime is eventually overcome by good." About a week later another woman came up after a lecture with a small bell in her hand—like the sort of bell that a cat is sometimes forced to wear so as to warn birds and other prey animals of approaching danger. "Jane," she said, "ring this bell when you talk of your hope for peace." And so I always do. It is made from metal that was part of a defused landmine from the "Killing Fields" of Pol Pot. And now Pol Pot is gone, the Khmer Rouge is disbanded, and the Cambodians are trying to put their country back together. And the mines, one by one, are being detonated.

March 19, 2003, was the fateful day when America and the United Kingdom began bombing Iraq. All around the world, millions and millions of people had taken part in peace marches and demonstrations, protesting against war. England had the biggest demonstrations in her history. None of this made any difference to the Bush administration or British prime minister Tony Blair. Saddam Hussein was given a deadline: Leave the country, with your family, by 8:00 P.M. American Eastern Standard Time and your country will be spared a war that you cannot win. That was a tense day, for until the first bomb was dropped, there was still the chance of a miracle. On that day I should have been giving lectures in Denver. But there were great snowstorms in Colorado, and the Denver airport was closed. Because of that I was able to extend, from two days to three days, my one tiny holiday in a nine-week tour. This holiday was planned so that I could see the migration of the Sandhill cranes and snow geese as they pass through Nebraska. I was with Tom Mangelsen, whose father had built a cabin by the Platte River where the cranes and geese stay for about a month before continuing on to their winter feeding grounds.

Each of the three days was fantastic, each was different. But it was the last day, the extra day that was like a gift, the day that a terrifying war against terror was set in motion, that was unbelievably significant. For it was on that day that I received, through the cranes, a powerful message: a message that will sustain me through the darkness and that I want to share. On the evening of March 18, which should have been my last evening, the sheer number of geese and cranes that passed us on the way to one of their roosts, about a quarter of a mile downstream, was staggering. For one and three-quarter hours they flew by, in great flocks, in family groups, in dense clouds, or delicate skeins that traced ever-changing patterns against the sky. Other groups were approaching the roost from different directions, like clouds of smoke in the distance. The noise of their calling was, at times, quite overwhelming. Theirs are voices that speak of wide-open spaces, the freedom of the skies, snowy wastes and distant lands. A group of Sandhills flew so close above us that I could see individual feathers. I looked directly into the eyes of one of them, and she gave the soft chuckling sound that indicates, Tom said, that she knew we were there. Calmly they flew on, to be replaced by another family, flying even lower. I was moved to tears. The sun sank low, turning the clouds golden and shell pink—and still the birds came in, wave after wave, dark against the darkening sky. The clamor of their wild voices from the roost was awe inspiring, tremendously exciting. It got dark and we went back into the cabin and lit a fire. And, still praying for a miracle, we lit a candle for peace.

March 19 dawned gray. We went out, as usual, about six-thirty but were soon driven in by the rain that blew in on the icy north wind. About ten o'clock a flock of Sandhill cranes circled above the cabin and landed in the cornfield just outside the windows. There were a couple of thousand birds, mostly cranes but there were snow geese too, creating patches of white among the gray. For the next hour and a half first one group of cranes and then another performed their graceful dance, wings outstretched, leaping high like feathered ballerinas, throwing bits of straw or clods of earth up into the air. Cranes are symbols of peace in many parts of the world. And there they were, dancing for us, closer to the cabin than Tom had ever seen them before. With their beautiful Dance of Peace they were, I believe, bringing a message for us humans. Animals, it seems, are often sent as messengers. Only they are so often not heeded, and those who listen are derided and considered slightly crazy. This message, brought by the cranes, seemed clear to me: "However dark the times ahead, keep the knowledge of peace to come in your heart." I shall keep the image of that Dance of Peace constantly in my mind over the coming months, for it is more important than ever to keep hope alive in these frightening times.

The days and its messages were not over. We searched the stubble for fallen feathers that I wanted to send as symbols of peace and hope to a few special friends who need them most. And that evening, forgetting for a while the fateful 8:00 P.M. deadline, we went downstream to the main roost. There we established ourselves in a small hut, built by the Platte River Trust. We were glad of the shelter it offered, for the wind was even bitterer, and we were cold despite our thick jackets and boots and gloves. Peering through the tiny window holes, camouflaged by pieces of flapping hessian, we watched the birds come in. Countless thousands had already landed a little way upstream. As more and more arrived, the gray and white feathered mantle that was settling over the shallows and sandbars of the wide river came closer and closer to our hideaway. After an hour the birds were landing right in front of us. A deer and her fawn passed by, picking their way daintily through the water, then disappearing into the vegetation that lined the bank.

The invisible sun sank lower in the west. Suddenly there was a deafening sound, as more than a million birds, calling at the tops of their voices, took off and circled round above us—all because a lone bald eagle had come cruising along the river. The eagle landed a few yards away from us, and soon the cranes and geese came down again, leaving a circle around the bird of prey. After a while he flew away, presumably to his own roost in the branches of a tree.

It was almost pitch dark when we left, but we could just make out the black shapes against the almost black sky as the birds continued to arrive. For more than two hours they had been flying to the roost. And that is but one of the roosts along the Platte. An estimated 12 million water birds spend about a month feeding in the area in order to acquire sufficient body fat to sustain them on their lone, long journeys. Some go to Alaska, many go as far as Siberia.

What an inspiring experience it was, that last extra day on the Platte. It left me with another important message, this time a call for action. Despite the harm that humans have inflicted on the land—the Platte River has never been so shallow; some farmers have begun ploughing the corn left from the harvest into the ground, thus depriving the migrating birds of this so important food, and fertilizers and pesticides are polluting the land and water here as everywhere—despite this, the stretches of the Platte and the surrounding fields and remnant prairie, where the birds stop each year, can still sustain this vast migration.

And so, as we turned on the TV and heard the horrifying but expected news—that bombs were even then being dropped on Iraq—we had images and messages to sustain us and spur us to even greater efforts to protect the environment around the world. For if we make valiant efforts to protect what is left, and work desperately to restore some of that which has been destroyed, then when peace comes, as it will, we shall be ready for it. We can never live in harmony with each other unless we live also in harmony with nature. When I was traveling around the United States after 9/11 I found that many people were afraid to admit that they cared about the environment, lest it made they seem unpatriotic. In fact, if we do not care MORE, and work HARDER, to help Mother Nature, the terrorists and other forces of evil will get the last word, for there will be nothing left for our grandchildren and theirs. We are shocked and horrified when we hear of atrocities practiced against children, yet if we do not become better, more passionate stewards, we are condemning all children of future generations to lives of increasing ill health, crime, despair, and poverty.

As I write, the assault on Baghdad is underway. As I have already said, one of the best ways to combat despair is by taking action. Our Roots & Shoots groups are working hard to develop and expand our Initiative for Peace. Students in many parts of the world are learning about people of different cultures and religions. They are learning the difference between moderate Muslims, Christians, and Jews, and the fanatical sects that spring up in all religions. They are learning that the Ten Commandments of Islam and Christianity are the same—and both include "Thou shalt not kill" and "Thou shalt not covet thy neighbor's possessions." (And "possessions" surely includes oilfields!) The students are studying conflict resolution, and writing scripts so that they can act out different solutions to a variety of problems—one solution based on aggression and violence, another on negotiation, respect, and understanding. One of our college members, Bob Cornett, has teamed up with Puppet Farms. Together they have created many giant puppets, including the Giant Peace Doves. There is a flock of 26 scattered across the United States, and they have appeared in many peace demonstrations across the country. Now the instruction kits have gone to our over 4,500 groups around the world, so that soon the huge doves, made of simple materials, largely recycled, will be seen everywhere.

In April 2002, the secretary general of the United Nations, Kofi Annan, named me a UN Messenger of Peace—a great honor, but also a huge responsibility, especially now. We shall continue to protest war. We shall create and fly the giant doves until the planet is covered and they can be seen from a satellite in space. Above all, we shall work to protect and restore the natural world, seeking ways to heal the wounds we have inflicted, and ways to live in greater harmony with Mother Nature, as well as with each other.

One real reason for hope is that the people of the world are uniting everywhere to speak out strongly, but for the most part peacefully, against war. We need more people to swell the ranks. We must remember, each and every one of us, that our voices and our actions make a difference, every day. Yesterday I saw a woman wearing a button I had not seen before. There was a small star-spangled banner depicted, with the words "PEACE IS PATRIOTIC." I really like that.

By the time this book arrives in stores, much may have changed in the world. We may have seen a proliferation of terrorist attacks around the globe, and the future may seem more grim than ever. But the worse it gets, the harder we must try to work for the future of the planet. I shall keep the images of the Sandhill cranes in my heart. I have asked Tom to make me some prints so that I can hang them on the wall in my room in the Birches. And he is offering to make these same prints available so that everyone who is moved by the scenes I described and the message that I believe the cranes have brought us can share the images.

I often think back to that glorious day of love and peace in Vermont on September 9, 2001. That is how the world can be. One day it will. We must be ready for peace when it comes.

AUTHOR'S NOTE

In 1984 Phillip Berman asked me if I would consider contributing an essay to a book he was editing, titled *The Courage of Conviction*. It was a difficult essay to write, but I did my best.

Twelve years later, Phillip approached me with another idea. Would I be prepared to undertake a joint venture with him that expanded on the themes I discussed in my essay? I told him I didn't have time, but he countered by suggesting that we produce a book of interviews—questions from a theologian to an anthropologist. All I would have to do was edit my replies.

Somehow, along the way, the scope and focus of the book changed. What was conceived of as an extended interview evolved into a more personal book, a "spiritual autobiography" that required digging deeply into my past and examining my present and future. This was a very different proposition, one that I knew would mean hours and hours of thought and writing.

In the early stages, Phillip interviewed me in America, at my home in England, and in Tanzania, in both Dar es Salaam and Gombe. He also interviewed many people who had played an important role in my life. Then he began the difficult task of going through and ordering miles of tape.

Writing this book was a daunting prospect, but one that, in a way, represented a challenge. Perhaps, I told myself, it was one of those opportunities that occur in life and that can be seized, or rejected, as we choose.

Based on the structure provided by Phillip, and his interpretation of our interviews, I set to work. Had I known how much time the writing would take, the sometimes painful searching of my soul that would be involved, I think I would not have accepted the challenge. It took up all my time when I was at my family home in Bournemouth—the only peaceful place I have for writing, since I am on the road lecturing nearly 300 days a year. I worked late into the nights, woke early in the mornings, and set aside everything else that was not desperately urgent. Still, it took far longer than I'd anticipated. Thank you, Vanne, for giving up so many precious hours when we should have been together.

Within the book there are certain passages that I have lifted almost word for word from my other books. In struggling to find the best possible way of putting thoughts into words, or describing especially meaningful experiences, sometimes what I wrote originally seemed to be the best I could do.

The book is now done, the photos selected, the title agreed upon.

But the journey never ends.

ABOUT THE JANE GOODALL INSTITUTE FOR PEOPLE, ANIMALS AND THE ENVIRONMENT

Every individual matters.
Every individual has a role to play.
Every individual makes a difference.

The Jane Goodall Institute (JGI), a tax-exempt, non-profit organization, was founded in 1977 to support field research and conservation projects involving chimpanzees and other wildlife in Africa, to improve the conditions of chimpanzees and other animals in captivity, and to raise awareness and understanding of these issues with as wide an audience as possible.

When Jane Goodall realized that chimpanzees across their range in Africa were becoming increasingly endangered due to habitat loss and hunting, she knew she must leave her forest paradise to help the remarkable beings who had given her so much. As she spent more and more time lecturing in different parts of the world, and as her visibility and interests grew, so JGI expanded its scope of involvement.

Roots & Shoots, a hands-on environmental and humanitarian education program, empowers young people, from kindergarten to college, to take action to make the world around them a better place for the environment, animals, and their local communities. ChimpanZoo researchers study and improve living conditions for chimps in captivity. Sanctuaries in Tanzania, Congo-Brazzaville, Kenya, and Uganda provide new homes for chimpanzees orphaned by poachers. The TACARE project in Tanzania involves villagers living along the shore of Lake Tanganyika and around Gombe in environmentally sustainable projects to improve the quality of their lives and reduce their dependency on remaining forests: it is the local people, ultimately, who will determine whether or not the chimpanzees survive. And, of course, the research at Gombe continues, providing new insights into the behavior of our closest living relatives. All the data from 1960 to the present is being computerized and analyzed by a team of dedicated students under the direction of ex-Gombe researcher Dr. Anne Pusey at the Jane Goodall Center for Primate Studies at the University of Minnesota.

For more information on our projects, or to become a member of JGI, visit our Web site at www.janegoodall.org or contact the JGI office nearest you.

JGI-USA, P.O. Box 14890, Silver Spring, MD 20911

JGI-UK, 15 Clarendon Park, Lymington, Hants SO41 8AX

JGI-Tanzania, P.O. Box 727, Dar es Salaam

JGI-Uganda, P.O. Box 4187, Kampala

JGI-Canada, P.O. Box 477, Victoria Station, Westmount, Quebec H3Z 2Y6

JGI-Germany, Herzogstrasse 60, D-80803 München

JGI-South Africa, P.O. Box 87527, Houghton 2047

JGI-Taiwan, 6F, No. 20 Section 2, Hsin Sheng South Road, Taipei

JGI-Holland, P.B. 61, 7213 ZH Gorssel, The Netherlands

Roots & Shoots-Italy, via D. Martelli 14a, 57012 Castiglioncello (Li)